Remaking *the* Urban Waterfront

Primary Authors

Bonnie Fisher
David L.A. Gordon
Leslie Holst
Alex Krieger
Gavin McMillan
Laurel Rafferty
Emma Stark Schiffman

Contributing Authors

Beth Benson
Peter Droege
Steve Fader
Anne Frej
Guy Gibson
William P. Macht
Virginia Sorrells

Urban Land Institute

About ULI–the Urban Land Institute

ULI–the Urban Land Institute is a nonprofit education and research institute that is supported by its members. Its mission is to provide responsible leadership in the use of land in order to enhance the total environment.

ULI sponsors education programs and forums to encourage an open international exchange of ideas and sharing of experiences; initiates research that anticipates emerging land use trends and issues and proposes creative solutions based on that research; provides advisory services; and publishes a wide variety of materials to disseminate information on land use and development. Established in 1936, the Institute today has more than 20,000 members and associates from more than 60 countries representing the entire spectrum of the land use and development disciplines.

Richard M. Rosan
President

For more information about ULI and the resources that it offers related to urban waterfront development and a variety of other real estate and urban development issues, visit ULI's Web Site at www.uli.org.

Project Staff

Rachelle L. Levitt
Executive Vice President, Policy and Practice
Publisher

Gayle Berens
Vice President, Real Estate Development Practice
Project Director

David Takesuye, AIA
Senior Associate

Nancy H. Stewart
Director, Book Program

James A. Mulligan
Managing Editor

Sandra F. Chizinsky
Manuscript Editor

Betsy VanBuskirk
Art Director

Byron Holly
Senior Graphic Designer

Diann Stanley-Austin
Director, Publishing Operations

Karrie Underwood
Administrative Manager

Recommended bibliographic listing

ULI–the Urban Land Institute. *Remaking the Urban Waterfront*. Washington, D.C.: ULI–the Urban Land Institute, 2004.

ULI Catalog Number: R40
International Standard Book Number: 0-87420-903-X
Library of Congress Control Number: 2004110832

Cover photo: Tourism New South Wales

About the Authors

Bonnie Fisher

Bonnie Fisher is a principal of ROMA Design Group, in San Francisco, where she also serves as director of landscape design. Her project experience ranges from planning for major open space preservation and restoration projects to planning for new urban districts to the design and implementation of urban open space, plazas, and streetscapes. Fisher is a registered landscape architect with a master of landscape architecture in urban design from the University of California at Berkeley and a bachelor of arts from the University of California at Los Angeles. Over the course of her career, she has taught and lectured at various educational and other institutions, contributed numerous articles and book chapters (she is currently working on her first book), served as a major speaker at a number of conferences, and served as the lead designer and planner on a number of projects both inside and outside the United States. In San Francisco, Fisher has played a long-standing role in the transformation of the urban waterfront from industrial and maritime uses to a vibrant, mixed-use urban district served by transit and connected by a necklace of diverse open spaces.

David L.A. Gordon

David L.A. Gordon, MCIP, AICP, teaches urban planning at Queen's University, in Kingston, Ontario. He has been a professional planner in the private and public sectors for 20 years, twice sharing the Canadian Institute of Planners' National Award of Distinction, and was a project manager for the Toronto waterfront redevelopment agency in the mid-1980s. Gordon received degrees in urban planning and civil engineering from Queen's University and holds a master's degree in business administration and a doctorate in design from Harvard University. His extensive writings on urban waterfront redevelopment include *Battery Park City: Politics and Planning on the New York Waterfront* (New York: Routledge, 1998).

Leslie Holst

Leslie Holst is a former senior associate in ULI's Policy and Practice Department, where she contributed to the writing and publication of many ULI books, including *The New Shape of Suburbia: Place Making and Town Center Development,* and the *Mixed-Use Development Handbook.* A contributing author to *Urban Land* magazine, Holst also served as editor of ULI's Development Case Studies subscription service, which highlights innovative and successful real estate development projects from around the world, and as project director for numerous ULI Advisory Services panels. Before joining ULI, Holst was a research librarian at Aspen Systems Corporation, in Rockville, Maryland. She has a master's degree in urban and regional planning from Virginia Polytechnic Institute and State University and a bachelor's degree in social work from Longwood College.

Alex Krieger

Alex Krieger, FAIA, is professor in practice of urban design at the Graduate School of Design at Harvard University. He is a founding principal of Chan Krieger & Associates, a 20-person firm that combines the disciplines of architecture, urban design, and public-space planning. An authority on the evolution of urban settlements, Krieger's publications include *Mapping Boston* (1999); *Design Concepts for Nippon-Daira and Its Region* (1993), *Towns and Town-Making Principles* (1991), *A Design Primer for Cities and Towns* (1990), *The Architecture of Kallman, McKinnell & Wood* (1988), *Past Futures: Two Centuries of Imagining Boston* (1985), and essays for various architecture, design, and planning periodicals. He is a contributing editor for *Architecture Magazine.* Krieger has served as director of the National Endowment for the Arts Mayors' Institute on City Design (1995–1998); commissioner on the Boston Civic Design Commission (1988–1997); design review architect for the Providence Capital Center Commission (1991–1998); vice president of the New England Holocaust Memorial Committee (1989–1998); and director of the National Leadership Institute for Planning Direction (1998 to the present).

Gavin McMillan

Gavin McMillan is a principal with Hargreaves Associates, Cambridge, Massachusetts, a landscape architecture and planning firm founded in 1985 and known for its explorative design approach to a wide range of project types and site scales. The firm provides special expertise in the areas of urban design and waterfront redevelopment. McMillan's work focuses on post-industrial site remediation and redevelopment, and his past projects include the redevelopment and design of waterfront projects in the cities of Chattanooga, Tennessee; Louisville, Kentucky; and Homebush Bay, New South Wales—the site of the 2000 Sydney Olympics. His award-winning work has led him to waterfront projects around the globe, and he has lectured and contributed articles on waterfront development to a range of trade and professional institutions and publications. McMillan is a graduate of Queensland University of Technology, in Brisbane, Australia.

Laurel Rafferty

Laurel Rafferty is the founding principal of Portscape, an international urban and coastal-area planning firm based in Lexington, Massachusetts. The firm specializes in coastal zone management, the city-port-waterfront relationship, and land use issues specific to waterfront areas. Among other projects, Rafferty has worked as a port- and harbor-planning specialist for the Massachusetts Coastal Zone Management Program—where, in partnership with the Massachusetts Institute of Technology, she created a model port/waterfront planning process used by the major ports of Massachusetts to produce development plans. Rafferty has made presentations on the implementation of this model at international conferences sponsored by the International Association of Cities and Ports and the International Association of Maritime Economists. In earlier private sector work, she was principal of a land use planning and development consulting firm.

Emma Stark Schiffman

Emma Stark Schiffman is a staff landscape architect with Hargreaves Associates, Cambridge, Massachusetts. Her work focuses on the ecological, remedial, and programmatic aspects of waterfront redevelopment projects, including the 21st-Century Waterfront in Chattanooga, Tennessee, and the Clinton Presidential Center in Little Rock, Arkansas. Schiffman holds a master of landscape architecture from the Graduate School of Design at Harvard University.

Acknowledgments

Remaking the Urban Waterfront started being shaped after a joint forum was held by the Urban Land Institute and American Rivers at ULI offices in Washington, D.C., on February 15, 2001. The forum was chaired by ULI full member Jim Heid; participants included Steven Apfelbaum, Beth Benson, Uwe Brandes, Ignacio Bunster, Pat Condon, Steve Durrant, Paul Fishman, Peter Harnik, Barry Hersch, Mark Johnson, Ilze Jones, John Knott, Nan Laurence, Jim MacBroom, Roy Mann, Betsy Otto, Michael Pawlukiewicz, Dan Redondo, Brian Reilly, Bill Wenk, and Joseph Zehnder. The all-day forum began a discussion of ecological design and practice issues as they relate to waterfront development and planted the seeds for this new book, intended to look at a new generation of waterfront development. ULI's first effort at exploring waterfronts was a 1983 book titled *Urban Waterfront Development*, written by Douglas Wrenn. The 2004 waterfront book draws from that earlier work, but contains almost all new material, including 13 new case studies.

Books like these are necessarily the result of work by many different people. In particular, I would like to thank Frank Uffen, of the New Amsterdam Development Company, and Laurel Rafferty, of Portscape, for reviewing the entire book. In addition, various sections were reviewed by Stanley McGreal, of the University of Ulster, and Leslie Holst and David Takesuye, of the ULI staff. I also would like to thank the following people for their assistance in other aspects of the book: Sandy Chizinsky, Marta Goldsmith, Byron Holly, Leslie Holst, Oliver Jerschow, Rachelle Levitt, James Mulligan, Laurel Rafferty, Nancy Stewart, Karrie Underwood, Joseph Zehnder, and especially David Takesuye. In addition, I would like to thank the many authors and their assistants for their work on this important new publication. And to those people I have forgotten to mention, I apologize and offer my thanks.

Gayle Berens
Project Director

Contents

Remaking *the* **Urban Waterfront**

Chapter 1

An Introduction to Urban Waterfront Development

Laurel Rafferty and Leslie Holst

he resurgence of waterfronts began more than 40 years ago, when waterfront areas became centers of intense redevelopment activity. In Boston and San Francisco, pioneers in the field transformed wharves into thriving commercial and recreational areas. Within 15 years, waterfront revitalization projects had been undertaken across North America, and the redevelopment of both old seaports and inland waterfronts had become a major industry. This turn of events signaled a remarkable change in the previously grim prognosis for these once-abandoned areas.

Now that nearly 50 years have passed since the first of these efforts to remake the urban waterfront, it is a good time to take stock, and to ask which of the factors that figured in these early transformations are still relevant today, and what new factors have emerged. This chapter reviews the historical development of the waterfront and the roots of its transformation. The intent is to provide a context for evaluating the past and a foundation for moving forward.

Historical Development of the Urban Waterfront

Throughout the past several centuries, as North America was transformed from a sparsely populated wilderness into an industrial force and trading center, the waterfront has been essential to economic life.

Coastal Seaports

The first permanent European settlers traveled to the Americas via water routes, and for several hundred years thereafter, oceangoing vessels provided the only means of transporting people and products to and from the New World. Thus, all the early settlements in North America were founded in or near a protective harbor. These safe harbors provided security, accessibility, and a starting place from which to explore and settle.

A place of anchorage safe from harsh winters and the storms of the Atlantic was of cardinal importance to early colonists. Despite its physical distance from the ocean, Philadelphia was considered a great seaport because the width of the Delaware River (at Philadelphia, it is virtually an arm of the sea) and the characteristics of the surrounding geography created a level of safety that could not be found in more

Philadelphia, while 102 miles (164 kilometers) from Delaware Bay, enjoys ideal anchorage on the Delaware River, which is over three-quarters of a mile (1.2 kilometers) wide at the port.

While a major factor in Philadelphia's growth as a seaport was its upriver anchorage, the growth of the harbor at Charles Town (now Charleston), South Carolina, was due to its relative safety from storms. Its coastal position, however, required a pronounced military presence, part of which was provided by the Battery, now a shoreline promenade.

open ports. Similarly, the fact that the port at Charles Town (later Charleston), South Carolina, could provide safe anchorage for oceangoing vessels easily outweighed the inconvenience of having to drop anchor at a distance from the land and use barges to load and unload.

As economic activity increased, safe harbors evolved into fully functioning seaports—which, in turn, stimulated growth in the surrounding region. By the 18th century, five of the early colonial outposts had developed into small but thriving towns: Boston, Newport, New York, Philadelphia, and Charles Town, each with its own increasingly active seaport. Over time, these seaports became more sophisticated, adding complete docking and cargo-handling and storage facilities.

Waterfronts eventually became the focal points of all activity in their regions. They were important not only economically, but also as conduits for ideas and information. Waterfronts became central to the social and intellectual life of cities.

In Boston, where it was said that all streets led to the sea, colonists gravitated to Long Wharf. Those that did not go to sea set up shops, warehouses, and offices along the

Factors Contributing to the Resurgence of Waterfront Development

Available Land

The movement of cargo-handling facilities and factories away from the downtown waterfront meant that the land, often centrally located, was available and ripe for development. Depressed prices for waterfront property also served as a stimulus for entrepreneurs looking for an opportunity, and for local government officials seeking to revitalize urban areas.

Cleaner Water and Land

The deindustrialization of the waterfront, coupled with increased environmental regulation in the 1970s and 1980s, led to a significant improvement in water quality, which in turn helped make waterfronts more attractive to developers and consumers. The reclamation of brownfields, many of which were transformed into parks or attractive residential or commercial developments, also increased the aesthetic appeal of waterfront areas.

The Historic Preservation Movement

The 1960s and 1970s marked the beginning of the historic preservation movement, which recognized the aesthetic qualities of previously ignored older buildings. Preservationists actively lobbied to prevent the demolition of historically significant architecture that, in past decades, would have fallen to the wrecking ball. Preservationists were among the first to recognize the beauty of abandoned waterfront areas, places with picturesque views of the water and a plethora of historically significant (or at least interesting-looking) buildings and waterside structures.

Citizen Activism and Leadership

Though they periodically opposed developments, citizen activists also played an important role in the revitalization of urban waterfront areas. Activism reflects a commitment to the city and to improving its quality of life. Input from citizen committees, citizen leaders, or both has given many urban waterfront developments their legitimacy and spurred the essential cooperation, and perhaps even financial involvement, of local governments.

Urban Revitalization

The rebirth of the cities in the 1980s and 1990s, after decades of neglect and decay, is certainly one of the great stories of our time and a central factor in the redevelopment of urban waterfronts. As downtown business districts came back to life and cities again became centers for entertainment, downtowns were transformed from places that were virtually deserted after 5 p.m. to districts with an active nightlife. Concomitant with this transformation of the downtown was the revitalization of the waterfront. Similarly, waterfront development frequently followed or accompanied the building of new residential areas (like Battery Park, in New York City) adjacent to waterfronts. Residential developments also provided a ready consumer base for retailers, restaurants, and upscale bars that opened in revitalized waterfronts.

Diagonal Mar is a 34-hectare (84-acre) development by Hines Interests España of a decaying seaside industrial site in Barcelona. The project consists of a superregional retail and leisure center, 1,400 apartments at buildout, 950 rooms in three hotels, and three Class A office buildings. *Verónica Escudero*

The Return of Certain Water Uses

Downtown urban waterfronts may no longer be centers for commercial shipping, but the return of certain water uses has played an important role in waterfront redevelopment. Ferries and other kinds of water transportation attract users and give character to a development, in addition to providing transportation to downtown workplaces, to parks, and to other waterfront attractions not easily reached by other means. As interest in small-craft recreation has increased, the construction of small-craft marinas has played an important role in waterfront development.

---

harborfront. By 1720, local shipyards and merchants dominated the economic life of southern New England.

West Coast seaports developed later than those on the East Coast. San Francisco's first major pier, Long Wharf, was not built until 1849, and San Diego's first commercial wharf was built a year later. But the evolution from safe harbor to major seaport followed a pattern similar to that of East Coast ports.

Top: Long Wharf in Boston, Massachusetts, once extended 2,000 feet (610 meters) into Boston Harbor. Today, a hotel, restaurants, and shops line the wharf, just as in the colonial days, when the wharf was an extension of King (now State) Street. "Long Wharf" today appears to be something of a misnomer: 300 years of landfill have effectively shortened the wharf to 800 feet (244 meters). *Lenny Domzalski*

Bottom: Pittsburgh, Pennsylvania, where the Allegheny and Monongahela rivers join to form the Ohio, successively was a military outpost guarding this important river junction, a mercantile center, and an industrial power. Today, the three rivers enhance the city's quality of life by providing recreational and environmental benefits. *Riverlife Task Force*

Inland Ports

Until the introduction of railroads in the mid-19th century revolutionized transportation in North America, navigable rivers and canals provided the easiest (and, often, the most economical) way to transport people, livestock, and goods over long distances. Overland transportation, when it was available at all, was difficult and dangerous: the few roads were rudimentary, unpaved, and rarely well maintained.

Happily, North America was blessed with a number of highly navigable rivers, including the Mississippi and its numerous tributaries. Naturally, port cities—among them Cincinnati, Pittsburgh, and St. Louis—emerged along

these inland waterways. Pittsburgh, built on the Ohio River, was an important starting point for the shipment of goods to the Mississippi River and to all the inland ports along the Mississippi, down to New Orleans. Many merchants in coastal seaports first shipped goods overland to Pittsburgh (via covered wagon) and then loaded them onto barges and rafts for river travel downstream.

After the Louisiana Purchase, in 1803, all the ports along the Mississippi—including the important, formerly French ports in St. Louis and New Orleans—became American ports. Farmers in Cincinnati, for example, could then send goods entirely by water: down the Mississippi, across the Gulf of Mexico, and north to cities along the Atlantic seaboard. Recognizing the importance of the inland waterways, the U.S. Army established forts along the waterways to maintain security—which, as an added benefit, improved the safety and reliability of waterborne transportation.

In the second decade of the 19th century, the introduction of the steamboat increased the efficiency and importance of inland water transportation, cutting upstream shipping time by two-thirds. This technological innovation also spurred urban growth by making viable waterfronts even more important.

New York City, an important commercial port since its founding, gained further importance with the opening, in 1825, of the Erie Canal, which connected the Hudson River to Lake Erie and created an east-west trade route over water. Nevertheless, by 1835, the value of exports moving through Louisiana—approximately $54 million—was higher than the value of exports moving through New York.

Like the Mississippi, the Great Lakes were an important inland water route. Port cities that developed along the Great Lakes followed the same pattern as coastal seaports. Since the Great Lakes are essentially inland freshwater seas, subject to the same dangerous storms and killing waves as the oceans, the first Great Lakes ports, like their coastal counterparts, were founded in safe harbors. Toronto Bay provided such a harbor for the early settlers of York (later renamed Toronto), who built their town around the bay's inland port. The completion of the St. Lawrence Seaway, in 1959, increased the importance of the Great Lakes by opening another all-water trade route from the interior of the continent to the Atlantic; this route was particularly important for the transport of grain.

Impact of the Railroad

Railroads were a double-edged sword for water transportation. On the one hand, because they could move freight more quickly and more cheaply than could older forms of overland transportation, railroads provided valuable support to inland and coastal ports. But port cities that could not accommodate railroads ultimately suffered.

In St. Louis, for example, the old port area known as Laclede's Landing, although perfectly suited to the steamboat age, lacked sufficient unused land for the construction of rail yards. Because St. Louis's considerable railroad complexes

Toronto, Ontario, is an important harbor for the St. Lawrence Seaway, which extends 2,340 miles (3,700 kilometers) from the Atlantic Ocean to the head of the Great Lakes.

were built southwest of the levee and a mile or more away, the port—inadequately served by rail lines—atrophied. More important, as commercial and industrial activity moved away from the riverfront, the city lost its connection to the levee, and the area was allowed to decline.

With roots in the City Beautiful movement, Daniel Burnham's Plan of Chicago (1909) proposed an extensive, six-county open-space system of parks, transit, and neighborhoods that has kept Chicago's lakeside public, open, and green—in keeping with the city's motto, *Urbs in Horto*, "City in a Garden." *The Commercial Club of Chicago*

In Chicago, in contrast, where there was enough land to integrate the port and the rail yards, each strengthened the other. In addition, city leaders recognized early on the importance of the lake for recreational activity and endorsed a plan, by Daniel Burnham, that turned much of the lakefront into parkland without sacrificing any of the city's considerable commercial and industrial potential.

Over time, the railroad opened up the parts of the continent that lacked serviceable water routes, thus creating competition for established port cities. Railroads also competed directly with water-based transportation for freight traffic.

Urban Waterfronts over Time

Urban waterfronts, always intimately tied to their surroundings, reflect any change in the social, economic, or industrial climate. New technology, for example, periodically transforms waterfronts; and, when a waterfront cannot adopt a new technology, as was the case in St. Louis, the waterfront loses some of its vitality.

Historically, waterfronts have not been carefully or coherently planned. Growth has been disjointed and incremental, the result of a complex matrix of decisions and actions undertaken by numerous entrepreneurs and political jurisdictions. Thus, each urban waterfront will have its own idiosyncratic history. Those who are interested in

exploring development opportunities in a particular waterfront area must make a point of understanding its history, as it will influence the incentives for, and constraints on, future development.

Nevertheless, ports do develop in a more or less typical pattern. It is important to remember, however, that the "typical" pattern does not correspond to any one city, and that the scale of development and pace of change will vary according to the physical characteristics and the unique past of each waterfront city.

During the 19th century, timber and shipbuilding were mainstay industries of the port of Seattle, Washington, which peaked with the Alaska gold rush. Seattle's shipping industry brought in merchant seamen, sailors, and prospectors. Whether passing through or working at the docks, they frequented the waterfront neighborhoods, turning them into undesirable parts of the city. It was in Seattle that the term "skid row" was coined. *Tony Koski/Centrifugal Media*

The Succession of Waterfront Uses

The uses and spatial arrangement of a waterfront change over time. At first the waterfront is only a docking area, a place where passengers and goods embark and disembark. As the region's economic life becomes more diverse, the waterfront becomes home not only to maritime industries, such as cargo handling, fishing, and shipbuilding and repair,

The Typical Pattern of Port Development

1. The first prerequisite for establishing a port is the existence of a safe harbor suitable for cargo and passenger ships. Within the harbor, a small wooden jetty is constructed. This jetty is not large enough, nor is the channel deep enough, to allow ships to dock at the jetty. Instead, ships anchor offshore, and cargo is transported to the jetty by smaller boats. At this time, inhabitants have direct contact with the natural shoreline, and the waterfront is little more than a point where rough inland trails converge at the jetty. Over time, a street pattern slowly emerges.

2. In the next phase, one of rapid growth and development, the physical configuration of the waterfront significantly alters. A larger pier is usually installed to allow ships to dock, and more buildings are erected along the street grid. Seawalls and bulkheads are constructed to stabilize the shoreline and improve anchorage. A shoreline road still provides the primary access to the waterfront.

3. At this point, the settlement is fast becoming a city, and its waterfront is emerging as a port. Maritime commerce stimulates urban development, and the shoreline road becomes a busy street providing services, supplies, and office space for merchants and the shipping trade. Rows of newly constructed warehouses and other buildings block access to the water's edge.

4. With the advent of steamships, commerce escalates. Bigger docks, made of stone and fill, gradually replace wooden piers. As docking and anchorage facilities expand, the distance between the city's center and its shoreline increases significantly. A governing body—a port authority or commission—is established to manage shoreline activities.

5. As more warehouses are built and the first railroads appear, the port continues to thrive. With the introduction of railroads, a great amount of waterfront land is required both for tracks and for specially designed docks. To meet that demand, the city must create more land (the fill used for this purpose is often generated by the dredging operations that are undertaken to deepen the channel). These changes effectively sever the central city from the waterfront.

6. As the waterfront continues to expand, the distance between the original shoreline road and the water increases, and the shoreline road becomes less useful. The central city is effectively detached from the shoreline, and the waterfront becomes congested and difficult to maneuver through. To alleviate the congestion, an elevated highway is built near the shoreline, providing limited access to the city. Offices and stores along the old shoreline road are converted to warehouses.

7. In its next stage, the typical port development scenario follows one of two paths. If shipping declines, then the shoreline remains unchanged, the buildings along the old shoreline road are eventually demolished, and the expressway is widened.

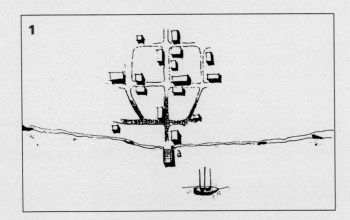

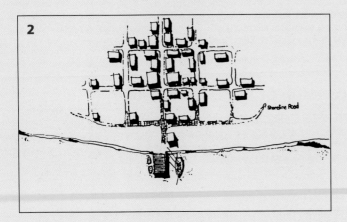

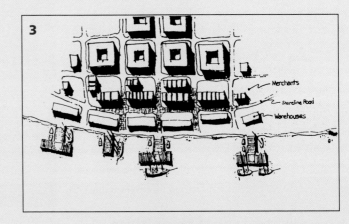

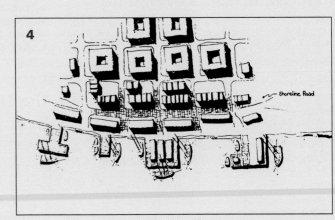

8. If shipping increases, then the port activities are expanded, more industrial uses are introduced, and wider piers are constructed.

9. Throughout this incremental development process, the scale of the waterfront increases significantly with the size of the elements of industrialization (trains, cranes, ships) in use. Today, the economically successful port resembles figure 9. In North America, however, the original port area rarely developed as a commercial shipping terminal because the ports were too constricted for modern container ships to maneuver easily and lacked adequate space for cargo storage.

10. An example of one pattern of contemporary mixed-use waterfront development.

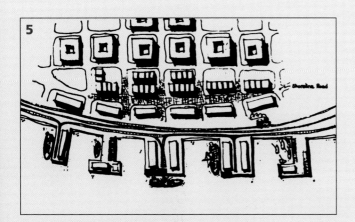

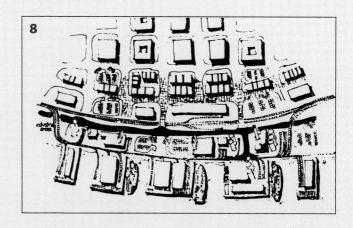

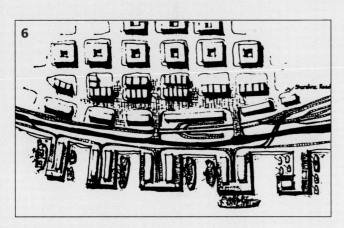

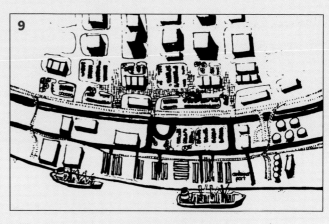

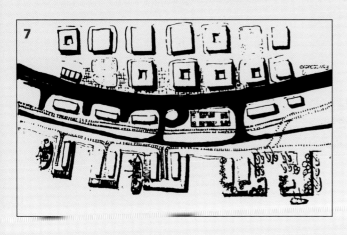

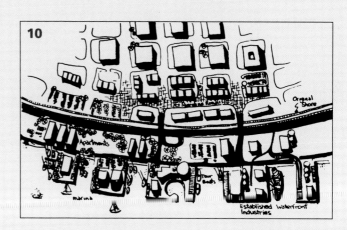

but also to other commercial ventures. Shops, inns, and small hotels spring up to serve the needs of the shipping industry; factories are built to manufacture the goods to be shipped; and warehouses are constructed to store both raw materials and finished products.

The industrial use of central urban waterfront areas reached its peak during the late 19th and early 20th centuries, with the development of a full network of railroads and the tight integration of rail and water transportation. This enhancement made waterfronts important centers for the movement of people and goods. As the 20th century progressed, however, a number of technological advances led to the decline of downtown waterfronts. Most notably, changes in shipping and cargo-handling methods made many older waterfront areas obsolete. Until World War II, ships spent substantial time dockside, as cargo holds were slowly emptied or filled. After the war, however, modern containerization techniques allowed material to be shipped in huge, but easily moved, containers, which considerably sped up the process of loading and unloading cargo. This shift necessitated the construction of larger warehouses to hold material that had previously been stored on board ships. Most older docking facilities also lacked the channel depths needed for the newer, larger ships used in the shipping industry. To gain access to deeper water and more land, ports moved downstream, to areas that were away from the downtown but still within the metropolitan area. The new port facilities built in these locations were equipped with advanced technology for loading and unloading and could accommodate the new shipping and warehousing techniques.

After World War II, a web of new state and federal highways and the rise of the trucking industry encouraged firms to leave the waterfront and the city for modern new suburban facilities, diminishing still further the importance of the waterfront. (It was no help that waterfronts had become, through years of industrial activity, areas of concentrated air and water pollution.) The automobile, too, encouraged cities and their surrounding suburbs to grow away from waterfront areas. And with the arrival, in the 1950s, of jet aircraft, passenger traffic on rivers, lakes, and oceans all but disappeared.

As downtown waterfronts were abandoned, the land was appropriated for other uses. Larger sites were leveled to make room for airports. On smaller waterfront sites, buildings were torn down for parking lots or transformed into storage areas. And many waterfront areas were stripped, or sliced apart, to make room for massive highway projects.

For many years, the prospects for abandoned urban waterfronts looked bleak. But in the 1960s, the resurgence of the urban waterfront began. As will be revealed in the rest of this book, waterfront redevelopment has evolved since the earliest efforts, and it continues to evolve.

As downtown waterfronts were abandoned, land was appropriated for other uses. In Tacoma, Washington, the Thea Foss Waterway became an industrial site and red-light district. Thea's Landing, completed in 2003, converted a full-block brownfield along the waterway to mixed uses, including 19,400 square feet (1,800 square meters) of retail space, a 423-car parking garage, and 236 residential units, both for-sale and rental. *Doug Scott*

In San Diego, competition between trade and tourism is intensified by the large presence of military bases and installations.

The Urban Waterfront Today

Today, cities across the world are striving to achieve many of the same objectives for their waterfronts—objectives that are striking both in their affirmation of earlier objectives and in their new emphasis. Cities seek a waterfront that is a place of public enjoyment. They want a waterfront where there is ample visual and physical public access—all day, all year—to both the water and the land. Cities also want a waterfront that serves more than one purpose: they want it to be a place to work and to live, as well as a place to play. In other words, they want a place that contributes to the quality of life in all of its aspects—economic, social, and cultural. Many waterfronts have already succeeded in achieving these objectives, and others are learning from their successes—a process this book is intended to facilitate.

Competition between Trade and Tourism

As the urban areas around waterfronts grow, the competition for the use of the waterfront is becoming more and more intense, and the demand for space is growing. The competition is especially keen between two key industry sectors: trade and tourism. With an increasingly global economy, international trade is booming. And, as trade grows, so does the transport of oceangoing goods and the demand for room at seaports to handle cargo.

At the same time, burgeoning trade produces economic growth, which often yields a rise in tourism. And as tourism increases, cities use an attractive, appealing waterfront as one way to help win this competition. Thus, tourism not only competes with port uses for waterfront space, but for control of the city's image: in the view of the tourism industry, industrial and other port uses damage the appeal of the waterfront. And, as limited waterfront space is fast being used up, the traditional practice of filling in harbors (to create more land for expanding uses and to buffer conflicting uses) is facing stiff environmental constraints.

The Changing Nature of Trade

Trade today is a more complex enterprise than ever before. Containerization is no longer the new story for ports. Instead, it is the increasing demand for door-to-door, just-in-time delivery of best-priced, custom-tailored goods. Modern trade means the transport not only of goods but also of information, to ensure efficient, seamless delivery to destination. Ports have become central to the logistics of transforming and transporting goods as they move from country to country, from raw to finished goods, and from generic products to made-to-order solutions to customers' needs—not incidentally, clearing customs and security as they go.

Advanced information and communications technologies are central to this new role: logistics is very much a "new economy" function of ports. And, as physical goods are being moved, tangible infrastructure remains as essential as the new "info-structure." The port's changing role translates into a need for space: to handle goods, to process them, and to move them, via connecting road, rail, or water links, across inland areas; and space along the way, if not in the port area itself, for the processing of goods and other logistics activities.

The Seaport Economy and Its Place on the Urban Waterfront

The seaport economy continues to shift in response to numerous trends. In some cases, the nature of modern shipping and cargo operations required ports to move to entirely new locations, sometimes many miles from the city where they began. Nevertheless, many seaports remain intimately tied, both physically and economically, to their surrounding cities. In fact, one of the most important trends in urban waterfront development is the effort to sustain traditional port uses while weaving connections between the seaport and the urban fabric. To this end, many cities are focusing on integrating their ports into the city, rather than allowing them to be segregated from other urban uses.

Integrating Port and City

Seattle's recently expanded and modernized container terminals are adjacent to its downtown. Sydney's first port remains in Sydney Harbour, near the central business district (CBD); when more space was needed, a second port, Botany Bay, was built within the city. And, though Botany Bay is nine miles (14.5 kilometers) south of the CBD, it has not escaped the march of urban development. Urban growth in this area has recreated the competitive pressures of the central harbor. Singapore's first three container terminals are within the densely developed city, a ten-minute drive from the downtown; its fourth terminal, recently constructed and state of the art, also within the city, is four miles (6.4 kilometers) to the west of the other three.

The Docklands notwithstanding, the Port of London is still one of the top three ports of the United Kingdom. While the 70 terminals and facilities within the port's authority extend 94 miles (151 kilometers) along the Thames to the North Sea, one-third of its facilities are maintained in London. As with most ports, however, London's major container terminals are located downstream of the city: Tilbury, one of the largest, is 20 miles (32 kilometers) from central London.

The Port of Genoa's newest cargo terminal is six miles (ten kilometers) to the west of the historic port. But cargo facilities were built as recently as 1988 at the immediate edge of the historic port; and, within the historic port, cargo functions were replaced by urban development and a passenger port: thus, port and city remain connected.

Genoa is not alone in linking port and city. In many parts of the world today, the growth of ports and their surrounding cities is leading to the integration of urban and port activities, including core port uses such as cargo handling; Kobe, Shanghai, and Rotterdam are notable examples. Kobe has built the new Port Island and Rokko Island, which combine port, port-related, manufacturing, housing, commercial, institutional, and green space uses. Shanghai, which is expanding its offshore islands to create a deep-water port, is connecting the port by bridge to a new port-city on the mainland. And in Rotterdam as well, the integration of port and city is key to the city's new vision for its port.

In fact, the integration of port and city uses is not such a new idea in Rotterdam or elsewhere. A long-time port expert with global experience has observed that Rotterdam, in the 1990s, and Ghent and Antwerp, in the 1980s, revitalized old port areas through new cargo-port uses. These initiatives indicate the cities' recognition that central urban areas can be good locations for small maritime firms, inland waterway barge operations, and cargo transport that relies on smaller-scale vessels (which, despite the trend toward larger ships, will continue to be used).

Sydney's primary port remains in Sydney Harbour, near the central business district. At right is the now-iconic Sydney Opera House, completed in 1973.

Port Island, in the harbor at Kobe, Japan, has been under construction since 1966. A new airport, under construction on additional landfill farther into Kobe Bay, is connected to Port Island by a causeway. *M. Murakami*

As many cities discover that low demand for port facilities may be temporary or cyclical, they are increasingly reluctant to make irreversible decisions to close port areas. The greatest risk of such closures is the inability to meet forecast increases in trade volume, which can threaten a port's ability to sustain its competitive position. Given the history of the Docklands, it is notable that for the 29 wharves east of the Thames Barrier, which are situated in close proximity to the Royal Alfred Dock and London City Airport, the British government has enacted measures that prohibit redevelopment for anything but port uses. Similarly, under a new investment strategy, the Port Authority of New York and New Jersey, whose major cargo terminals have long been in Newark, New Jersey, has identified terminals in Staten Island and Brooklyn as priority redevelopment areas for container facilities. Many ports around the world are struggling with and debating similar issues.

The Seaport as Cluster

The seaport economy is a classic cluster industry, consisting of multiple subsectors that, in the aggregate, make a significant contribution to the regional economy. In addition to cargo handling, these subsectors include the cruise industry; seafood harvesting, processing, and distribution; shipbuilding and repair; warehousing; marine services; and marine technology.

Cruise and ferry operations are a growth industry not only in the major U.S. cruise ports of Miami and New York, which serve the Caribbean, the largest market, but also in numerous other ports, which serve other geographic markets. Seattle, Miami, New York, and Boston are national centers for the distribution of seafood products, a growing segment of the seafood industry, which includes other subsectors such as commercial fishing (harvesting) and processing. Significant shipbuilding and repair operations, both government and commercial, can be found on the waterfronts of Philadelphia, San Diego, and New Orleans, to

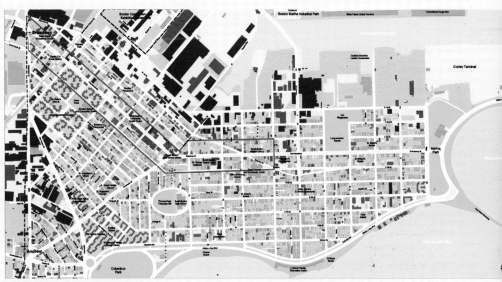

Source: Boston Redevelopment Authority

name but a few urban locations. Warehousing, a major marine service supporting cargo-handling operations, is generally found wherever there are cargo terminals.

Because of their proximity to world-class marine research institutes, the waterfronts of southern New England host a marine technology subsector. Maritime institutes themselves are part of the revitalization strategies of places such as Venice and Genoa. One such institute was started in Venice to decrease the city's dependence on tourism and to make productive use of the infrastructure of the historic shipbuilding site known as the Arsenale.

Key industries of the seaport economy, such as logistics, are part of the so-called new economy. The logistics capability of a port, with regard to both products and transport, is decisive in determining its competitive position; and, according to the Massachusetts Institute of Technology, logistics is the biggest industry sector in the world today—bigger than the health and life sciences industry.

As with any cluster industry, the seaport economy depends on the health of its individual elements. Competition for waterfront space—between the seaport industry and other industries,

such as tourism, and among seaport industries themselves—can cause some subsectors to be displaced, undermining the health of those that remain. In Oakland, for example, cargo terminals and urban uses are crowding out other port-related activities that are needed to support primary port functions.

Boston's Seaport Economy

Although the makeup of the seaport economy varies by location, a close look at one harbor will reveal the importance of the seaport economy. The Boston waterfront has been well publicized as an example of successful urban revitalization, and its continued success is reflected in the city's current plans for the South Boston and East Boston waterfronts. As indicated in a 1996 economic development plan jointly developed by the Massachusetts Port Authority and the city, Boston's waterfront offers not only a mix of residential, commercial, and recreational uses but also a thriving seaport economy that encompasses, in addition to the expected tourism and cargo-handling operations, cruise and ferry operations, seafood industries, ship repair, and marine service and support activities.

The Seaport Economy and Its Place on the Urban Waterfront (Continued)

The accompanying map shows that these activities are spread across the various waterfront neighborhoods of East Boston, Charlestown, and South Boston, and extend as well to the North

Source: www.mbta.com

End/Downtown Waterfront—which, while designated for mixed residential and commercial uses, plays an important role in water transportation. Rowes Wharf and Long Wharf, for example, are terminals for water taxis; cruises of all stripes; shuttles to Logan International Airport; commuter and excursion ferries to Boston Harbor communities and various Inner Harbor wharves; and recreational ferries to the Boston Harbor islands, Cape Cod, and Rhode Island.

According to the economic impact analysis undertaken as part of the 1996 economic development plan, Boston's seaport economy makes a major contribution to the overall regional economy: in the aggregate, the port and its associated indus-

tries handle $800 billion in goods annually and employ 9,000. While these numbers are impressive, the seaport economy's leading sector is cargo operations, which provides timely, reliable, safe, and cost-effective transport of the goods that consumers and businesses depend on. With increasing globalization, the port plays a more vital, "new economy" role in logistics: specifically, in the door-to-door delivery of just-in-time, made-to-order products.

It is commonly believed that commercial fishing is the principal activity in the seafood industry, and that because of the decline in fishing stocks, commercial fishing is, perhaps permanently, in decline. But the seafood industry is a much broader industry—and in Boston, it is not commercial fishing but distribution, a large and growing sector of the seafood industry, that has the greatest economic impact. By exploiting global sourcing networks, Boston has succeeded, despite the decline in fish stocks, in providing a steady supply of seafood to restaurants, hotels, fish markets, and processors—and in gaining a global competitive advantage.

Boston's seaport economic development plan first assessed the various subsectors of the seaport economy to identify those with significant growth prospects, then recommended actions to strengthen this growth. The economic impact findings, by sector, were as follows:

■ In the four years prior to the study, cruise-ship calls had tripled. The study predicted that during the next ten years, the impact of the cruise industry would double, and that by 2006, it would have $18.6 million in sales, employ 200, and yield $26 million in indirect revenues.

■ In direct impacts, the seafood industry contributed $724 million in annual sales, $177 million in income, and 1,900 jobs.
■ The ship repair industry employed an average of 175 and had the potential to expand.
■ The marine services industry consisted of 250 private businesses.

The objective of the Port of Boston, and the basis of its competitive strategy, was to establish itself as a full-service niche industrial port. The ship repair and marine service industries were identified as essential components of that strategy. The ship repair industry offered a means of providing employment for blue-collar workers, retaining a shrinking but important pool of skilled labor, and capitalizing on an enormous economic investment: the port's publicly owned dry-dock infrastructure. (It is worth mentioning that Boston's Drydock #3, a vast inverted pyramid made of granite, appears on lists of the most notable architecture in the city.)

Much of the seaport economy is dependent on a waterfront location, and it is essential to strike a balance among the many activities that compete for limited waterfront space. Boston's planning efforts have demonstrated that these uses do not have to be in conflict. Boston is promoting its port as an element of its tourist trade, designing pedestrian access routes to weave through the port. While up-close views of the port are interesting in their own right, they are intended to serve an important additional purpose: fostering awareness and appreciation of the port. Port uses—with their cargo and fishing vessels, dramatic industrial cranes, monumental drydocks, and gritty ship repair yards—add vitality and authenticity to urban waterfronts, enhancing their aesthetic appeal. In the words of a Sydney port official, absent a port, a waterfront is little more than a "dormitory beside a pond."

Boston's Seaport Economy

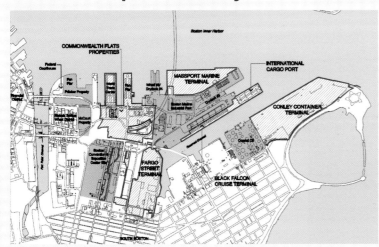

South Boston Waterfront Seaport Uses

- Seafood processing, distribution, wholesaling, importing, exporting
- Marine industrial park
- Conley Container Terminal
- Black Falcon Cruise Terminal
- Warehousing, distribution, freight forwarders
- Bulk cargo operations
- Light industrial
- Free trade zone
- Lobster fleet

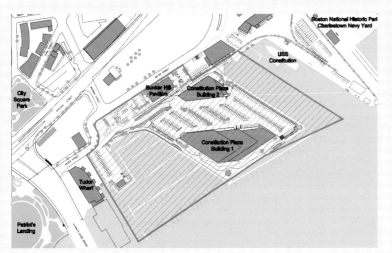

Charlestown Waterfront Seaport Uses

- Bulk cargo operations—mostly dry bulk, some liquid
- Moran Autoport
- Warehousing, distribution
- Light industrial

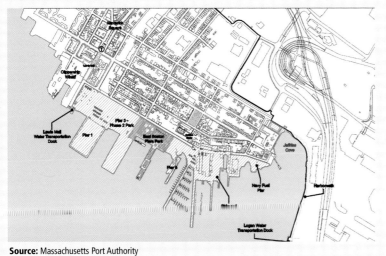

East Boston Waterfront Seaport Uses

- Smaller-scale marine services and support industries
- Harbor pilots' base
- Small lobster fleet
- Ferry terminal
- Petroleum-handling facilities

Source: Massachusetts Port Authority

As a loading dock and warehouse, then as a ferry terminal, and finally as a parking garage, Pier 1 symbolized the decline of San Francisco's old economy in favor of the new. The redevelopment project that converted its 90,000-square-foot (8,360-square-meter) footprint to a multitenant, two-level office building was the first in the Port of San Francisco's master plan of 1997. The development scheme underwent a 14-month entitlement process that had to gain the approval of 21 separate local, state, and federal agencies. *SMWM*

an increasingly important and effective means of achieving such a vision and ensuring that the public interest in the waterfront is honored. For example, early and frequent consultation with key stakeholders (waterfront users, civic groups, representatives of the multiple jurisdictional interests, and so on); well-advertised public participation programs in which input is sought at critical milestones; and other, similar measures have succeeded in producing agreement among conflicting interests. Planning processes stand to become even more effective through the application of new technologies, especially the Internet, which can be used to present information, gather input, post results, reach a global audience, and convey lessons learned.

The chapters that follow are testimony to the increasing expertise of planners and urban designers, who have successfully absorbed the lessons of the past and learned to formulate development programs that are not merely feasible but that achieve new, ever-increasing standards.

Today's Trends

Some of today's trends suggest what the waterfront of tomorrow may look like.

For innovative plans, China may be a place to watch. To relieve heavy congestion in urban areas, China is looking to establish new towns and cities in waterway locations; this approach would exploit the potential for seaport trade and waterfront tourism—and, by increasing the use of waterways as an alternative mode of transportation, would reduce demands on roadways. China has launched major international urban design competitions to attract world-renowned experts to the task of creating cutting-edge master plans for these new towns.

Major port cities, such as Rotterdam, Shanghai, and Kobe, see the integration of port and city uses as the solution to conflicts between uses; and in the United States, New York City may soon be following suit. With waterfront space at such a premium, this may be a trend to watch.

The movement toward integration is being helped along by other trends. The port and tourism industries, while competing for space, intersect more and more, par-

The port infrastructure that is essential to trade in consumer goods cannot readily be moved from its existing location because it represents too large a public investment. For transport to be cost-effective and for goods to remain competitively priced, ports must be situated in urban areas, in proximity to a critical mass of consumers. Thus, a major issue for the urban waterfront today is to ensure that ports can coexist harmoniously with their urban neighbors.

The Role of Planning

Experience has shown that the best plans for the urban waterfront—indeed, for any area—come from balancing interests and fashioning win-win scenarios. The goal is to strive for a coherent overall vision, rather than to settle for piecemeal, ad hoc solutions. Public planning processes, which have a demonstrated capacity to resolve conflicts between the port, the waterfront, and the city, are becoming

Riverfront development in Shanghai reflects the Chinese belief that the more the river is used, the more the river is valued. Shanghai takes pride in its 2,400 buildings that are over 20 stories high, and they extend the urban edge to the Huangpu River, mixing with port facilities. *Sasaki Associates*

ticularly as ports have begun to enter into the real estate and development business. To further progressive policies—that is, to be "good neighbors" on the urban waterfront—ports are developing some of their own real estate for urban uses, many of which are tourist based. The revenues generated are a source of income for port operations, and the new commercial and recreational activities revitalize previously underused port lands.

Ports are also coming to appreciate the appeal that their own industrial sites offer to tourists. While mindful of security needs, port authorities are removing barriers that had cordoned off such sites physically and visually, and are inviting public access, sponsoring guided tours, and providing observation decks for viewing harbor activities.

The burgeoning cruise industry is another critical intersection between the port and tourism sectors. According to the cruise industry, North American cruise ship travel is increasing in rough accord with cruise ship capacity, at an average of over 8 percent a year since the 1980s. Near cruise terminals, ports and cities are fostering synergistic commercial development that is compatible in use and scale with adjacent landside neighborhoods and is interdependent with water uses.

Not just cruise ships, but all manner of vessels once again ply the harbors and dock at the waterfront, including water taxis and ferries of every sort—freight and passenger, recreational and commuter, and interharbor; in many cases, waterfronts are intermodal junctions where waterborne

The port at Miami, Florida, calls itself "the cruise capital of the world." Air passengers flying in from throughout the United States to embark on a cruise vacation get a glimpse of what awaits them as their flight path into Miami International Airport takes them over the port and the American Airlines Arena, pointing them to an auspicious start of their holiday. *Basketball Properties, Ltd.*

Integrating Land- and Water-Based Perspectives and Diverse Waterfront Uses: The Portland, Maine, Experience

Balancing the range of critical interests in the waterfront—the public interest; the interests of those who live, work, play, or own property there; the economic interests of the surrounding community and region—is an art. The master-planning process for the Eastern Waterfront Project, in Portland, Maine, is an example of this art in practice. Recognizing that the preservation of a range of perspectives and uses was crucial to the economy, culture, and identity of the community, Portland has undertaken an exemplary initiative.

Background

Protecting its working waterfront is important to Portland, a city with a strong identity as a fishing community. Like many other communities, Portland faced pressure from heightened interest in mixed-use waterfront development. And, like many other communities, Portland attempted to use zoning measures—often hotly contested—to strike the right balance between competing interests. One of the biggest lessons of Portland's experience may be that success is defined not by whether individual zoning or development proposals are approved or denied, but by whether, after a period of years, a community can create an overall vision of which uses shall be allowed where.

By 2001, when Portland initiated its new master-planning project for the Eastern Waterfront, the waterfront was considerably different than it had been 15 years earlier. In addition to an active traditional fishing industry, there were marinas, condominiums, and commercial, non-water-dependent uses at the water's edge (some of which, by 2001, would no longer have been allowed in their current locations). Through extremely rigorous zoning, an extensive zone had been reserved exclusively for working waterfront uses. The new zoning reflected an understanding that there can be competition not only between water-dependent and non-water-dependent

The harbor at Portland, Maine. *Shannon Doyle*

activities, but also among water-dependent uses, and that working waterfront uses, in particular, can easily be displaced in both competitions.

Portland's current zoning consists of two key waterfront districts: (1) the new zone reserved for the working waterfront and (2) a more flexible zone. The more flexible zone, at the heart of the city's waterfront and abutting the historic downtown, is the Waterfront Central Zone (WCZ). It sits on the shore side of Commercial Street, the main public way along the waterfront, and sets the boundary between waterfront zoning and the upland areas covered by a variety of business districts. The Waterfront Port Development Zone (WPDZ), the area that provides maximal protection to working waterfront uses, flanks the WCZ to the east and west.

Within the WCZ, uses are assigned priority: top priority is given to water-dependent uses, and second priority to marine and marine-related support uses. Other specified uses are allowed to the extent that they do not interfere with, and are com-

patible with, the high-priority uses. Permitted uses include seafood loading and processing, shipbuilding and repair, marine product distribution, and cargo handling, among others. Uses such as hotels, residences, and convention facilities are prohibited. Other non-water-dependent uses, such as restaurants and offices, are allowed under various conditions intended to ensure a harmonious relationship with the desired water-dependent uses (for example, if such uses are within 35 feet [11 meters] of Commercial Street, or are above the ground floor and meet certain other requirements). Uses in the WPDZ are limited to those that are dependent on a deep-water location and contribute to port activity.

Zoning in the core WCZ and WPDZ districts prohibits any uses that would have an adverse impact on future marine development opportunities. The prohibition reflects the value that the community places on preserving the option of using the waterfront for port activity in the future. The zoning ordinance specifically identifies impermissible impacts. One, critical to the protection of the fishing industry, is designed to prevent a reduction in the amount of berthing space available for commercial vessels.

The protection of berthing space for commercial fishing was the subject of a long struggle for Portland. A 1996 comparative study of fishing communities revealed the value of Portland's working waterfront; in particular, the study found that the fishing industry was a central component of the city's industrial sector. Interestingly, the study also found that the working waterfront had a synergistic value in attracting other waterfront uses:

Much of the development of the harbor in the past ten years has been the growth of condominiums and other real estate development that often competes with commercial fishing for space and aesthetics. Despite these changes, commercial fishing in Portland remains a core industrial segment, important in the city's identity and history. Indeed, those responsible for monitoring waterfront development see non-marine-related uses of space along the waterfront as directly tied to marine-related uses in positive ways.[1]

The Eastern Waterfront Master Plan

When Portland undertook the development of the Eastern Waterfront Master Plan, it ushered in a new, comprehensive planning effort that offered a chance to absorb the lessons of past experience and redefine standards. The first phase of the project concentrated on the easternmost waterfront, an underutilized area threatened by increasing vacancies. Of particular concern was the fact that an existing port industry situated on city-owned property had indicated that it might not renew its lease, which was about to expire.

A major element of the master plan called for the relocation of an international ferry operation to the area. The ferry operation currently shared space with a container cargo facility on Portland's western waterfront, in an area no longer large enough for the two operations. The new eastern waterfront location, which had been recommended by a 1999 cargo and passenger study, offered two advantages: (1) available, publicly owned property and infrastructure, and (2) a location that was closer to both the harbor entrance and the historic downtown area, which would bring both navigational and economic development benefits.

A second element of the plan involved the creation of a redevelopment program to support the new terminal facility. The program was to focus on an area that was adjacent to the terminal and that included both publicly and privately owned property. The goal was to develop a cohesive program of complementary uses that would optimize benefits for the community and region and minimize negative impacts; special regard was to be given to the effects on surrounding neighborhoods.

As was characteristic of Portland, the entire master-planning process was marked by vigorous public debate. There were numerous scheduled opportunities for public comment, beginning in the scoping phase, continuing through the public design charrette at the initiation of the planning process, and including committee meetings, hearings, and Internet exchanges throughout the process.

As the planning effort progressed to the key task of identifying alternative proposals, questions focused on how best to address the significant parking and security needs of the international ferry terminal while responding to a range of important interests—namely, those of (1) island residents, who wanted to preserve parking in proximity to the island ferry operation located in the project area; (2) owners of property in the vicinity of the project; and (3) trail enthusiasts, who were concerned that security barriers might be proposed between customs and the terminal that would disrupt existing public access to the waterfront network running through the site. While these interests posed challenges, they were known and attention was directed at addressing them; a larger difficulty was uncertainty about whether all interests were being identified, understood, and responded to.

In parallel with the issues posed by the various alternatives, three persistent questions emerged that challenged some of the very premises of the planning process. The first was whether the eastern waterfront was indeed the best relocation option for the international ferry operation. This question was serious enough to lead, midway through the planning process, to a reassessment of the location possibilities, which ultimately confirmed the original decision. The second question, which concerned the economic benefits of the ferry operation, led to calls for an economic impact analysis, and to efforts to reverse the decision to include this costly component.

The third question loomed large. While one of the goals of the project was to develop a plan that would create synergy between the ferry terminal and other development, there was concern that waterfront rezoning would likely be necessary to accomplish this objective. And, because the community's memory of previous zoning conflicts was still fresh, rezoning was anathema.

Treatment of the Water's Edge

With two existing piers in the project area, there were substantial physical waterside assets to work with, allowing a range of alternative development proposals. The State Pier, also known as Pier One, was the larger of the two. It was 1,000 feet (305 meters) long and included a 100,000-square-foot (9,290-square-meter) cargo shed that extended virtually the length of the pier. Since 1983, the 600-foot- (183-meter-) long Pier Two had been the site of a private ship repair and overhaul facility, but this activity had come to an end when the Bath Ironworks decided to consolidate its operations at its main facility rather than to renew its lease.

The organizational structure of the planning effort foreclosed some of the options that might have been considered for the integrated treatment of the piers and uplands. Two committees were involved, each with its own consultants: one was focused on the development of the ferry terminal and the other on the area master plan and its impact on the uplands. Unfortunately, the terminal committee and consultant began their work in advance of the master-planning committee, and thus the structure and timing of the process prevented important early collaboration between the consultant for the master plan and the facilities consultant.

Nevertheless, later coordination between the two committees led to the recommendation to create an intermodal transportation hub that would maintain the flexibility of the pier infrastructure to accommodate changing trends in port industries. The State Pier would, for the time being, remain in its current use, as an island ferry terminal facility (decisions about the eventual future of the State Pier were deferred to a subsequent planning phase). The international ferry terminal would be located on an expanded Pier Two, and parking needs for that facility would be met on adjacent uplands. On the uplands, a phased buildout was recommended to allow for different possible building scenarios, depending on the nature of the public/private partnership that was to be arranged for the development of city-owned and privately held land.

Within this overall framework, the plan recommended guidelines that are a model for the treatment of the water's edge. The guidelines promote the integration of land- and water-based perspectives, recognizing that it is the interaction between land and water activities that will continue to create the value and identity of the Portland waterfront.

As an intermodal transportation hub, the project site will handle a broad range of waterside craft—not only the international ferry but also other passenger boats, and private and emergency vessels. The marine passenger terminal will be located where the waters are deepest and capable of accommodating the ferry; to the east of Pier Two, where the water is more shallow, berthing space will be available for smaller vessels. The transition from deeper to shallower water provides the basis for the guidelines for the water's edge. Just as the size of the vessels to be berthed shifts from larger to smaller according to water depth, the corresponding landside development changes in use, scale, access, and intensity of impact.

Integrating Waterfront Uses

Since the vision of the master plan is to create not only an intermodal transportation hub but also synergistic, mixed-use development, the challenge was to achieve both objectives, given current zoning.[2] The WPDZ, which applied to an extensive portion of the project area, essentially restricted uses to those that were dependent on deep water and contributed to port activity. In addition to encompassing Pier One and Pier Two, the zone extended deeper into the uplands than did the other waterfront districts. Consultations suggested that a zoning change that permitted mixed uses that were economically or operationally supportive of port activity would meet the plan's dual objectives and would also be consistent with the plan's guidelines for the water's edge.

Because of the community's strong sentiments about zoning change, the analysis that was undertaken as part of the planning process explored rezoning alternatives that were (1) the simplest possible and (2) had a precedent in existing zoning. Precedents that already existed in the WCZ became the basis for a rezoning proposal and were adapted to allow a limited percentage of specified mixed uses in the WPDZ. Though the rezoning proposal was not formally incorporated as a recommendation of the master plan, the plan laid firm groundwork for making the regulatory change. (It should be noted that the current zoning already provides for some mixed uses and for public access, and that pedestrian use and bicycle trails are both permitted. When the next step is taken, the zone would allow a viable and vital integration of working waterfront, water-dependent, non-water-dependent, and public access uses).

As further steps in the development of the plan will take time, Portland—true to its character, business culture, and principles—has found a temporary, revenue-generating use for Pier Two. The Eastern Waterfront Master Plan responds to the need for increased public access to the water through increased park development, relocation of the eastern promenade trail to the water's edge east of Pier Two, and design guidelines that promote direct access and use of the water by the general public wherever safe and reasonable.

Given the general underuse of the Eastern Waterfront, a new generation of zoning regulations for the area could ensure a mix of uses—landside and waterside, water-dependent and non-water-dependent—that better represent the community's current vision of its waterfront.

Notes

1. David Griffith and Christopher Dyer, *An Appraisal of the Social and Cultural Aspects of the Multispecies Groundfish Fishery in the New England and the Mid-Atlantic Regions* (Institute for Coastal Marine Research and Aguirre International, 1996).

2. While a significant component of the project addressed rezoning for the envisioned upland development, the focus here is on the use of the water's edge, within the existing WPDZ.

transportation meets various land-based forms of transport. Other more rare, but important, vessels are also found on harbor waters—hospital or research ships, for example.

The design and construction of state-of-the-art ferries is one element of a new marine technology industry that is appearing on the waterfront. The elements of this industry that are water dependent, like ferry terminals, are particularly suited to a shore-area location. These activities that make use of both the water and the land are also mixing up the categories of work and recreational pursuits.

Contrary to common perception, elements beyond the cargo-handling, cruise, and tourism industries still make a significant contribution to regional economies. The example of the seafood industry is telling. Even in cities known for their high-tech sectors and knowledge-based industries, the comparative economic impact of the seafood industry is significant. Studies done in Boston in the 1990s, for example, showed that the seafood industry in the aggregate contributed $4 billion at the time that the booming high-technology sector generated $5 billion.

Power plants and petroleum-related uses have long been situated in waterfront areas, but the activities related to the alternative energy industry are now finding a place there as well. For example, waterfront sites may serve as staging areas for the development of ocean-based wind farms, or may host facilities that support these developments.

The future always has a way of surprising us. One wild card for the waterfront is the high-speed ship. Advanced technology is making possible the construction of ocean-going vessels of such speed and economy that they have the potential to fill a niche between fast but expensive air transport and slower but cheaper waterborne transport for the delivery of high-value, time-sensitive goods. It is difficult, though intriguing, to speculate about the impact of the mega-ship, with its mega-requirements, on international trade and the movement of consumer and business goods.

The remaining chapters of this book focus on the issues involved in transforming the areas of the waterfront that are outside the realm of the port. Chapter 2 looks at the important considerations in undertaking such transformations. Subsequent chapters look at the urban design, implementation, and environmental issues related to such efforts. The book concludes with a collection of case studies.

The chapters that follow reveal just how much has been learned about remaking the urban waterfront. They are a reminder, most importantly, of what is perhaps an old lesson, expressed aptly by Bonnie Fisher in chapter 3: because of its singular characteristics, "the waterfront needs to embody dual realms of land and sea; it needs to speak two languages."

Chapter 2

The Transformation of the Urban Waterfront

Alex Krieger

I t was known for centuries as "Genoa the Superb," not simply for its leading role in the seafaring culture of the Mediterranean but for its unforgettable silhouette as seen from the sea. As it embraces its harbor in an amphitheater-like form, the city of Genoa appears to have been carved from the coastal mountains, and the mountains themselves seem to rise straight from the sea. To visit Genoa is to immediately feel the power of place made possible by inhabiting a portion of the earth at water's edge. While Genoa is blessed with a particularly memorable geography, it is hardly alone among cities whose waterfronts provide indelible images of place—and that have, periodically in their cities' histories, become catalysts for dramatic urban change and renewal.

Urban waterfronts are unrivaled in their potential for providing an exceptional or celebratory enterprise. Imagine the Sydney Opera House, or the Guggenheim Museum in Bilbao, or even Cleveland's Rock-and-Roll Hall of Fame not juxtaposed against each city's body of water. The London Eye, London's majestic Ferris wheel, actually sits in the Thames. Much of contemporary Chicago's identity and self-image, not to mention wealth, comes from the spectacular, 20-mile- (32-kilometer-) long facade that stretches along the shore of Lake Michigan. Where else but along the mighty Mississippi would the citizens of St. Louis have constructed their monumental Gateway to the West? Humanity, it seems, delights in and finds inspiration at waterfront settings, but increasingly asks more of them than mere spectacle.

As Americans, recalling urban pleasures, seek to recover the virtues inherent in city living, and return to places that had been nearly abandoned during a century of suburbanization and industrial relocation, urban waterfronts are more appealing than ever, and for a broader array of reasons. Along the waterfront, it seems possible to accommodate the changing needs of today's urban dwellers, as modern society continues its shift from an industrial-based economy, with its attendant spatial demands, to a service- and lifestyle-based economy, with its own requirements.

Ten Principles of Waterfront Development

To take advantage of the opportunities afforded at the water's urban edge and to succeed in new development there, the following issues must be considered:

1. The transformation along the urban waterfront is a recurring event in the life of a city, and tends to occur when major economic or cultural shifts lead to conflicting visions of contemporary urban life.[1]

Without water in sight, this image is instantly recognizable as belonging to Venice, Italy. A powerful identity of place is inherent in most urban settings near water. *Alex Kreiger*

A view from one of London's newest landmarks, the London Eye, which is quite naturally located along—actually, standing in—the Thames. *Alex Kreiger*

2. The aura of a city largely resides and endures along its waterfront, allowing substantial changes to occur without inevitably harming its enduring qualities of place.

3. Despite periodic and sometimes rapid change, a waterfront preserves for its bordering city some inherent and unalterable stability.

4. As valuable and often contested realms, urban waterfronts bring forth the opposing, though reconcilable, human desires to preserve and to reinvent.

5. Even though a waterfront serves as a natural boundary between land and water, it must not be conceptualized or planned as a thin line.

6. Waterfront redevelopments are long-term endeavors with the potential to produce long-term value. Endangering this for short-term riches rarely produces the most desirable results.

7. Underused or obsolete urban waterfronts come alive when they become desirable places to live, not just to visit.

8. The public increasingly desires and expects access to the water's edge. This usually requires overcoming historic barriers—physical, proprietary, and psychological—while persuading new investors that there is merit in maintaining that valuable edge within the public domain.

9. The success and appeal of waterfront development is intrinsically tied to the interrelationship between landside and adjacent waterside uses—and to the environmental quality of both the water and the shore.

10. Distinctive environments, typically found at waterfronts, provide significant advantages for a city's competitiveness in its region or in relation to its rival cities.

These ten considerations provide the framework for the remainder of this chapter, which examines how a number of cities are responding to the challenge of their waterfronts.

Principle One

The transformation along the urban waterfront is a recurring event in the life of a city, and tends to occur when major economic or cultural shifts lead to conflicting visions of contemporary urban life. Consider Boston.[2] Its history demonstrates two important lessons regarding waterfront development: (1) the re-planning of a waterfront is a recurring need, and (2) undue caution is rarely the proper course.

As it has throughout its 370-year history, Boston is redesigning one of its waterfronts. The newly renamed South Boston Seaport District, an area exceeding 700 acres (283 hectares) in size and lying directly east of the downtown, is poised to receive the next expansion of downtown Boston. Following substantial public investment in regional access, including a new harbor tunnel that brings the airport to the district's doorstep, the Seaport District is brimming with anticipation, plans, and potential investors, although negative fluctuations in the economy take their toll. The area is also brimming with worries and political controversy.

View of central Boston: much of the city's present perimeter was captured from the sea through two centuries of land making. *Alex McLean/Landslides*

The area now known as the Seaport District was created a century ago through a massive landfill. The goal was to create a modern boat-to-rail port that would replace the historic central port, which was by then too congested to accommodate new infrastructure of the scale required for modern ships and efficient rail connections. However, since it reached its peak during World War II, the South Boston waterfront has undergone major changes in land use: some large areas are still underused, while others are being redeveloped to meet the needs of a competitive contemporary port. Shipbuilding, military, transatlantic passenger, multistory warehouse, and narrow-apron cargo operations have given way to a modern container port, cruise terminal, logistics center, marine industrial park,

and seafood industry. But areas that were once the site of major rail yards have for some time hosted large parking fields and similar supporting uses for the nearby downtown. Though a world trade center and some landmark restaurants occupy piers and other nearby space, the vast parking lots and other areas used during the construction of the new harbor tunnel have for years essentially served as a land bank, awaiting better regional access— and, more important, demand for renewal.

Seemingly overnight, the area is becoming home to convention venues, hotels, luxury housing, parks, and a cultural amenity or two. But some wonder whether, once the planned array of tourist and residential uses is realized (more than 20 million square feet—1.8 million square meters—are in various stages of planning or design), the locally and regionally important seaport economy can still be sustained. And the concern is not only about the survival of the seaport economy and the preservation of a harmonious port-city relationship; it extends to overbuilding, traffic congestion, gentrification, affordability of housing, and the long-term effects on the adjacent South Boston community—long a cohesive, predominantly Irish-American, working-class neighborhood that is generally intolerant of outside influence.

Maintaining industrial jobs for the residents of South Boston—jobs that are competitive in pay with those being lost, and for which South Boston residents are or can become qualified—is another concern. There is also concern about the preservation of public waterfront space and public access to the water; about the balance of uses being planned; about the public's ability to guide the actions of large and powerful landowners; about whether too much history will be erased; and about who stands to gain or lose, both politically and economically.

Similar concerns have arisen during prior periods of Boston's waterfront development history. Few of the world's cities have witnessed as substantial a change to their natural geographies as has Boston. As one walks around central Boston, it is nearly impossible to imagine that the original Shawmut Peninsula was virtually an island, or that four out

Photomontage of Boston: a contemporary aerial view shows the areas of filled lands; the reddish tint depicts today's actual land configuration, showing that 80 percent of the land area depicted in this map is landfill. *Chan Krieger & Associates*

nearly 40 years, from the late 1850s through the 1890s. The effort, which produced one of the nation's most distinctive residential districts, was further augmented in the 1930s, with the completion of the Charles River Esplanade. Indeed, the Charles was eventually graced with a continuous, 18-mile- (29-kilometer-) long public domain along both its Boston and Cambridge banks. Frederick Law Olmsted's late-19th-century work on Boston's park system produced Day Boulevard, Pleasure Bay, and Marine Park, a continuous open space along the southern and eastern edges of the South Boston Peninsula.

of five acres (1.6 out of two hectares) have been created by human intervention. To prosper amid a geography of steep hills, tidal flats, and marshes, the city had no choice but to make land. Beginning in the mid-18th century, an expanding seafaring economy led the city to push outward into its harbors and bays to gain usable land.

Land was made in two ways: by "wharfing out" (filling the slips between wharves) and by dumping into the harbor the land that had been scraped from the steepest hills to make them easier to settle. These efforts foreshadowed the much larger 19th-century land-making ventures that created the topography of modern Boston. In all, some 3,500 acres (1,416 hectares) of land were created (including much of the land on which Logan Airport is built), through more than a dozen major landfill initiatives spanning a 200-year period.

Among the remarkable waterfront environments that these efforts yielded is Quincy Market, an "urban renewal" project that dates not to the 1970s, when the market was reimagined by James Rouse as the first "festival marketplace," but to the 1820s, when a town dock was filled to create the land on which the first market buildings were built.

The venture that called for 600 acres (240 hectares) of the Back Bay to be filled preoccupied Bostonians for

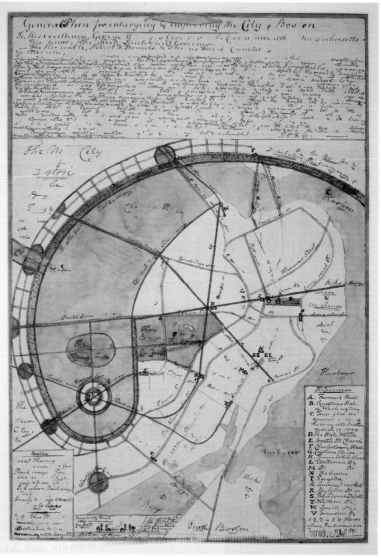

Boston's Charles River Basin, imagined as a continuous public open green space lined by residential districts, as depicted by Robert Gourlay, in 1844—nearly a full century before its contemporary implementation. Dreaming of pleasurable public access along the natural edge of urban waters is not a new human tendency.

While the end of the 1940s brought construction of the Central Artery, severing the waterfront from the city, the beginning of the 1960s ushered in the adaptive use or reconstruction of Boston's oldest wharves, including Long Wharf, Central Wharf, Lewis Wharf, and a number of others in the North End. The effort yielded one of America's earliest transformations of old and obsolete wharf architecture into a modern, mixed-use waterfront area.

The confluence of the Monongahela, Allegheny, and Ohio rivers (the "Rivers of Steel"), circa 1950, toward the end of Pittsburgh's mighty industrial era. Before long, the city's six riverbanks would no longer be lined with factories and steel plants, and the long search for a different relationship to the rivers would begin. *Pittsburgh Riverlife Task Force*

It is Boston's impressive record during prior eras of waterfront renewal—generally eschewing conventional wisdom while producing striking and distinct environments—that should prepare the city well for succeeding with the Seaport District, despite current worries. Nevertheless, a sense of impending loss currently pervades, as if the future about to unfold will prove less desirable than present circumstances. And this uneasiness constrains vision. During past renewal efforts, however, conflicting interests and competing visions were eventually reconciled on behalf of larger public purposes, such as expanding the landmass or accommodating new uses in neglected waterfront areas. Maintaining the status quo was not a high priority—nor should it be, at moments of impending economic change.

Pittsburgh's current vision of its future: a city facing and embracing, rather than receding from, its rivers. *Chris Ritter/Chan Krieger & Associates*

Principle Two

The aura of a city largely resides and endures along its waterfront, allowing substantial changes to occur without inevitably harming its enduring qualities of place.

There is an enduring quality to a city's waterfront as it bears witness to—and often takes the brunt of—the ebbs and flows of a city's prosperity. Seizing upon this aura during a period of change is key to successful waterfront planning.

Take Pittsburgh and its three rivers—the Rivers of Steel, as they were called. As in many cities that thrived during the industrial age, the main role of Pittsburgh's rivers was, until recently, to buttress the city's industrial might. For miles, the banks of the rivers were places of production, and of transportation infrastructure to support that production. At the height of the steel era, few even recalled that the initial reason for the city's siting was to gain territorial control over the strategically important confluence of the Monongahela, Allegheny, and Ohio rivers—not to facilitate the processing of raw materials.

In terms of economic well-being, the rivers were essential; but in terms of living, recreating, celebrating, governing, socializing, touring, siting cultural institutions, entertaining visitors, communing with nature—all the varied urban functions that are found on waterfronts today—the Pittsburgh rivers were secondary. Such activities took place elsewhere, as far from the industrial banks as possible (or at least downwind of the stacks), or far above, on the hilltops, where the soot was less pervasive.

Today, Pittsburgh (and it is hardly alone) is trying to determine how to turn itself "inside out." In the city's next iteration, its industrial backyard is to become its frontyard. The Riverlife Task Force—drawn from the leaders of the corporate, cultural, philanthropic, real estate, and political communities—is charged with the task of overseeing the transformation. And the task will be a difficult one—physically, emotionally, and fiscally, especially since the metropolitan area is not in an era of substantial growth.

Nevertheless, it is clear that for the city to thrive again, a metamorphosis must occur along its rivers. Those who will be drawn to the city in the future, or who will choose to remain, will do so not because steel mills and rail yards once dotted the riverfronts but because the riverfronts will be accessible, green, beautiful, and clean; will offer great places to live; will support modern expectations for quality of life; and, finally, will preserve important moments of Pittsburgh's history—minus the unhealthy air and industrial din.

Valuable as they have been for two centuries of intensive and vital use, the three rivers of Pittsburgh are also proving to be the best catalysts for the city's renewal. In the past several years, more than a billion dollars has been invested in the proximity of the six riverbanks. A new baseball park and football stadium have opened, along with several riverfront parks. Along the Allegheny, the Alcoa Corporation has built an architecturally impressive headquarters; across the river is a new convention center that is not only an architectural landmark but is also renowned for its "green" engineering. The Carnegie Science Center is in the midst of a sizable expansion designed by Jean Nouvel. The Mon Wharf expressway is being partially recon-

An aerial view of Pittsburgh, 2004, in the process of bringing to reality the city's vision of its future. The riverbanks are dedicated to parks, to public spaces, and to places of assembly, recreation, and culture. *Pittsburgh Riverlife Task Force*

structed in a way that will permit public access to the Monongahela, which has been blocked by the highway since its original construction.

These projects are complemented by more modest though hardly less important improvements, such as a riverbank trail system. While seeking broad economic investment, Mayor Tom Murphy (an avid runner and cyclist) has also doggedly advocated extending the riverfront trail and water-access system, mile by mile, to eventually form a continuous public way along the entire urban segments of the three rivers and even beyond.

A change in local attitudes toward the rivers is well under way. Pride no longer stems from their faded glory as the Rivers of Steel, but resides instead in their power to enhance the daily experience of living or working in the city. Geographically, the great confluence of the three rivers remains, but it is now surrounded by emblems of today's idea of the good urban life: great places to live and to assemble, to enjoy nature, and to encounter culture.

Redesigning the character of the rivers and the roles that they serve is enabling Pittsburgh to recapture the magic, magnetism, and even exoticism that all great cities must have as they compete with their sprawling peripheries and a world economy. The Riverlife Task Force is aptly named, for it recognizes the life-giving powers of the city's oldest asset.

Now consider Shanghai, a city at a very different point in its evolution. Rome may not have been built in a day, but Shanghai appears determined to prove that such a thing can be done. In a little over a century, the city has been transformed from a major commercial port city to a multifunctional megalopolis whose population is soon expected to reach 20 million. The full impact of the city's extraordinary growth is being felt today. While Americans worry about sprawl and about disinvestment in their core cities, in Shanghai, it is as if Manhattan and Los Angeles are emerging concurrently. Incredibly, Shanghai is committed to constructing 1,800 miles (2,900 kilometers) of elevated highways in the metropolitan area over the next decade. Exuding optimism about its future, the city takes pride in the more than 2,400 buildings (and counting) that are over 20 stories high, and shows none of the sentimentality, so common today in the West, about the "good old days."

Amid such confidence in the city's capacity to absorb massive change, can the DNA of Shanghai's earlier incarnation survive, much less sustain relevance? Many in the city answer affirmatively, as they rally around a series of ambitious plans to reorient modern, cosmopolitan Shanghai to its ancient river, the Huangpu, and to clean up its principal tributary, Suzhou Creek. While there will be many future highways, points out Zheng ShiLing, vice president of Tongji University, there will only be one river. Precisely because everything in Shanghai (which means "upriver to the sea" in Chinese) is currently in flux, recommitting to the river is vital, and culturally reassuring. After all, as Professor ShiLing notes, "Water reflects the morality and wisdom of our nationality." Such near-mystical associations are not unique to Asian cultures, and are valuable for waterfront planning anywhere.

Welcoming modernization and growth, yet sure of the river as a stabilizing force and an enduring amenity, planners in Shanghai are less concerned than their North American counterparts about precisely determining the most appropriate scale and uses along the riverbanks. In North American cities, a general unease about the effects of growth has led to a belief that certain uses—commercial spaces, or perhaps tall buildings—will forever damage the proper relationship between a city and its harbor. In Shanghai, such concerns are at the moment secondary to the belief that the more the city focuses on the river, the more faithful it will remain to its own heritage.

Principle Three

Despite periodic and sometimes rapid change, a waterfront preserves for its bordering city some inherent and unalterable stability. When compared with present-day Shanghai, Boston and Pittsburgh seem stable and unchanging. Yet imagine an expatriate returning to Boston after an absence of 50 years, not a particularly long period in the life of a city. He would have left a mid-20th-century city where the historic waterfront was emptying; where the port, once thriving, was diminishing in size; where maritime infrastructure had been abandoned; where the not-so-busy wharves were being used to store a different kind of commodity—parked cars for the downtown; and where pollution and decay were clearly evident. Of course, the waterfronts of many industrial-era cities experienced similar fates, and many have yet to recover.

Could our hypothetical expatriate have predicted that within a generation, the bustle at the waterfront would return—not in the form of warehouses, customhouses, longshoremen, or clipper ships, but in the form of residences, cultural institutions, tourists, and pleasure craft? Boston's oldest waterfront is a center of action once again, but this time for redefined uses and desires. Our expatriate would surely be surprised that Rowes, Burroughs, Lewis, and Mercantile wharves were elegant residential addresses, not places of industry; that life in the Charlestown Navy Yard was being directed by homeowners' associations instead of naval protocol; that 47 miles (76 kilometers) of shoreline were being steadily converted to a continuous public promenade; or that some of the most valuable local real estate was situated along wharves that had been dilapidated not so long ago.

Despite the surprises, this returnee would have little trouble finding his way along Boston's historic waterfront. Amid all that has been lost or transformed, continuity persists. The particular geometries of piers and wharves largely survive, as do many of the streets leading inland. The general shape of the outer and inner harbors is familiar, as is the disposition of the 33 harbor islands and the silhouette of high grounds and hills seen across the water. Even with the extensive topographic changes that Boston has undertaken, enough of the particular configuration of land, water, and human artifice remains to immediately suggest that, yes, this is still Boston. Likewise, the infrequent traveler to Pittsburgh, New Orleans, Cairo, or London will feel that he or she is in familiar territory in the vicinity of the waterfront, regardless of architectural changes over the years. It is this capacity for geographic persistence, despite the periodic transformations of built forms, that is one of the most valuable qualities of urban waterfronts.

Principle Four

As valuable and often contested realms, urban waterfronts bring forth the opposing, though reconcilable, human desires to preserve and to reinvent. Cities that are exploring new uses for their waterfronts often have to measure grand expectations against the realities of local markets and traditions, and resistance to change. A period of collective self-reflection often ensues before a plan can be made definitive and advanced.

To what end should the waterfront or the economy be repositioned? Should planning for reuse support traditional maritime industries or promote new forms of economic activity? Should the city seek new markets and status through a refurbished waterfront, or maintain the

Boston's historic waterfront in 1964, at a time of transition: the maritime industries are largely gone, but the rich mixture of today's harborfront uses is not yet in evidence—perhaps not even anticipated.
Mapping Boston Foundation

area's traditional character? Should public investment favor current residents' needs, attract newcomers, or cater to tourists? Should it be used to shore up adjoining neighborhoods or to encourage gentrification? Should it increase public access or leverage private development? Should traditional navigation channels be maintained, or should they be altered to accommodate recreational boating? Should redevelopment favor business expansion or civic and recreational needs, especially those that private initiatives do not readily provide? Should the city seek to profit from the scale of modern development attracted to the waterfront, or should it restrict density while enlarging recreational space? Should the city preserve the heritage of the waterfront, or risk losing its traditional character to new development?

A Vision and Strategy for Distinguishing and Connecting Waterfront Neighborhoods

There is increasing consensus among planners that the creation of diverse, mixed-use neighborhoods is a reliable recipe for enduring waterfront revitalization. Since there is always a learning curve in moving from reliable recipes to reliable results, considering the experience of others may help to smooth the way—and, not incidentally, may help to avert the risk of overapplying an idea that works only in limited circumstances.

The Seattle Experience

In terms of both content and process, Seattle offers a textbook case that demonstrates how to create a vision and strategy to distinguish and connect waterfront neighborhoods. With an expanding downtown and a mosaic of distinct neighborhoods, defined by individual plans for areas both on and off the waterfront, the city went in search of a unifying vision.

In 2000, the city launched a major urban design effort that is still underway. The effort began with a look back at what had been done to date. In 1999, the city formulated its Downtown Urban Center Neighborhood Plan, covering five neighborhoods; this plan, combined with other planning efforts undertaken since 1998, yielded a total of ten neighborhood plans for areas within the center city, some of which encompassed waterfront areas. Two critical findings from the city's review of these previous efforts are driving the current initiative: First, the waterfront is a major community resource—specifically, an urban design resource—that is "critical to defining the character and identity of Seattle's downtown," but it has not received sufficient planning attention. Second, the plans for the downtown and for the waterfront neighborhoods need to be connected in a coherent overall framework. Thus began the development of what is dubbed Connections and Places, an urban design strategy for the center city and the waterfront.

The Olmsted brothers' Green Ring plan interconnected Seattle's parks and boulevards; the Blue Ring proposes to do the same for neighborhoods and the waters of the city's largest open space, Elliott Bay.

The 100-Year Vision: The Blue Ring

Declaring that a great city needs an accessible public realm, Seattle proposed an open-space strategy as the vehicle for connecting neighborhoods and places of importance. Water is central to this strategy. Water is conceived as open space—and, in that it surrounds the city, it is viewed as a defining feature, community asset, and elemental component of the public realm. Seattle's major water bodies—Elliott Bay, to the west of the center city, and Lake Union, to the north—are considered two of the city's most significant open spaces. Within view everywhere but largely inaccessible by land, water became the basis of a three-pronged strategy that would (1) improve its accessibility, (2) link the various neighborhoods of the center city, and (3) reinforce the role of water in creating the city's image and sense of place. The strategy is intended to "make real" the strong public belief that the downtown should

be linked to the water in any direction.

The vision behind this strategy is called the Blue Ring. Significant both in its literal form, as a connecting course, and in its abstract form, as an organizing principle, the Blue Ring is intended to replicate the Green Ring, which was created for Seattle in a 1903 plan by the Olmsted brothers, and to echo the precedent-setting landscape design of the Olmsted legacy, the Emerald Necklace of Boston.

It is a way of conceiving, designing and creating Center City open spaces that build on each other, and on one of the city's most profound assets—its water. The Blue Ring will not be one continuous place but rather the aggregation of varied and interconnected places and spaces that will add up to the equivalent of a much larger open space. The Blue Ring will be unique to Seattle—our Central Park, our Rambla, our Golden Gate.[1]

Shoreline improvements to two parts of Seattle's Blue Ring, the Waterfront and South Lake Union Park, will provide direct access to water. At the same time, the Blue Ring—true to its name—will bring water inland through a series of water features. *Seattle citydesign*

Like the city's Green Ring—which, after 100 years, is now complete—the Blue Ring is a 100-year vision that is expected to become reality over time. In its role as an organizing principle for a 100-year agenda, the goal of the Blue Ring is to create (1) a "legible and cohesive Blue Ring system"; (2) an "umbrella for open-space plans and policies"; (3) a "living document" that will be updated periodically; and (4) a "comprehensive

urban design framework." The Blue Ring is viewed as providing a vital foundation, linking individual projects to the experience of the whole.[2]

Process

The planning process to develop Connections and Places followed best practices. It was also exceptionally well documented, an important factor in conveying to the public the purpose of the plan, critical steps, opportunities for participation, and outcomes.

One of the early and important steps in the plan development process was the creation of a report: *A Center-City Mosaic: A Summary of the Plans, Gaps, and Outcomes Since 1985*. In addition to providing the summary promised in the title, the report also provided design guidance for filling the gaps and exploiting the opportunities that it had identified. One of the important audiences for the report were the participants in the public design forum that would take place next.

The Center City Design Forum 2000, a three-day conference, was open to all stakeholders, broadly construed. The presentations, by people from both within and outside the area, made for a healthy and open exchange of ideas—not simply reinforcing planning assumptions, but raising provocative questions about them. Ray Gastil, for example, executive director of the Van Alen Institute, in New York, asked

Does context matter in the way it used to be understood? Can city districts still be thought of as neighborhoods, or are their identities global and regional? Do

design regulations hinder or enrich the opportunity for new types of uses and forms? Is it the market or planning that will yield the optimum results? How can you plan for the unexpected, for the future you can't define?

After the forum, a two-part report was produced to summarize the outcome; Part 1 summarized the principles and proposed actions, and Part 2 summarized the keynote presentations and reports. The Blue Ring, the proposed vision and strategy for the city center, was also presented in a two-part document: the first part described the 100-year vision and the second part the implementation strategy for the next decade. Particular care was given to the design of these documents so that the strategy would be clear to a broad audience.

In keeping with the Blue Ring implementation strategy for the next decade, the city is proceeding with the development of a plan for the Central Waterfront.

Implementation

The new Central Waterfront Plan is currently in the early stages of the planning process. The main goal is to make good on the waterfront's value as a "front porch" for the community. Distinct segments of the shoreline and uplands, whose boundaries were established in former waterfront planning efforts, are the foundation of the new initiative. The main task is to confirm or reassess the character and functions of these areas, identify potential new uses, and build on the plans for public improvements that have come before.**—Laurel Rafferty**

Notes
1. City of Seattle, *The Blue Ring: Connecting Places, 100-Year Vision* (Seattle: City of Seattle, June 2002.)
2. City of Seattle, *Connecting Places*, 9.

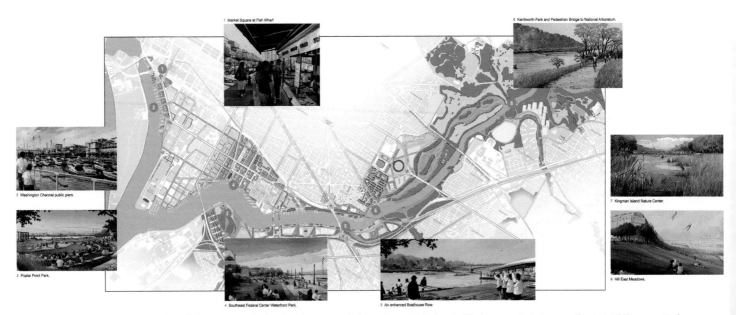

A portion of the Framework Plan for the Anacostia Waterfront Initiative, in Washington, D.C. Seven miles (11.4 kilometers) of a long-neglected river are being converted to a world-class urban environment that will be the center of 21st-century growth in America's capital. *Michael McCann/Chan Krieger & Associates*

These are precisely the questions confronting the leaders of Washington, D.C., as they embark on a plan to reengage the capital and the Anacostia River. For most of the 20th century, the Anacostia was hardly regarded as a city-building amenity. Quite the opposite; both geographically and symbolically, the Anacostia stood for demarcations—between the national monuments at the core of the District and its peripheral settlements, between economic well-being and poverty, between more and less desirable neighborhoods, and between largely white and largely black population centers.

Over time, the Anacostia yielded its natural beauty to industrial (primarily military) infrastructure, absorbed too much of the region's surface runoff and pollutants, gave its banks over to highways and railroad corridors, and even began to disappear from local maps—which, of course, focused on the monumental core. Long assumed to be less important to Washington than the Potomac, the Anacostia saw its fortunes—and image—steadily decline.

But what if the neglect and the negative image could be reversed? Under the leadership of Mayor Anthony

Williams, and by agreement among 20 District and federal agencies, the Anacostia Waterfront Initiative (AWI) was launched in 2000. The AWI is not simply about compensating for a history of poor decisions about land development. The initiative is equally motivated by the realization that the Anacostia River and its environs offer one of the best opportunities for the District to accommodate growth and remain competitive with its burgeoning region.

Along and near the shores of the Anacostia are more than 900 acres (364 hectares) of land—nearly 90 percent in public ownership—ready to be transformed into a model of 21st-century urban life. There is space to add between 15,000 and 25,000 new, mixed-income households; to build 20 million square feet (1.8 million square meters) of commercial and retail space; and to create miles of trails and parks and connect them to neighborhoods, existing parks, and natural areas. There are historic neighborhoods to be revalued and renewed. There is even the opportunity to enlarge the territory on which government agencies, national institutions, and monuments can locate, lessening the burden on the core. Such efforts are important for a city that has spent the past several decades losing population and business to a prospering region, and that is now in the early stages of a comeback.

New Jersey Avenue, one of the grand diagonal boulevards of Washington, D.C., shown reaching (as L'Enfant intended) with urban vitality toward the Anacostia River. This rendering was commissioned as part of the Anacostia Waterfront Initiative Framework Plan. *Michael McCann/D.C. Office of Planning*

The District today is experiencing modest population and job growth, a market for urban housing, and the demand for lifestyle amenities and unique places that often accompanies growth in service and knowledge economies. Yes, there is concern that a new focus on the Anacostia will hasten gentrification and displacement rather than sustain adjoining neighborhoods. But there is also great optimism. At one end of the river are the Washington Channel marinas, Hains Point, and the Tidal Basin; at the other are Kenilworth Park and Aquatic Gardens and the National Arboretum. With such cultural and geographic anchors, the history of prior uses, and a capacity for change (that springs, in part, from having been neglected for years), the Anacostia River is wonderfully poised to serve the city anew. The key will be to reconcile unnecessarily polarized views about the river's future, through a common conviction that plans for its eight-mile (13-kilometer) length can successfully accommodate both preservation and reinvention.

Principle Five

Even though a waterfront serves as a natural boundary between land and water, it must not be conceptualized or planned as a thin line. Land-water relationships are often thought of in terms of opposites, or of the edge between the two. Metaphysically, this edge is razor thin. In terms of city building, the opposite is true. Places like Amsterdam, Sydney, or San Francisco make this quite evident with their complex land-water weave. Even when geography offers limited variation, the broader the zone of overlap between land and water, the more successfully a city will capture the benefits of its water assets.

It is generally easier to attract investment to the water's very edge, and to construct (even overbuild), over time, a facade along the water. And indeed, most cities possess at least one great avenue along their waterfronts: think of the Bund, in Shanghai; the Malecon, in Havana; the Avenida

Two "thin lines": the Malecon, in Havana (left), and upscale apartment towers lining the Nile in Cairo (right). Such grand, urban-scale facades at water's edge are powerful symbolically and generally irresistible to investors, but the allure and economic value gained along the edge does not always extend (without careful planning and policy) very deep into the adjacent neighborhoods behind. *Right photo: Alex Krieger*

Maritima, in Las Palmas. These avenues certainly deserve much attention: even when they are forced by traffic demands to evolve into highways, they continue to serve as prominent addresses, to house visitor accommodations, and to host celebratory events. Nevertheless, the allure of the "thin line"—think of Miami Beach as seen from the air—must be balanced by a conception of the waterfront that incorporates perpendiculars to the water's edge. Many cities that have opted for a tall or dense edge of development right at their waterfront experience a precipitous drop in land value a block or two away from the edge—and with it a drop in the quality of the urban environment.

Managers of harbors and port authorities advise "getting into the water": figuratively, by blurring the suddenness of the edge, and literally, by ensuring that any existing or planned industrial, transportation, or recreational uses of the water itself influence landside planning. To avoid the less desirable consequences of a thin line of development, a city must create perpendicular streets and civic corridors that are as desirable as the shoreline drive. Bostonians, for example, hold dear their "fingers to the sea," the colonial streets (many of them still prominent today) that were a vir-

tual extension of the piers and wharves and that reached far into the Shawmut Peninsula. Developing the potential of such perpendiculars is often the key to comprehensive planning for both landside and waterside improvements.

Because of the seasonal flooding of the river, Cincinnati's thin line developed at some distance from the Ohio. And, as in many American cities, the local street grid to the waterfront was severed by highways that were expected to *ease* access to the waterfront.

But a new planning agenda is emerging. In three famous examples, Boston's Central Artery has been replaced by a tunnel; San Francisco's Embarcadero Freeway, which was partially destroyed by an earthquake, has been removed; and New York's West Side Highway has been partially demolished. Cincinnati is following suit: in the 1960s, the downtown was cut off from the riverfront by the construction of Fort Washington Way, which has a benign-sounding name but is actually a segment of I-75/I-71. The highway has been partially depressed, and its 600-foot (183-meter) right-of-way narrowed by two-thirds. These changes allowed five streets of the downtown grid to continue directly across the highway, reconnecting the downtown with the Ohio River. The addition of a planned major riverfront park, the new ballpark (replacing Reds Stadium, which sat on a high podium of parking obstructing even a view of the river), the new football stadium, the National Underground Railroad Freedom Center, and supporting mixed uses are helping to restore the connection between city and river.

Principle Six

Waterfront redevelopments are long-term endeavors with the potential to produce long-term value. Endangering this for short-term riches rarely produces the most desirable results. One of the most poignant observations about the seductiveness of the "thin line" was made by Mario Coyula, the director of planning for the Havana

This proposed riverfront park, currently in the design stage, is the future open-space anchor of downtown Cincinnati, in its new embrace of the Ohio River. *Hargreaves Associates*

Downtown Cincinnati's rather unbecoming relationship to the Ohio River, circa 1998. Not long after this photo was taken, the narrowing of Fort Washington Way and the construction of two new ballparks and the National Underground Railroad Freedom Center (all now completed) would begin, as part of a major riverfront planning initiative designed to once more orient the city toward its river. *Hargreaves Associates*

capital region, at a waterfront conference. Confronted with a dire need to improve (indeed, to create) an economy, Havana sees international tourism as a very tempting vehicle, and is struggling to decide how much of itself to offer and how quickly. "Do not lead with your best sites," Coyula advised. "The early investors want the best locations but do not do the best projects." Coyula is right: too many cities attempt to jump-start waterfront renewal by accepting second-rate development proposals or engineering entire redevelopment

plans around specific sites that they believe will enhance commercial real estate.

Among the current development trends yet to be proven of durable value is the introduction of very large draws—such as stadiums, convention centers, and casinos—at the water's edge. Cincinnati, Cleveland, Detroit, Pittsburgh, and San Diego are a few of the cities that have followed this trend or are trying to do so. Such big projects do have the capacity to attract substantial public resources and to energize (for a while) local leaders and the public. The problem comes when a city feels that simply attracting one of these facilities to its waterfront is enough: its job is done. In San Diego, for example, the introduction, more than 15 years ago, of a huge convention center and tall hotels to the South Embarcadero bayside brought many conventioneers, but also a palpable emptiness when they were inside the facility (as was usually the case), or not in town at all. Stadiums, too, animate their immediate environments only sporadically, and when the surrounding mixed-use development is insufficient, as is often the case, the area feels empty once the sporting event or concert ends. Even cultural facilities—whose "action," with a few notable exceptions, takes place largely indoors—require extra attention to their grounds and to other nearby uses before their presence can sufficiently animate a waterfront.

Perhaps strategically, Boston's new convention center was built about a half-mile (0.8 kilometers) from the water but is being touted as a Seaport District attraction. The expectation is that a vibrant mixed-use corridor, perpendicular to the waterfront, will evolve between the waterfront and the convention center's front door. And in San Diego, a new master plan for the one-mile- (1.6 kilometer-) long North Embarcadero area features, in contrast to its South Embarcadero neighbor, many more perpendicular street connections and view corridors; a more continuous esplanade at the bay; and a much broader variety of uses, including more housing.

In a different context, consider how unusual—and, so far, successful—Bilbao's efforts have been. First, and quite consciously, the city set out to improve local self-esteem and to improve the region's image internationally through several cultural projects, most notably the Bilbao Guggenheim Museum. Now the city is pursuing more conventional redevelopment efforts, including a substantial commercial development at the river, between the Guggenheim and the even newer opera house. Josu Bergara Etxebarria, the president of the provincial council of Bizkaia, often speaks about the strategic goal of using culture, not just real estate development, as a tool for redevelopment. The Bilbao lesson is that competing globally may require substantial recasting of, rather than more narrowly preserving, a city's waterfront image and uses.

Many cities are paying attention and responding. At the end of Wisconsin Avenue, facing Lake Michigan, the wingspan of the great *brise-soleil* of Santiago Calatrava's addition to the Milwaukee Art Museum presents an image

A precursor to the "Bilbao effect": Frank Gehry's Weisman Art Museum (completed four years before his Guggenheim Museum in Bilbao, Spain) on a portion of the University of Minnesota campus that runs along the Mississippi River. *Alex Krieger*

that is reminiscent of Frank Gehry's Bilbao Guggenheim— and just as compelling. Nevertheless, it remains unclear whether cities are drawing sufficient insight from Bilbao's experiment, or are pinning their hopes too narrowly on the catalytic potential of an arresting architectural icon along their waterfront.

Principle Seven

Underused or obsolete urban waterfronts come alive when they become desirable places to live, not just to visit. The mayors of many prominent waterfront cities— Mayor Frank Sartor, former Lord Mayor of Sydney, among them—argue for the importance of maintaining a "living city" despite pressure to yield to more lucrative commercial development. With a number of American cities experiencing increasing demand for both market-rate and luxury housing, waterfront sites are naturally appealing. Minneapolis, for example, after decades of almost no new downtown housing construction, has recently built over 5,000

housing units along its central riverfront. Cities on both coasts are experiencing similar trends.

It is Vancouver that has undertaken the most determined campaign to increase housing; the city's "'Living First" slogan proclaims that residents are as important to cities as anything else. Particularly in North America, where industrial-era cities have been losing population to their suburban peripheries for half a century, this is a crucial insight. In the 1980s, Vancouver began to shift its multiple downtown waterfronts away from industrial and rail uses. The city's intent was to add as many as 25,000 mid- to high-density housing units, and by century's end it was well on the way to achieving this goal.

The city's planning director, Larry Beasley, speaks of using waterfront locations to create a competitive advantage for downtown living that is capable of offsetting the allure of the suburbs. He refers to density, congestion, and even high-rise housing as "our friends," in that they create lively, mixed-use, urban lifestyles. Beasley notes that in

Vancouver's motto of downtown for "Living First" is clearly in evidence in the residential towers shown in this 2004 aerial view.

order to make it harder for people to commute from the periphery—and to thereby induce them to select in-town housing—the city has adamantly and deliberately refused to upgrade its highway system. Until recently, such talk would have seemed naïve in most American cities—and, perhaps for some, sounds improbable still. But to experience

Milwaukee Riverfront Redevelopment

Milwaukee, Wisconsin, like many U.S. cities, has been experiencing a wave of multi-family residential development, including both new construction and the adaptive use of historic buildings. And much of this development is taking place along the Milwaukee River, a once-neglected amenity.

As in many Rustbelt cities, Milwaukee's river was the hub of the local industrial economy. The Beer Line B site, known by that name because of its earlier use as a rail yard serving the thriving breweries, was first developed in the early 19th century. This former industrial corridor is situated just north of downtown and along the west bank of the Milwaukee River, from Pleasant Street to Humboldt

As one looks south along the Milwaukee River, Bradley Center (Milwaukee's indoor professional sports arena) is visible beyond the Holton Street Bridge. The vantage point is at River Homes, where 41 rowhouse units and 21 condominiums have been completed to date. *Milwaukee Department of City Development*

The Milwaukee River is just under 200 feet (61 meters) wide along the 3,400-foot (1,036-meter) water frontage of the Beer Line B plan area. This view, looking back to Beer Line B, shows the riverside elevation of Trostel Square, an upscale residential project of 99 apartments and 27 condominiums and boat slips on the Milwaukee. *Milwaukee Department of City Development*

Avenue. The current plan for the area lays out a scheme for converting 60 acres (24 hectares) of former industrial property to high-density development, including new and redeveloped parkland, a riverwalk, significant neighborhood connections, and a boating facility in the Milwaukee River Valley, north of the central business district.

The Beer Line B redevelopment project, which is being overseen by the Milwaukee Department of City Development, evolved from a series of investigations that explored the potential for revitalizing the area, which for 20 years had consisted primarily of abandoned buildings, coal piles, and vacant, blighted parcels. The land was initially acquired for a

major public works project and became available for redevelopment when the project was completed.

In 1999, the city completed the planning study that now provides the blueprint for the area's redevelopment. Under this plan, any new development along the waterfront requires the provision of public access to the river through the construction of a section of the riverwalk. The new sections of riverwalk will connect with the existing riverwalk system, which was started in 1994, and will provide a pedestrian link both to the nearby Schlitz Park office complex and to downtown.

The Beer Line B plan relied on a high degree of public involvement to create a vision, a development plan, and design standards that provide investors with a predictable environment for development. The city held six public meetings to discuss the goals of the development plan and to get feedback on various proposals.

The city's method of sale on a parcel-by-parcel basis created competition among developers, which resulted in high-quality products and innovative design, and also allowed for a variety of housing styles, including condominiums, apartments, townhouses, stacked flats, and rowhouses.

Because of Beer Line B's prior industrial uses, the city was required to convert and upgrade the infrastructure to accommodate people instead of factories and machines. The land immediately adjacent to the river consisted of fill and marsh deposits, which required deep foundations that are not customarily used for townhouse residential development. Approximately half the site consisted of bluff land, which meant that significant cutting and filling was necessary to accommodate new development.

The city of Milwaukee has worked closely with the private sector to create recreational space and public access to the Milwaukee River, entering into development agreements with individual developers to receive permanent public easements along the river. In exchange for the easements, the city participates in the development by funding 50 percent of the private improvements to the riverwalk.

The overall goal of the Beer Line B plan is to create a pedestrian-friendly riverfront and a new, traditional neighborhood, and to integrate them into the downtown, the surrounding neighborhoods, and the riverwalk system. Brewer's Hill, which is adjacent to much of the new development, offers a traditional neighborhood grid, complete with two-story duplex units and midblock service alleys, a common pattern in many Milwaukee neighborhoods.

"The Beer Line neighborhood really has something for everyone," says former mayor John O. Norquist, now president of the Congress for New Urbanism. "The amenities that developers are capitalizing on, such as the RiverWalk and new parks, are also available to residents of the surrounding neighborhoods. Not only are we adding value along the Beer Line, but we're adding value to our more established neighborhoods such as Brewer's Hill and Riverwest as well."

As of fall 2002, more than 650 units had been completed, were planned, or were under construction, representing more than $120 million in new investment in Beer Line B.—**Gayle Berens**

While the scale, site planning, and architectural ambitions of this new housing development in downtown Jacksonville, Florida, may be modest, what is clear is the nearly universal appeal of urban living near an amenity such as a river. *Alan Mountjoy/Chan Krieger & Associates*

Vancouver today is to understand what "living first" means. Housing has created demand for virtually everything else: new services, shopping and entertainment, public transportation, and open space.

The creation of great places to live in the heart of Vancouver and Boston was an early policy priority, not the later consequence of other initiatives. Curiously, however, there is concern that planning for a lot of housing in the emerging South Boston Seaport District will crowd out other uses, create excessive density, and privatize the waterfront. However, in all but the most extreme circumstances (that is, truly excessive density, or incompatibility with still-vital port uses) having more people living in proximity to the waterfront creates a long-term competitive advantage for a city. Regulations can control building mass and how and where shadows are cast, and can ensure that the edge is maintained continuously for public purposes (as is, indeed, the law in Boston). To once more evoke the miles of dense housing that stretch along Chicago's lakefront, the idea of living coming first seems to be a very urbane one.

Principle Eight

The public increasingly desires and expects access to the water's edge. This usually requires overcoming historic barriers—physical, proprietary, and psychological—while persuading new investors that there is merit in maintaining that valuable edge within the public domain. The cities that limit public access to their waterfronts outnumber those that provide generous access. Various impediments—from physical barriers to riparian rights, flood zones, and long-standing uses and habits—have made this so. But the citizens of those cities that have made their waterfronts accessible to the public—as Chicago began doing, nearly a century ago—do not regret the results. Nor has Chicago's real estate community, which continues to build at as large a scale and in as close proximity to the public lakefront as regulatory processes allow.

Gdansk, Poland, along the Motlawa River. Public access to the river's edge is enjoyed in a variety of forms. *Alex Krieger*

Providence—which, during the 19th century, entirely covered long stretches of the Providence River to create roads and freight yards—has gone so far as to "unbury" its river. The resulting investment in the vicinity of the river has helped reinvigorate a downtown that had struggled for

decades, and the river has itself become a star attraction for various events and celebrations, including a remarkable bonfire and musical spectacle that attracts tens of thousands of people from around New England twice each summer month.

In Louisville, Kentucky, a new 100-acre (40-hectare) park on the flood banks of the Ohio River has, similarly, begun to pull the downtown closer to the river—not with buildings, but with a wonderfully varied recreational landscape. Because of the propensity of the Ohio to flood, the city had historically protected itself from the river with broad banks—on which, predictably, it later built an elevated highway, making the water's edge even less accessible. The new park, ingeniously designed by Hargreaves Associates, passes beneath the highway and remains part of the city's flood-protection system; at the same time, it has transformed a stretch of the flood banks into an environment that makes people more aware of the river's seasonal movement and its indigenous riparian plant life.

The park's popularity was immediate, and pride in the accomplishment led the Jefferson County School Board to publish *Waterfront Park: A Curriculum Guide.* The manual uses the new park and its design as a springboard to describe to schoolchildren the environmental and social history of the river and the city. It is distantly reminiscent of the famous *Wacker Manual,* read by generations of Chicago schoolchildren and based on Daniel Burnham's 1909 Plan for Chicago—which, not incidentally, first pointed Chicago's cultural and recreational life toward Lake Michigan.

Along the Canadian shore of Lake Ontario, Toronto, in cooperation with its 31 sister communities, is engaged in one of the most sweeping current endeavors to reclaim a waterfront for public use. Over the past decade, a deceptively simple, shared vision of a continuous trail has yielded over 100 separate projects that, collectively, have produced over 215 miles (346 kilometers) of public trails—along with the determination to double this figure, and connect the entire, 400-mile (644-kilometer) shore of Lake Ontario. Motivated by the twin goals of regeneration and public access, the greenway trail already links nearly 200 natural areas; 150 parks,

Left: A public swimming pool on Wool-loomooloo Bay, in Sydney, Australia, expands the range of public enjoyments available at the urban water's edge. *Alan Mountjoy/Chan Krieger & Associates*

Below: Boston's historic mercantile wharfs, once known as "fingers to the sea," provide a simple way to experience the river along the Charles River Esplanade, and a new "finger to the sea": a direction to the good life in an urban setting. *Alan Mountjoy/Chan Krieger & Associates*

promenades, and beaches; dozens of marinas; and hundreds of historic places and cultural institutions.

An organization called the Waterfront Regeneration Trust, founded in 1990 as the successor to the Royal Commission on the Future of the Toronto Waterfront, has acted as facilitator, partner, conscience, cajoler, and primary promulgator of the regional vision. Its kindred organization, the Toronto Waterfront Revitalization Task Force, published its own plan in 2000—supported by a commitment of $1 billion (in U.S. dollars) of public funding—to invest $7 billion more along a several-mile-long stretch of the city's waterfront.

Again, the ambition is stunning. In addition to reclaiming obsolete or marginal industrial and port properties and creating green space, the plan anticipates a new work and living environment for 100,000 people on 2,000 acres (809 hectares) of land adjacent to the downtown. Toronto's determination to substantially expand its lakeside public realm will surely continue, as will the same determination in Cincinnati, Louisville, Pittsburgh, Providence, San Diego, Washington, D.C., and numerous other cities that are coming to realize the value of attractive and public shores.

Principle Nine

The success and appeal of waterfront development is intrinsically tied to the interrelationship between landside and adjacent waterside uses—and to the environmental quality of both the water and the shore. Like Toronto's waterfront, Detroit's river—the water link

between lakes Erie and Huron—has been designated as one of 42 Great Lakes areas of concern by the International Joint Commission on the Great Lakes. In the course of its history, Detroit has used its river to great benefit, and abused it thoroughly. As a result, the only development that the river has hosted during the past several decades was designed to face away from it. When Henry Ford's Renaissance Center opened—around 1980, and to great fanfare—signaling a major corporate reinvestment in the city, the complex ignored the Detroit River entirely, though it

View along the Detroit River as it was used for much of the 19th and 20th centuries. *Alex Krieger*

With the industrial glacier long in recession, the recently formed Detroit Riverfront Conservancy, a public/private corporation armed with a $50 million challenge grant from the Kresge Foundation and substantial local corporate support, has been empowered to create and maintain the six-mile- (9.7-kilometer-) long RiverWalk, which will be this century's public point of contact between city and river. *Chan Krieger & Associates*

was located next to it. The "Ren Cen" was equally rude along its city side, barricading itself behind highway-scaled approaches and fortresslike service structures at street level. Such defensive tactics helped neither the downtown nor the riverfront—nor, ultimately, the status of Ren Cen itself.

Along the river, a downward spiral had been set in motion. Exhausted from its long service to heavy industry, the river was unsightly and terribly polluted, and the city recoiled ever further from its untended edge. Even Belle Isle, the majestic, 1,000-acre (404-hectare), Olmsted-designed island park, began to deteriorate and lose visitors—partly because of inadequate maintenance and partly because park visitors had to negotiate the unattractive environment along the river.

The degradation did not occur all at once, and neither will the regeneration, especially given Detroit's still-fragile overall economic recovery. Nevertheless, a half-dozen initiatives are being pursued, thanks in part to the fact that the river was designated as one of 14 American Heritage Rivers, a status that enables bordering communities to seek federal funding to preserve, protect, and restore rivers and their associated resources important to history, culture, and natural heritage. The work is focused on recovering brownfields; reducing contaminants in the river and along its banks; replanting native trees and grasses to help stabilize the shoreline; cleaning a natural bayou (dubbed the Black Lagoon for its toxicity); and reintroducing several native habitats on Belle Island, as part of its revitalization. The long vision, not unlike Toronto's, is of a continuous string of public open spaces and greenways stretching some 20 miles (32 kilometers) along the river; part of that vision, a downtown waterfront park, opened in 2001, in commemoration of Detroit's 300th anniversary.

As in Pittsburgh and other Rustbelt cities—from Gary, Indiana, to Gdansk, Poland—the painstaking, slow, and expensive process of redefining the role of a body of water is under way. Each initiative in Detroit is intended to prepare the river edge to receive, rather than repel, both new investment and urban life. (A recent plan—probably permanently squelched—to place several large casinos at the river would not produce as lively or as public an edge.) And the Ren Cen's new owner, General Motors, responded

Woodward Avenue, Detroit's main street, reached right to the edge of the river early in the 20th century. Such direct perpendicular connections are just as necessary today, to fully benefit from the presence of a public waterfront. *Detroit Riverfront Conservancy*

properly to the river's regeneration by adding a monumental wintergarden as part of a major transformation of the complex, which—miraculously, and at long last—opens out directly to the river.

Principle Ten

Distinctive environments, typically found at waterfronts, provide significant advantages for a city's competitiveness in its region or in relation to its rival cities. In Detroit, the eventual civic and economic gain from the recovery of the river will be no less—and likely more long-lived—than what was initially achieved by tapping the water's industrial potential alone. In the post-industrial era, geography is more than the opportunity to extract natural resources or command a trade route. Beautiful places today attract people and investment. And

keeping them beautiful—taking advantage of their distinctiveness—is one way to minimize the tendency of modern development to produce generic environments.

While Genoa's natural (and historic) harbor is not large enough to accommodate modern cargo shipping, its shape creates a powerful, centripetal force that brings the sprawling, modern city to focus on the old harbor. Over a decade ago, in anticipation of the commemoration of the 500th anniversary of Columbus's first voyage to America, the city began to reinvent itself as a cultural and tourist destination, and the harbor's "centering" effect proved very useful. In a prior epoch, the unique geography of land and sea had facilitated the creation of a well-scaled, well-protected urban port. Today, the same geography accommodates

A view of the architectural offices of Sir Norman Foster & Partners, which are perched on the banks of London's Thames River. During the 21st century, urban living and livelihoods will gradually be oriented toward lifestyle amenities—among which proximity to the water is one of the most prized. *Alex Krieger*

sions of place. The value of these "postcard views" is not to be dismissed. For cities and nations seeking access to broader markets, globalization represents both opportunity and the risk of cultural homogenization and the loss of local identity. Local geography, uniquely reinforced by a special pattern of urbanization—especially in relationship to a body of water—can facilitate the goal of competing globally while avoiding the generic and the mediocre.

Increasingly, the makers of emerging economies decide where to work and where to live on the basis of the lifestyle amenities offered by a locale. Surveys tracking locational choices among knowledge workers consistently show that, in addition to job-related characteristics, other important factors influencing the choice of one urban area over another include the presence of culture and

and highlights a diverse and spatially contained realm of businesses, institutions, residences, and visitor facilities— all in view of, and surrounded by, the layers of Genoa's prior incarnations.

The canals of Amsterdam, the intricate pattern of docks and quays in Sydney, the more recently constructed forest of residential towers in Vancouver, and the impossibly dense wall of skyscrapers facing Hong Kong Bay are the counterparts, in those cities, of the distinctive land-sea relationship in Genoa. Indeed, as they have for centuries and in various incarnations, cities located on major bodies of water leave visitors with powerful impres-

Dallas's Trinity River—long maligned, dumped upon, and (being flood prone) sequestered from its host city by vast levees—is about to be reinvented as Dallas's version of New York's Central Park. Like many cities seeking to become "world class," Dallas has come to appreciate the essential role that its most prominent natural feature will have to play in the city's quest to become a superb urban place. *Dallas Trinity Commons/Landslides*

arts; a healthy environment and natural amenities; opportunities to pursue an active lifestyle; a strong "sense of place"; and socially diverse and progressive-minded populations. In other words, the various ingredients that allow a blending of work and leisure in one locale are proving to be important to prospective workers. Access to water, both for recreational purposes and for the ambience that waterfront settings provide, is a key attractor in cosmopolitan venues. A lively waterfront will attract global markets and possibly forestall the "this could be anywhere" syndrome of much current development. Just about every waterfront city should aspire to be called, like Genoa, superb.

For myriad reasons, waterfronts always have been attractors par excellence. If access to water was long essential for sustenance, transportation, commerce, and industry, it is now necessary for less tangible, though hardly less important, human needs. Toronto lists its three "pillars of city living" as community, economy, and environment. These are also the cornerstones of those who champion more sustainable urban futures.

Community, economy, and environment: where else but along a city's waterfront can these so propitiously come together? As usual, Jane Jacobs expressed it most succinctly: "The waterfront isn't just something unto itself," she pointed out, "it's connected to everything else." Waterfronts are those places in a city where nature and culture best meet; and, thus, will remain the most dynamic territories for urban—and, one hopes, urbane—development.

Notes

1. Some of the principles outlined in this chapter were based on presentations made at a conference entitled "Waterfronts in Post Industrial Cities," which was held at the Harvard Graduate School of Design, October 7–9, 1999.

2. The portions of this essay that review the history of Boston's waterfront were based, in part, on "Experiencing Boston: Encounters with the Places on the Maps," which appears in Mapping Boston, eds. Alex Krieger and David Cobb (Cambridge: MIT Press, 1999).

Chapter 3

Waterfront Design

Bonnie Fisher

Great urban waterfronts can be found throughout the world and throughout history. Over the broad sweep of time, port cities such as Alexandria, Amsterdam, Istanbul, Shanghai, St. Petersburg, and Venice have captivated the imaginations of urban dwellers and called to mind the romance of a distant past, when water offered routes for transportation and trade and the waterfront shaped a city's identity, stature, and economic vitality.

In antiquity, harbors were the sites of some of the greatest public works in history—renowned wonders such as the Pharos, in Alexandria, and the Colossus of Rhodes—that defined the edge of land and sea and underscored the role of the waterfront as a gateway to the mysterious unknown. Flooded cities; marooned harbors, such as Ostia; and submerged towns, such as Atlantis, evoke a rich trove of mythic imagery and recall the glories of past civilizations long lost to the modern world.

In the past few decades, there has been great interest in reclaiming the urban waterfront. Changes in transportation technology have left vast tracts of urban waterfront land vacant, underused, abandoned, and separated from the cities that they once nourished with trade and commerce. Today, cities across North America and throughout the world have embarked on planning efforts designed to reevaluate the role of the waterfront and to determine how the waterfront can best be reintegrated with the city. Although design decisions having to do with spatial, structural, and urban form may have the greatest effect on the image and identity of the urban waterfront, they are often neglected in favor of financial objectives by private developers, fiscal feasibility by cities, congestion management by traffic engineers, or community values related to parks and public access. This chapter asserts the importance of urban design in bringing together all these objectives in rebuilding the waterfront, making it a more meaningful part of the city and a more appropriate and effective setting for economic rebirth and revitalization.

The chapter focuses on the artful composition of activities and elements that intensify the sense of place, produce an emotional response, reveal the underlying physiographic structure and the dynamics of natural processes, and give the urban waterfront its timeless appeal and memorable qualities. The intent here is not to delineate strict rules and standards or to control design, but to inspire creative design solutions that will heighten the intrinsic qualities that distinguish places. The urge to duplicate what has worked in one place and apply it to the next has seldom led to the creation of a great waterfront—and, in fact, has contributed to the failure of many waterfronts in recent years. Amid increasing globalization and standardization, the waterfronts that stand out are those that have found their own special identity, that neither throw away nor exploit their history, and that leave an indelible imprint on our memory—by playing up the eccentricities of the physical setting, the juxtaposition of elements, the relationship between contrast and harmony, and the complexity that comes from multiple experiences that touch the mind, the senses, and the emotions.

The approach to urban waterfront design outlined in this chapter is based on a number of premises. Some are broad and tied to urban design concepts; others have to do with specific physical elements—buildings, open spaces, and edge treatments—that characterize the waterfront zone:

■ No waterfront is exactly like another, nor should be, and the design should recognize the intrinsic qualities of each site.

■ Features that recall the underlying structure of the landscape should be used to reinforce spatial form and identity.

■ Barriers to the waterfront need to be removed, but should not be replaced by new hindrances such as large, unactivated open spaces or inward-facing complexes.

■ Multiple linkages to the waterfront should be created, along with multiple reasons for going there.

Changes in transportation technology have left vast areas of urban waterfront lands vacant, underused, and abandoned, separated from the cities that they once nourished with trade and commerce. The influx of automobiles as commuter vehicles is one form of change. In San Francisco, the Ferry Building became obsolete with the completion of the Bay Bridge, in 1936; the Embarcadero Expressway (top) further isolated the dockside from the city until the viaduct was torn down (bottom) following the 1989 Loma Prieta earthquake. *Top: Boris Dramov; bottom: Ira Kahn*

Avalon's harbor at Santa Catalina Island, California, recognizes the spatial dimension of the Pacific Ocean offshore, which gives form to the semi-circular harborfront.

■ While remnants of the past are necessary to cities' social and economic diversity and add to the character of the waterfront, change and adaptation are of greater value than slavish historicism.

■ Single-purpose transportation systems should be redesigned to create multimodal corridors at the water's edge, affording pedestrian, bicycle, transit (landside and waterborne), and vehicular access.

■ Improvements in infrastructure along the shoreline should be designed to serve multiple purposes simultaneously.

■ The city should be extended to the waterfront; a mix of urban uses, including residential, can also play an important role in reuniting the city with its waterfront.

■ At the same time, the influence of the waterfront should extend inland to establish greater amenity and value for redevelopment and renewal.

■ The spatial dimension of offshore water should be recognized for its power to shape adjacent land areas.

■ The transitional space between land and water should be designed with care and consideration, as a provocative environment that engages the land-bound urban dweller and provides a place to sit, view, and linger as well as a space to move through.

■ Waterfront buildings should be permeable—open to views and public access—and designed with consideration of the scale, form, and character appropriate to the public orientation of the waterfront.

■ Civic and community leadership—whether grassroots or through formal channels—should be established to guide the implementation of large-scale projects and to care for them over time.

Before engaging in an expanded discussion of planning and design considerations, it is essential to recognize the unique characteristics of the urban waterfront.

Whereas natural waterfronts are constantly changing environments, the urban waterfront seeks stability in form and treatment. It is not a place of gradual progression along a descending route from land to water, but rather a place where the marginal zone is more often minimized; where engineered structures create an abrupt interface, preempting a series of natural transitions; where an intricate trace work of natural process is no longer evident in meanders and eddies; and where the edge is seldom defined by the lowest low tide but by proximity to the deepest deep water. While there are many different kinds of waterfronts—along rivers, bays, estuarine marshes, sandy oceanfront beaches—and different kinds of cities with different traditions and

Top: Underlying every urban waterfront is the imprint of the natural systems that once gave it form and identity. Here, the sloping street of La Rambla, leading to the Barcelona harbor, follows an ancient underground drainage course.

Bottom: Pier 7 in San Francisco established a new water-oriented identity and thus attracted new uses to the waterfront. On axis with the pyramid-spired Transamerica Tower, Pier 7 projects 840 feet (256 meters) into the bay. *San Francisco Chronicle*

the land, and can sometimes be discovered on close inspection. Reading the waterfront, one can see that the gentle slope of Barcelona's La Rambla follows an ancient underground drainage course as it leads to the harbor; that the lighthouse in Portofino, Italy, punctuates a promontory peninsula; and that the pier at Aquatic Park, in San Francisco, extends the natural sweep of the historic cove.

The most engaging built elements on the shoreline retain the essential qualities of what came before, and treat nature not as an adversary but as an accomplice. As the urban waterfront undergoes a cycle of transformation from industrial service area to more valued urban land, the opportunity to uncover and reveal natural systems asserts itself. Drainages that were covered, beaches that were filled in, shorelines that were straightened: all have the chance to be reclaimed and redefined. While full-scale restoration is often not feasible, it may be possible to bring to light waterways long buried, to reconfigure the land to reflect below-grade influences, or to heighten physiographic structure.

Extant remnants of ecological systems can also be found along the urban waterfront. These areas escaped full-scale alteration because they had little economic value for maritime or commercial development, or were set aside and protected because they served larger public roles—for military defense, for flood control, or for watershed management. Today, as military installations are decommissioned and sites taken out of industrial use, many are being made more visible and accessible to the public. In these cases a light-handed approach is required to integrate them into a new context;

economies, all urban waterfronts must address common issues involving the transformed natural landscape and its potential to fulfill a variety of human purposes.

Underlying every urban waterfront is the imprint of the natural systems that once gave it form and identity. Though not always immediately apparent, old beaches, wetlands, stream courses, and sloughs reside in the memory of

special attention must be given to the design of the edge, to linkages to other areas, and to expanding visitors' awareness of and engagement with the natural world.

The Urban Waterfront

The urban waterfront—in particular, the working waterfront—has long been the site of intensive development and alteration of the natural realm. No single place within the city has been subject to greater demands and expectations or experienced more dramatic and rapid metamorphoses. Waterfront cities, whether on a river, lake, bay, or ocean, reveal a succession of shoreline edges, each attesting to shifts in economic opportunity and technological innovation.

The shoreline of the Inner Harbor at Oakland, California, facing the channel shared with Alameda to the west (left), has undergone a succession of changes with shifts in economic opportunity and technological innovation. Today, it is the nexus of trade by sea (container ships), air (Oakland Airport), and land (rail and interstate highways). *Patrick Carney*

Traditionally, port cities grew through incremental extension outward: gaining ground on deep water, capturing the amenity of the shoreline, and building improvements for stabilization, reclamation, and flood control. With the advent of the industrial age came shifts not only in the rate but also in the nature of change. The waterfront became home to a growing number of increasingly specialized facilities (first railroads and rail yards, then bridges, freeways, ramps and tunnel portals), and piers dedicated to specific types of cargo handling replaced the multipurpose quay. Piers, wharves, and docks were moved farther and farther out over the water, where they became less visible; on the inland side, parking and support areas distanced the city from the water. These physical barriers made the waterfront appear subservient to the city's larger economic interests—and off-limits to the public.

Over the past several decades, with shifts in transportation technology and the decline of industry in the historic urban center, opportunities to reunite the waterfront with the city have emerged. Today, for example, there are significant prospects for the removal of railroad tracks, rail yards, and elevated arteries and freeways that had—often for many decades—separated the urban waterfront from the surrounding city. In some cases, these opportunities are opening up as cities attempt to decide the fate of 50- or 60-year-old freeways that are reaching the end of their useful lives. Boston; Portland, Oregon; San Francisco; and Seattle, among other cities, recognizing the detrimental effects of transportation systems built right along the water's edge, have faced the prospect of their removal. Removal is an expensive and disruptive proposition; it is complicated, within an urban setting, to replace traffic capacity. Moreover, the removal of barriers, no matter how appealing it may be, is not always feasible. Whether the barrier remains or is removed, however, it is essential to address the fundamental issue of isolation through creative solutions that will integrate the waterfront with the city and make it a more meaningful part of urban life.

Today, the more enlightened cities are those that conceive of freeway removal and infrastructure development not as single-purpose transportation projects but as acts of city rebuilding; these cities realize that the investment involved must achieve multiple objectives not only for a variety of modes of travel but also for development, open

The Singapore Urban Redevelopment Authority issued a public tender to solicit proposals for the redevelopment of the Fullerton Building, a landmark remnant of Singapore's colonial days. The Far East Organization won the development rights and restored the eight-story, classically inspired post office building as a five-star luxury hotel, connected under Fullerton Road to a two-story, 86,115-square-foot (8,000-square-meter) dining and entertainment complex built on reclaimed land on the waterfront of Marina Bay. *Far East Organization/Sino Land*

space, shoreline stabilization, and public access. While the removal of infrastructural barriers is a major step in the right direction, tremendous effort is still needed to reposition the newfound resource of urban land. Areas long occupied by transportation facilities or other significant barriers need to be physically restructured so that they do not simply remain as leftover space.

Civic Responsibility and Leadership

To successfully implement change requires not only large-scale thinking about the nature of the city and the role of the waterfront within it, but also sufficient leadership and commitment to make major public improvements over a long period of time. Confronting the new is often difficult—and cities faced with big challenges tend, like people, to gravitate toward familiar ground. Some cities invest millions and millions of dollars in waterfront improvements without necessarily improving the fundamental relationship of city and water. Other cities, with a clearer sense of where

they should be headed, have made great strides, capitalizing on leadership, innovation, and available funds to accomplish multiple ends.

When a city is considering how to make the most of its waterfront, a design competition is often proposed as a means of eliciting creative ideas and solving thorny problems. The disadvantage, however, of design competitions is that juries are too often seduced by what looks good on paper and represents the latest stylistic predilections; the winning entry may not reflect what can actually be built with limited funds or, more importantly, what might be best in reality and stand the test of time.

The success of a competition depends on the jury that is selected, the clarity of the objectives and parameters, and the seriousness of the intent to follow through and build the project. At the same time, even the best of competitions can fall short: unlike the design that may be developed for an individual building, the design of a large

Faneuil Hall Marketplace, renovated in 1976 by developer James Rouse and architect Benjamin Thompson, of Cambridge Seven Associates, Inc., was a pioneering development in waterfront-oriented festival marketplaces. *The Rouse Company*

Meaning and Identity

Urban waterfront redevelopment involves building a new meaning and identity for a place that has experienced decline and that is now undergoing a transformation. Acquiring new meanings as physical conditions change, though, can be difficult. Projects that were initiated in the late 1960s and early 1970s, such as Ghirardelli Square and the Cannery, in San Francisco, and Faneuil Hall Marketplace, in Boston, were instrumental in setting a new standard for historic preservation and in bringing new activities to the waterfront. But when they were reproduced en masse across the country, they lost their special appeal. The fisherman's wharf, the waterfront landing, and the festival marketplace are now familiar kinds of specialty commercial developments that are based on a superficial sense of connection with the past—a kind of ersatz historicism. Ultimately, such places became more attractive to tourists than to residents.

Throughout urban history, there have been shifts in the popularity and appeal of different types of building projects, particularly those that give status to a community or involve large numbers of people engaged in some type of recreational activity. At the turn of the 20th century, for example, a boardwalk, pier, or amusement park was considered an essential feature of any self-respecting coastal resort. The difference today is in the much larger size and scope of the projects that are undertaken, and in their prepackaged sameness from one place to the next. As new markets emerge in the global economy, it becomes much easier to offer the same kinds of products in the same kinds of settings—the result being that the redeveloped waterfront in Sydney might feel very much like the one in Baltimore. Business strategies that emphasize economies of scale (achieved through industry consolidation and product standardization) are strengthening this trend, and have come to play an increasing role in the development of projects.

At the other end of the spectrum are those waterfronts that have become great, memorable places by establishing a special identity and character. In such cases, a different problem can arise, however: with the success of the initial proj-

urban project and its public spaces needs to address complex public issues and reflect community values. The urban waterfront should not be conceived as a "set piece" made by one hand; instead, it needs to be designed as a series of creative and well-planned interventions, in the form of numerous building projects, that take shape over a long period of time.

The cities that have been most successful in envisioning and realizing large-scale urban waterfront transformations are those that have had the advantage of strong leadership: that is, committed groups of people with clear goals, and with the authority to make decisions and to work toward the common good over time. The cities that seem least equipped to implement plans are those that have adopted open-ended processes, in which ad hoc committees lack the authority to assume responsibility or leadership. In these cases, the process itself overwhelms the possibility of creatively developing a reasonable project.

ect, many other projects—spurred by the hope that they will succeed by association—are drawn to that same place, until the individuality of the place, the very thing that made it so inviting to begin with, is obscured. This is a common phenomenon in successful commercial developments: instead of building on their successes by extending them along the length of the waterfront, these developments allow too much to be crowded into one area and ultimately limit their own appeal.

Extending the Urban Fabric

Introducing a mix of new activities is, of course, one of the most effective strategies for revitalizing the urban waterfront and making it a more vital part of the city. However, public policies have at times gotten in the way of urban revitalization by preventing the urban fabric from being extended to the waterfront. As the result of certain natural resource policies, for example, large habitat preserves are sometimes set aside for wildlife but made inaccessible to the general public, or are reserved for special, visitor-oriented uses that do little to make the waterfront a part of daily life in the city. Although appropriate to many environments, the preservation of waterfront lands as open space can be counterproductive in urbanized areas, where the waterfront offers a tremendous opportunity for the types of infill development

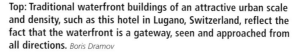

Top: Traditional waterfront buildings of an attractive urban scale and density, such as this hotel in Lugano, Switzerland, reflect the fact that the waterfront is a gateway, seen and approached from all directions. *Boris Dramov*

Middle: San Francisco's Northeast Waterfront was acclaimed by the *San Francisco Chronicle* as "the most striking success to date anywhere in this country and perhaps the world . . . of citizen participatory planning turned into a work of civic art. The result is not a patched-up popular compromise but a lordly urban vision." *Herb Lingl*

Left: The preservation of waterfront lands as open space can be counterproductive where the waterfront offers a development opportunity that will improve the city's image, character, and quality of life. While most of the frontage on the Willamette River, in Portland, Oregon, remains an open-space park, the 73-acre (30-hectare) RiverPlace development extends city activity to the river. *Randy Shelton*

that will improve a city's image, character, and quality of life. While environmental values are important in any setting, when they are implemented at the expense of the urban environment and the livability of the city, they need to be reconsidered.

Similarly, although visitor-oriented commercial uses play an important role on the waterfront, they cannot be solely relied on to transform the waterfront into a living, working part of the city. In fact, such uses may intensify the sense that the waterfront is separate from the city, by making it appear to be reserved for special occasions. No place can be sustained by occasional events and activities: what is needed is not a single use, no matter how successful, but diverse neighborhoods that extend the fabric of the city to the waterfront. It is the common, day-to-day activities—waiting for the ferry, catching a cab, buying a

newspaper, getting a cup of coffee—that add layers of meaning to a place.

Perhaps the most common mistake in waterfront redevelopment is allowing the amenity of the waterfront to be experienced only at the water's edge. Whether buildings have introverted or extroverted functions, they should be designed to promote public access to and visibility of the waterfront. High-rise developments that block the shoreline, private residential complexes that turn toward the waterfront and away from the city, gated developments that afford their residents views of the water but limit accessibility for others—all are examples of the kinds of injustices wrought along numerous shorelines. By claiming the waterfront as its own exclusive domain, such development takes away the benefits that the waterfront can provide to the city as a whole.

Public policies that limit residential use reflect the legitimate concern that such use can produce a private enclave reserved only for a select few. Such concerns are particularly serious in the case of lower-density developments, where one single-family house on a large lot can effectively seal off a long stretch of shoreline from public access. Urban-density residential development can be an entirely different affair, however. By its very nature, it is more publicly oriented, bringing large numbers of residents and guests, as well as activity, to the waterfront. Residential buildings that are designed as part of a neighborhood and conceived as part of a larger urban pattern, that are made more open to the public through first floors that are dedicated to lively commercial uses, and that are set back from the water's edge, with respect for inland views and public access, are among the best means of reuniting the waterfront with the city.

Diversity in building heights is an important means of giving the urban form an interesting composition and a good balance of fabric and monument. In reaction to the high-rise towers that can block views, and in order to create a gradual stepping down in height as one approaches the water, a number of cities have established relatively low height limits along the waterfront. But over time, this approach can produce a flat, undifferentiated, "pancake" effect, with buildings that lack variety and interest. Fur-

Buildings facing the Coal Harbour area of downtown Vancouver respect the public nature of the waterfront by stepping well away from the shoreline. At left is Canada Place, a convention and exhibition center and cruise-ship terminal; at center is Portside, or Crab, Park; and at far right is Dead Man's Island, a causeway-connected part of Stanley Park. *Waite Air Photos, Inc.*

Rowes Wharf, in Boston, was built on pier structures. Completed in 1987, the complex contains 230 hotel rooms, 100 luxury condominiums, and 345,000 square feet (32,000 square meters) of office space. The archway covers a public plaza that leads to the harborfront. *Steve Rosenthal/Skidmore, Owings & Merrill LLP, Adrian D. Smith, Design Partner*

thermore, the shorter buildings may occupy a large footprint; thus, although they allow views from taller structures inland, they do not do so at grade. Particularly for the pedestrian, the grain of development parcels and the orientation of individual buildings on the parcels are often as significant as height in determining visibility and access. Furthermore, contrary to conventional wisdom, taller buildings are not necessarily more visually obstructing than shorter ones, as evidenced by the small-footprint towers used to create a vital urban neighborhood on Vancouver's northern waterfront.

Waterfront Buildings

The design of the buildings that are constructed along the shoreline, whatever their use, should reflect the fact that the waterfront is a gateway, seen and approached from all directions. In other words, because buildings in a waterfront setting are uniquely visible, they should be designed with balanced facades, one facing the city and the other the water. In practical terms, this means, for example, that uses that demand privacy may not be able to achieve it at grade, but may instead have to be elevated on terraces overlooking the waterfront and the city.

Creativity will also be required in meeting the servicing requirements of large and complex buildings. Because of the size and orientation of the sites, the significant support needs of resort hotels and resort residential developments can often be absorbed into the overall form and massing of buildings. In an urban waterfront context, however, incorporating the "back of the house" functions in such a way as to ensure that one face of the building is not celebrated at the expense of another requires careful planning.

The task of integrating modern activities into waterfront buildings is even more difficult on pier structures, which are being increasingly adapted for new urban uses. Maritime piers recall the age of break-bulk cargo handling and contribute to the historic character and identity of the waterfront; but, depending on their size and landside relationships, they are often ill suited to reuse and redevelopment. Manhattan's Chelsea Piers and Boston's Rowes Wharf provide two different examples of what can be accomplished on pier structures, but few pier redevelopment projects have been able to replicate their success.

One problem is the high cost of rehabilitating aging pier structures. One of the grandest historic piers in the world—the West Pier, in Brighton, England—had been falling into the sea for decades, and ultimately collapsed because the necessary funds could not be obtained to repair it. The physical condition of any underused cargo pier must be critically assessed before plans for reuse are begun. It may, for example, be preferable to demolish selected piers and open up the waterfront to public view. Although this way of thinking can be a challenge for governmental entities seeking to transform outmoded facilities into new revenue sources, in cities where the waterfront is hidden behind maritime structures, the removal of piers and wharves can be an important step toward reclaiming the waterfront and integrating it with the city.

Even more significant than cost and condition is the issue of how to integrate maritime structures, such as piers, into the fabric of a city. New and redeveloped buildings present an opportunity to mend the urban fabric and overcome the isolation that can be found in transitioning waterfront districts. The buildings that are most effective in helping to achieve these goals are integrated into a larger pattern of streets and public spaces, creating a viable district or a neighborhood that feels like a part of the city as a whole. This way of thinking underscores the importance of preparing urban design plans that will not only guide overall development but also give close consideration to development grain and scale; the height, massing, and configuration of individual buildings; the activation of ground floors; and the integration of parking into the building envelope.

Too often, preservation and replication of the past are the only criteria applied to plans for the reuse and revitalization of the waterfront. It is important, however, to balance continuity with the past with the challenge of bringing new life and meaning to an area that has been neglected and, in some cases, abandoned. At the same time, it is important to recognize that not every waterfront setting can accommodate a grand new landmark like the Sydney Opera House; the Guggenheim Museum Bilbao; the Tenerife Opera House, in the Canary Islands; or Canada Place, in Vancouver. There are only a few locations in any city where such momentous architecture can be sustained, and these need to be carefully reserved for key structures, in consideration of the identity of the city as a whole.

Bringing the Amenity of the Water Inland

Waterfront designers need to give attention not only to what happens right at the water's edge and over it, both landside and waterside—that is, to the area encompassed by the waterfront in its totality—but also to the progression of experiences that lead into the embrace of the city. Strong connections between the waterfront and the surrounding inland districts are what differentiate a city with a waterfront from a true waterfront city. These con-

Not every waterfront setting can accommodate a grand new landmark building like Santiago Calatrava's addition to the Milwaukee Art Museum. *Timothy Hursley/courtesy of Milwaukee Art Museum*

nections can be forged through a system of public spaces that opens the city up to the water's edge and at the same time extends inland, through esplanades, leafy boulevards, plazas, and promenades. Connections can also be realized in the form of portals through buildings, arcaded structures, extended canopies, stairs, railings, bridges, and piers, as well as through a carefully structured continuum of activities that draws people to the waterfront and into the city. Opening up the waterfront, making it more visible, establishing strong visual and physical linkages to it, stepping development down toward the waterfront, massing buildings to create a distinctive urban form with views to the water, and drawing residents and visitors to a vibrant new neighborhood are all examples of measures that can effectively enlarge the size of the waterfront district, and bring about accompanying increases in value and benefit to the surrounding city.

Up until and immediately following World War II, the maritime waterfront was a lively, active place that offered employment to large numbers of workers and served as a point of embarkation for people and goods. When activities such as shipbuilding and transatlantic passenger service declined, and cargo-handling facilities shifted to container operations and relocated outside central downtown waterfronts, efforts were begun to seek alternative uses for over-water areas. During the postwar years, as leisure time increased, the marina became a popular replacement for defunct maritime uses. Beginning in the 1960s, marinas ranging in size from 500 to over 10,000 berths (at the largest facility at Marina del Rey, in California) began to be built, along with residential development on nearby inland sites. The marina was an effective way of bringing additional boats to the waterfront, satisfying growing recreational demand, and improving an environment characterized by decaying docks and wharves. At the same time, offshore waters began to fill up with fixed berths and slips that were not always active

views. Each body of water has a distinctive spatial form and character that, more than any other feature, gives the waterfront its temperament. Rivers, for example, are linear corridors, confined spaces where water flows continuously between flanking banks, often at some distance below the prevailing grade of a city. Bays and coves are protected enclosures set off from a larger body of water. Ocean beaches offer an immediate, unobstructed connection to the vast expanse of the sea.

In the 1930s and 1940s, aquatic parks, natatoriums, swimming structures, and improved beaches provided

Marinas are paired with residential development to satisfy a growing recreational demand. At Walsh Bay, in Sydney, Australia, Mirvac/Transfield built 140 luxury apartments on the original footprint of a finger wharf. Pier Apartments has under-pier parking for 387 cars and moorings for 49 boats. *Rowan Turner*

because, although boating is a popular sport, few people devote all their leisure time, or even a majority of it, to this one activity. Instead of enlivening the waterfront, marinas can look like parking lots for boats.

The Spatial Dimension of Water

To truly activate the water in conjunction with landside urban revitalization, waterfront redevelopment plans must consider offshore waters in spatial terms, taking into account the inherent fascination of ever-changing

models of recreational design that relied on protected water spaces and incipient coves to enhance the accessibility of the waterfront. Throughout the United States, the Works Project Administration was particularly instrumental in building projects that would open up the shoreline and the water beyond for public recreation. Water remained an open plane and "stage" for activity, not a site to be filled up with fixed, permanent facilities. The more

Often, the waterfront is the only place in a city that is capable of hosting a major event. In Louisville, Kentucky, 1.5 million people visit Waterfront Park each year. Seventy-two acres (29 hectares) of the eventual 85 acres (34 hectares) have been completed.
Hargreaves Associates

open the water space, the more flexible it remained—and the more intensively it could be used for a variety of purposes, including boating.

In places that are intensely boat oriented, like Sydney, boats typically anchor in or are tethered to buoys in protected coves that are adjacent to beaches used for swimming, sunning, and recreation. Creating destinations and safe anchorages for boaters to sail and motor to is essential to support recreational boating. Thus, planning for recreational boating must give consideration not only to permanent boat storage but also to temporary mooring at a variety of interesting destinations that can attract boaters and add lively activities to waterfront locations. Boating in smaller, individual vessels—sculling, kayaking, rowing, or canoeing—has increased in popularity and has brought new focus and interest to waterfront sites. The Head of the Charles Regatta, in Cambridge, Massachusetts, an event that focuses on this form of recreation, transforms the Charles River into a linear corridor for viewing the races, with activities spilling onto both banks and over the bridges.

The ability to attract special events and celebrations, such as the Head of the Charles Regatta, is a valuable characteristic of waterfronts. Often, in a built-up city, the waterfront is the only place capable of hosting a major event that draws large numbers of people. One city after another has begun to recognize the value of a parade, bicycle race, festival, celebration, market, or circus in changing the image of a place and initiating the process of cultural adaptation to new urban uses.

Large-scale urban change never takes place suddenly. It involves putting in place a physical framework that will allow activities to evolve over time. Special events can set in motion a series of incremental changes that will establish new traditions and bring new meaning, new activities, and a new identity to the waterfront. This was case with the farmers' market that established itself on a parking lot in front of the Ferry Building, in San Francisco: the market brought new life and focus to the area, creating a kind of new town plaza in spirit, and enabled people to envision the waterfront as a place to gather. Now that the Ferry Building renovation is complete, the Ferry Plaza Market has a more permanent home within it, contributing significantly to a setting that it helped to transform.

Waterborne Transportation

Anything having to do with waterborne transportation is a welcome addition to the waterfront and is key to bringing activities and people to it. Waterborne transportation is an authentic maritime activity that relates back to the historic role of the waterfront as a center for the movement of people and goods. Today, waterfront cities have a competitive advantage in being able to offer an alternative to automobile and truck transportation and their accompanying congestion and pollution. With the recent development of faster, nonpolluting and more energy-efficient vessels, the opportunities for waterborne transportation have expanded enormously. In New York, ferries efficiently carry large numbers of commuters to work, and a new inland distribution network uses barges to transport freight to inland ports such as Albany, taking trucks off the highway. Recent catastrophic events, such as the Loma Prieta earthquake and the destruction of the World Trade Center, further highlighted the importance of waterborne transportation. After these events, ferries emerged as the only reliable means for commuters to move from shore to shore; in New York, barges also carried away enormous quantities of debris.

Ferries can bring transit patrons directly into a city, facilitate transfers to bicycle, or serve as the first leg of a journey that will be completed by shuttle, taxi, or on foot;

in appropriate settings, they can simultaneously transport freight. Travel over water is highly pleasurable, providing expansive views and the opportunity to experience an impressive approach to a city. For all its advantages, though, waterborne transit cannot be expected to succeed if it is not visible or if it is poorly located—stuck in an old abandoned pier, for example. Public and semi-public agencies need to demonstrate their commitment to ferry service, and to provide high-quality facilities that reflect consideration of the comfort and convenience of the transit patron. In this way, ferry ridership will continue to increase along with other vital, genuine activities on the urban waterfront.

Movement and a Sense of Place

Whether waterborne or landside, transportation is an integral part of the urban waterfront. Embarkation, arrival, and movement through and to the waterfront are an essential part of its identity. In recent years, many people who were concerned about the impact of the automobile—and, in particular, about the development of freeways and other major corridors on waterfront land—concluded that movement should be eliminated altogether from the waterfront environment. But such a step would deprive the waterfront of one of the basic activities that give it life.

Lakeshore Drive, in Chicago, and Storrow Drive, in Boston, are two examples of once-elegant waterfront boulevards that, with the advent of the automobile, were transformed into freewaylike corridors. Like the freeways that they presaged, these drives replaced urban-scale streets used for driving, viewing, and promenading with single-purpose facilities that provided through-passage at the expense of a sense of place. These roads create the sense that the waterfront is a service area—a place to pass through, but not to linger.

Current transportation practice relies on measures such as "level of service" to determine how facilities should be designed. But demand-driven design, based solely on the automobile, is fundamentally flawed, and usually produces

Lakeshore Drive, in Chicago, was once an elegant boulevard that automobiles have transformed into a freewaylike corridor, creating the sense that the waterfront, cut off from the city by a ten-lane expressway, has become a service area—a place to pass by or through, rather than to actively use. *Boris Dramov*

something that no one wants to live with. Experience has shown that attempts to "build your way out of congestion" will fail. New capacity is almost always swallowed up by insatiable demand for automobile travel (most often in single-occupant vehicles), and the physical changes required to increase traffic capacity inevitably degrade and diffuse the street-level pedestrian experience. At the same time, there is increasing recognition that a certain amount of congestion is fitting to a healthy urban center, and that successful solutions to transportation issues consider a number of factors beyond the capacity available to a single mode of travel.

Design approaches to transportation and circulation need to be based on the appropriate size and scale of the site and facilities, and on a determination of how much is desirable to fit within the facilities. On the urban waterfront, redundancy in movement systems is critical, as is the integration of a mix of transportation modes; in particular, it is important to provide adequate space for certain modes, such as the bicycle, that are well suited to the typically flat topography and continuity of the shoreline. Even more than in other parts of the city, waterfront transportation corridors should serve as mixed-use public spaces, providing for the movement of bicycles and pedestrians as well as vehicles, and for various forms of public transit.

In designing the urban waterfront, emphasis must be given to its role not only as a place to move through but as a destination in itself. As a general rule, no more than 50 percent of the public domain of the street right-of-way should be devoted exclusively to automobile movement. Open space should be incorporated generously into transportation design. In this way, the waterfront will not only "read" as a public place; it will also have the opportunity to truly become one.

The Sensory Experience

Creating places for people is a necessary part of restructuring and reclaiming land. In recent years, the predominant view of the waterfront as a service area has been supplemented by another view, in which it is a place not only to work but also to live and play. Too often, however, current trends in landscape design defeat these values, producing spaces that are intended to be complete without any people in them. Even if aesthetically composed, such places appear two-dimensional—unengaged, and standing apart from the environment and context.

However, the social use of public space determines its value over time. Getting people to engage in a range of experiences—social and solitary, active and quiet—means more than creating visual and symbolic meanings; it also means embracing the sensory qualities of the environment, the features that enliven and exhilarate but that are not necessarily visually explicit. The sensory experience, key to the unique spirit of the waterfront, might come from the feel of saltwater spray against the skin, from the sense of dappled shade along a leafy promenade, from the scent of water-saturated soil, from a breath of humid air, or from the sensation, when walking on a pier or breakwater, of being on a boat at sea, imagining remote and distant destinations.

The well-designed urban waterfront heightens the sensory experience and enhances the natural enjoyable features of the environment. The contrast between land and water is heightened, and the natural scale of the setting is recognized. Essential features are expressed simply, allowing the place to reveal itself and be "discovered" by individuals on their own terms. Good waterfront design is both engaging and flexible, offering meaning in layered experiences, leaving something for the imagination and room for direct, personal experience. There should be no attempt to design around a single purpose; instead, good

waterfront design seeks a multiplicity of purposes and meanings, and allows a place to change, adapt, and gain in value over time.

Heightening Awareness of the Waterfront

Some of the most memorable interventions are those that reveal, through their appearance, the intrinsic qualities of the landscape—and, in doing so, heighten awareness of the waterfront environment. The massive bulk of the stone breakwater at Lyme Regis, in England, tells a story about the power and turbulence of the Atlantic coast. At Aquatic Park, built in the 1930s by the Works Progress Administration on San Francisco's northern waterfront, an enclosing breakwater was used to extend an incipient cove, creating a bay beach and an amphitheater for aquatic sports. The light and transparent cast-iron piers high above the water in Brighton, England, give the visitor a sense of being on a sea voyage, far from land and earthbound concerns. The sense of enchantment ignited by *WaterFire,* an art installation in downtown Providence, Rhode Island, captures the magic and mystery of

Started in 1994 in Providence, Rhode Island, Barnaby Evans's *WaterFire* has expanded to 97 braziers and some 25 lightings a year—an eloquent testimony to the power of public art and a moving symbol of Providence's renaissance. *Barnaby Evans*

The perimeter trail at Vancouver's 1,000-acre (405-hectare) Stanley Park follows the 5.5-mile (8.85-kilometer) seawall, drawing people to the outermost reach of land into water space.
Boris Dramov

flowing water, the darkness of the water at night, and its reflective, prismatic quality when used as a backdrop for light and fire.

Contrast is an effective tool for heightening awareness of the waterfront environment. The Shinto custom of venerating a sacred island by encircling it with rope, Christo's installation of *Running Fence* along the California coast, Robert Smithson's *Spiral Jetty*, and Andy Goldsworthy's *Red Ponds,* as well as more anonymous constructions—a curving breakwater extending a headlands promontory, a diving platform at the edge of a rocky cliff, an ephemeral set of stepping-stones that disappear when the tide is high and reemerge when the tide is low, a cove that serves as an amphitheater for aquatic performances, a lower-level promenade along a river corridor, a floating platform that appears to be an island to swim to—all of these are elements that offer two realities: one that is closely connected to the everyday life of the city, and another that reflects a more intense consciousness of the natural world.

The Line of Force

The water's edge is a line of force in the landscape, expressing the interaction of the shore with the water body: whether it moves inland or pushes outward; whether it is straight or sinuous; whether it adheres tightly to the form of rugged outcroppings in a fortification of solid rock or arcs broadly around a flattened perimeter of filled land. In the urban waterfront, this line is reinforced by a seawall or floodwall placed at the outermost reach where land can feasibly encroach into the water space—that is, deep water on a bay, as far forward as the nearest dune on the ocean beach, to the top of the channel on a river. The energy that is concentrated within this urban line has a strong magnetic quality, bringing people to and along the edge.

Urban waterfronts are linear in nature, and the simplicity of the line creates tremendous appeal. This is a positive feature, yet there is often a tendency to negate the bold linearity of the waterfront with the thinking that it is just "not enough" on its own. Instead, this linear simplicity is replaced by a plethora of created shapes intended to create variety and "interest." City after city has made the

A timber deck encloses a shallow beach in Honolulu. This simple gesture celebrates the duality of the water's edge by blurring the distinction between land water. *Boris Dramov*

mistake of building confectionary embellishments at the water's edge that compete with the power and majesty of the waterfront. In successful waterfront design, humility plays an important role, along with the recognition that it is often the simple "moves" that are most long-lasting.

The Duality of the Water's Edge

The urban waterfront gains its identity, to a great extent, from its condition as an "edge." It is the boundary between one world and another, the ultimate demarcation of the city and of the land. It is a transitional space that holds great latent potential—the suggestion of adventure, of settling in; of embarking, of arriving; of entering into and coming out of. It is the juxtaposition of the realm of land with that of water, and the heightening of the contrast between the two, that uniquely characterizes and defines the urban waterfront.

Often, in intensely developed cities, the waterfront is the most powerful representation of the presence of the natural world, a place outside the ordinary dominion of urban dwellers. The sensory experiences that it evokes, the temporal influences that it asserts, and the spatial expanse that it creates are all a part of an environment that breathes life and vitality into the urban world. Understanding the special qualities of the waterfront, and heightening the sense of nature

within the city, are fundamental considerations in waterfront design. Public access to the water should not only imply direct linkages, but also embrace the larger form and structure of the city and its associated physical, visual, and cultural dimensions.

The waterfront needs to embody dual realms of land and sea; it needs to speak two languages. Artistic juxtaposition and dramatic heightening of these two "characters" will reveal the essential identity of a place and enhance its meaning. The waterfront is temporal: the ebb and flow of the tides; the seasonal changes in water level; the periodic inundations; the erosions and accretions; the tsunamis, seiches, and high waves—all are characteristic of water bodies. Whether the body of water is a lake, river, or ocean, the dynamic qualities of the water's edge should be made visible. This is an important part of the individuality of place that needs to be built on as waterfronts are improved. Places such as the Malecon, in Havana; the Charleston promenade, in South Carolina; the Strandvagen, in Stockholm; the bulwark in St. Malo, France; the beach boardwalk of Atlantic City; the Strand, in Los Angeles; the leafy promenades of alpine lakefronts; the Children's Pool, in La Jolla; Pier 7, in San Francisco; and the lowered quays along the Seine, in Paris: all celebrate the changing nature of the water's edge and the ephemerality of the relationship between land and water.

The principles that guide the design of the urban waterfront are not unique. In most cases, they are relevant to public spaces and urban design as well. However, circumstances today place the urban waterfront at the front line for redevelopment and renewal in cities. The opportunity is to seize the potential that now exists—to reclaim waterfront lands and integrate them into the city, and, in so doing, strengthen the identity of the city and the quality of urban life.

Chapter 4

Environmental Issues in Waterfront Development

Gavin McMillan and Emma Stark Schiffman

aterfront sites with the greatest potential are often among the most ignored sections of our cities. Not only are these sites simply dirty; they are abused, derelict, and plagued by environmental issues: unstable landfills, contaminated soils and water, lost habitats, disturbed artifacts, trapped sedimentary pollutants . . . the list goes on. Nevertheless, urban dwellers and developers alike still value these waterfronts: nothing quite compares to the experience of being close to the water's edge. In the cycle of urban development and redevelopment, waterfronts are once again environments of opportunity. And this time around, with a greater understanding of the environmental issues inherent in waterfront sites and a commitment to an environmentally sensitive approach, it is possible, in the process of redeveloping the waterfront, to improve the environment rather than degrade it.

Helped by increased community awareness and education; by the enforcement of local, state, and federal regulation; by progress in science and technology; and by positive built examples, the development community is able to identify and effectively address the environmental issues associated with waterfronts. Such progress has led to a reexamination of the waterfront's natural and cultural systems, opening up entirely new possibilities for working with and reconfiguring those systems while enhancing their ecological performance, cultural significance, and economic value. This chapter offers a framework for exploring these possibilities. It is not a regulatory checklist for approaching and surmounting environmental "obstacles." Instead, it examines the principal environmental issues that affect the front end of waterfront development and describes approaches to addressing them. The goal of the chapter is to present options that can help inform strategic waterfront development decisions.

A Systems Approach

Developers, designers, planners, and citizens tend to see the waterfront as a discrete site to be acted upon. From this perspective, waterfront sites are bounded physically and temporally and are generally defined in relation to a particular set of uses (industry or trade) or a specific locality (the city). But from an environmental perspective, the waterfront is part of a much larger context and is complicated by the intricacy of its ecosystems. Ecosystems contain millions

Typical Environmental Issues

The following environmental issues are among those that typically arise at waterfronts. They can be considered in terms of their physical, cultural, and ecological impact on the site.

Soils
Sediments: Deposits from upstream sources may contain debris and can limit water depth, constrain navigation, and convey pollutants.
Soil: May be contaminated with toxins such as heavy metals, oil and grease, pesticides, dry-cleaning fluid, industrial chemicals, and dust and ash.

Water
Groundwater: Level may fluctuate; may be contaminated by leachate.
Surface water: May be contaminated by bacterial pollution and by discharges from boats.
Stormwater: May be polluted from catchments; flow may be disrupted.
Floodwaters: May limit habitable building elevations and setbacks.

Structures
Foundations: May be unstable; may have settled unevenly because of poor fill; may be corroded from chemicals or aeration.

Buildings: May contain contaminated materials or asbestos.
Marine bulkheads, piles, and piers: May have been damaged by weather, moisture, salts, or expiring design life.
Remnants: Historically significant buildings and structures may be present.
Relics: Sunken marine craft may be present.

Sensitive Materials
Waste: Gas or landfill soil may be present.
Energy sources: Waste or spills from energy sources may be present.
Artifacts: Historic or prehistoric artifacts may be present.

Flora and Fauna
Plants: Loss of habitat from clearing and filling, weed invasion, remnant wetlands, species loss of sea grass.
Animals: Invasive animals (e.g., zebra mussels) may be present; protected or endangered species or habitats may be present or at risk.

Uses
Transportation: Negative impacts may be present from infrastructure and navigation structures;
site may be affected by vessel speeds, wakes, or pollution.
Dumping: Pollution or contaminated fill may be present.

Relationship between Environment and Development
Although environmental issues are often viewed in terms of their effect on successful development, it also possible to consider the reverse: the ways in which a successful development will affect environmental concerns. Here are three ways of approaching the relationship between environment and development:
1. How might the current environment affect potential development? Waterfronts have been reworked many times, and usually come with a cultural inheritance from previous uses and abuses.
2. How might the potential development (e.g., increased boating, canalization, more hard surfaces) affect the current environment?
3. How might the future environment (e.g., a change in sea level, weather, or river management) affect any potential development?

of entities—living species, chemical compounds, forms and fluxes of energy—that are dynamically linked on different scales. In this view, the waterfront becomes defined through the continuous overlapping of land and water: its scale billows beyond the site to encompass the river, the harbor, the bay, the estuary, and the coast. Regional in scope, environmental concerns about waterfronts must take into account the effects of any particular development choice on a vast ecological system. Changes in both the form and function of a site can affect ecosystems downstream, upstream, or offshore. Thus, urban waterfront development entails examining the relationship between development and regional water ecosystems, as well as codifying in ordinances the desire to respect the water ecosystems.

Because ecosystems are immensely complex, environmental issues are among the most difficult to deal with in waterfront development. Dealing with such complex systems requires a systems approach. Through awareness

The seasonal Guadalupe River, which supports the migratory patterns of steelhead and Chinook salmon, courses through the heart of San Jose, California, where a flood-control project integrates urban open space, cultural events, and habitat restoration.
Hargreaves Associates

and understanding of the operating principles of systems, it becomes possible to emulate, in our own decision-making processes, the way that systems work: that is, to be multifaceted, interdisciplinary, and integrative in our understanding, treatment, and design of site systems.

The Major Issues

When it comes to land use decisions for waterfront development, the most significant issues fall into one of four major categories: flooding, natural resources, cultural resources, and contamination. These categories are not only useful in the abstract, as a means of conceptualizing the concerns associated with waterfronts, but are also regulatory imperatives: local, state, and federal regulatory structures all require that these four categories be addressed through research, planning, and design technology.

Flooding

Flooding is a process that has literally made waterfronts. It is an issue both timeless (seasonal and epochal flood trends have given geological shape to waterfronts) and immediate (recurrent flooding affects use and short-term development).

Flooding is a natural phenomenon within the hydrologic cycle of a region, and is a necessary occurrence through which nutrients and fine-grain sediments are returned to soil systems. Natural flood events of varying scales can be predicted—or at least expected—at certain temporal junctures: rainy-season high water, for example, and ten-year and 100-year floods. These cycles have been affected by an increase in the amount of waterfront development and the infrastructure that is needed to support it, which vastly increase surface runoff and lead to concomitant spikes in flood pulses. As more water runs off hard surfaces into storm drains (and, hence, into waterfronts), less is infiltrated back into local groundwater systems; the result is that the speed, volume, and force of runoff are less predictable and more damaging.

Flooding leaves its mark at the waterfront on both built and natural systems. It can cause erosion of river and estuarial edges because of flood pulses. On sites where the water's edge has long had structures such as levees and walls, the effects of floods can be seen in the layers of sedimentary deposits and refuse that collect and build in the floodway channel.

Federal regulations require municipalities to map floodplain and floodway boundaries. Although the regulations distinguish between urban and rural floodways, habitable development is generally restricted to the floodway fringe—that is, to the area outside the major conveyance route of a 100-year flood. Development within the floodway could exacerbate the effects of storms by raising water levels. Within the floodplain, fringe development must still adhere to flood-sensible design guidelines regarding building elevation and materials.

Davenport, Iowa, and Rock Island, Illinois, offer examples of two different responses to flooding. In the Quad Cities area, where these cities are located, the Mississippi River floods regularly, with great vigor and spread, with resultant devastating effects on property and infrastructure; in the summer of 1993, for example, the river level rose seven feet (two meters) above normal crest and remained high for 43 days.

Rock Island and Davenport sit on opposite sides of the river, normally divided by 2,000 feet (610 meters) of placid water. Rock Island, to the west, boasts a vast network of levees and dikes designed and constructed with help from the U.S. Army Corps of Engineers. Although these structures ensure that the city is largely protected from flood effects, they have also cut off this river city from its river, both physically and visually, and have led to the false assumption that it is safe to develop up to the edge of the river.

Davenport, on the eastern side of the Mississippi, chose to accept the cycles of flooding: the city bought out the remaining residential areas in the floodplain and retained governmental control of the riverfront. In addition, the city encourages (and provides financial incentives for) flood-sensitive development on the floodplain; here, parking and other nonessential functions are placed on the first, floodable, floors of buildings within the floodplain. As a result of its flood policies, Davenport experienced minimal actual property damage from the 1993 flood, despite its severity, and most of this damage was to recreational and industrial areas.

Nonetheless, the city has, on several occasions, considered constructing a levee and floodwall system similar to Rock Island's. However, the average annual maintenance costs for such a system would be only slightly outstripped by the liability costs resulting from the 1993 floods. Moreover, there has been some suggestion that the existing containment structures—

Davenport, Iowa, and Rock Island, Illinois, cities across the Mississippi River from each other, represent two opposite approaches to the mitigation of river flooding. This satellite image taken after the flood of April 2001 shows Davenport (upper, to the north) with its submerged riverfront, and Rock Island (lower, to the south) protected by its system of levees.
spaceimaging.com

miles and miles of levees up and down the Mississippi, extending along significant portions of the floodplain and floodways—have exacerbated the effect of flooding on both sides of the river by raising the waters in the unprotected portions of the floodway.

One could argue, then, that though Davenport's approach seems foolhardy, it is the more economical tactic in the long term because it takes into account both the physics of flood events and the economics of large-scale engineering. Moreover, Davenport's policy reflects no naïveté about the realities of flood events—events that, even when mitigated by containment structures, will always damage property built on the floodplain.

Natural Resources

The interplay of land-based and water-based environmental systems renders waterfronts unique. Waterfronts are what they are because of the interaction between hydrological and geological systems (water on rocks); wherever land meets water, there is life in its full variety.

Instead of regarding the interaction of land and water as a line, it is helpful to think of it as a zone—a unique entity in itself as well as a transition between diverse systems. The overlap of two ecosystems is referred to as an ecotone, and the range of soil conditions, nutrients, and flora and fauna that occur here, at the water's edge, are among the richest in the world. Common waterfront ecosystems include salt marshes, mudflats, salt- and freshwater wetlands, and sea-grass habitats.

Many potential waterfront development sites appear to be no more than weedy lots or shorelines clogged with waste, and it is easy to miss the more nuanced ecosystems

operating within these environments. Often, even in the most degraded spaces, remnants of the original systems survive. Small patches of remnant wetlands or sea-grass habitat may linger in inaccessible corners or depths. More likely still, these original systems have found the means of adapting to their changing environment. Though no

"Natural looking" and "natural acting" do not necessarily go hand in hand. Sitting atop a reclaimed landfill at the edge of San Francisco Bay, Byxbee Park helps to restore ecological function while encouraging human activity without creating a "natural-looking" project. Here, hillocks atop hills provide both refuge from the wind and prospects of San Francisco Bay. *Hargreaves Associates*

longer pristine or textbook examples of estuarine or marine ecologies, these adaptive systems, which combine elements of both urban environmental systems and the original ecosystems, can be rich as well as rugged. They are home to a surprising number of sensitive populations and fulfill important roles as habitats for both urban wildlife and migratory species.

The current regulatory framework requires mapping—and, sometimes, preservation or conservation—of remnant systems, but often gives little attention to the potential value of adaptive natural systems. A preservationist approach requires the protection of species and landscape types without regard to the contextual realities of site and regional systems. Thus, under such an approach, local site species and habitats would be protected and supported even if the

Byxbee Park's concrete chevrons control erosion while extending the axis of the adjacent Palo Alto airstrip into the park. The chevrons are visible from the air, forming an aeronautical symbol meaning "Don't land here." *Hargreaves Associates*

regional habitat and wildlife populations have been degraded to the point where the site is unable to function independently. In effect, preservation often places value on the protection of endangered species without asking whether local or regional systems remain capable of providing the necessary support and encouraging actual growth.

A conservationist approach pursues a more open-ended goal: to maintain environmental quality and resources, or a particular balance among the species present in a given area, regardless of whether these resources

At the waterfront in Louisville, Kentucky, modern technology and the integration of industrial with urban design have created thriving ecosystems that serve the region without requiring the waterfront to be returned to its original state. *Hargreaves Associates*

are physical, biological, or cultural. With either approach, however, the regulatory structure often gives priority to natural systems technology that has the appearance—or, at least, the hallmarks—of "nature."

In reality, the functioning of an ecosystem may have little to do with its outward appearance—with the aes-

thetics of "nature" that are held dear. Natural looking and natural acting do not necessarily go hand in hand. Natural systems incorporate a range of chemical, biological, and climatic processes that can be both revitalized and regulated via modern industrial technologies, producing ecosystems that reflect human design and influence but retain the natural functions that are their raison d'être.

Postindustrial sites offer the opportunity to rethink traditional dichotomies and to consider *both* the preservation of rare or site-specific species *and* the support of adaptive, but effective, natural systems. One key to working with such sites is the willingness to adopt nontraditional aesthetics in natural systems. Using modern technology and industrial design frameworks, it is possible to create thriving ecosystems that serve their regions without necessarily being returned to their original form.

At Landschaftspark Duisburg-Nord, a former steel refinery in the Ruhr Valley, in northeastern Germany, planners, designers, scientists, and citizens have made possible the regeneration of multiple natural systems. Focusing on function rather than on form, using a variety of technologies, and pursuing differing standards and goals for different elements of the site, the restoration at Duisburg-Nord serves a broad range of audiences and constituencies, human and otherwise.

Here, the effort to reclaim a postindustrial site and to revitalize natural resources and systems has taken two distinct tracks. A number of site systems projects are geared toward human use—visual and recreational. But other regeneration projects focus on the systems themselves, giving every advantage—technical and policy-oriented—to system health rather than human use.

Two restoration efforts that focus on human uses are a farm school, sited on the most open parcel of land, and a series of horticultural interventions that have created unique and exquisite small gardens in former ore storage bunkers. These projects honor a history of cultural landscapes specific to the region and address human interaction with nature according to a particular vision of the connection between the two. The farm school reinvigorates the historical relationship between people and the land that was prevalent before the intervention of industry. The gardens, where former industrial infrastructure has been used to create microclimates in which exotic and exciting species can thrive, evoke an emotional relationship between visitor and site. These exotic plants and plant communities owe their presence on the site to the transport of industrial resources to Duisburg-Nord—a process that, unintentionally, also brought seeds and spores from places far and wide.

In contrast, proactive water reclamation and wilderness protection projects focus on systems that do not result from human activities. The Old Emscher stream, which runs across the site, had been systematically degraded by industrial use and urban expansion, channelized, and used as a dumping and sewage conduit until it was little more than a nightmarishly contaminated open drain. The drain was sealed and buried and is now routed to cleaning facilities off site. Above the former footprint of this black watercourse, a clay liner collects grey runoff from the rest of the site, channeling the runoff into on-site tanks, where it is cleaned and then released. The system is powered by a wind tower constructed out of a former mill tower, and the cleaning tanks are former bunkers, tanks, and cooling ponds. The result is a system whose primary function is the restoration of site hydrology, but that is

The Musée de Pointe-à-Callière, on the St. Lawrence River, in Montreal, is a museum of local history and archaeology that exhibits the city's economic, cultural, and environmental relationship to the river. *Pierre Langlois*

also didactic, visibly explaining the process of surface water collection and cleaning.

A huge percentage of the site is actually closed to human use. In these "wilderness" areas, passive land-farming techniques are being used to remediate contaminated soils, and the natural regeneration of secondary urban growth is allowed to progress unchecked. The resulting thick, brushy growth and secondary forest provide valuable habitat to both native species and migratory populations. This habitat is by no means a strict re-creation of any original, pre-industrial system; in fact, it contains many exotic and urban species. The "wilderness" area demonstrates the ability of adaptive systems to support native fauna and ecological function, albeit without appearing outwardly to be in a classic, "natural" condition.

The longer-term processes of soil farming, wilderness regrowth, and watercourse cleaning are not compatible with human uses, as the risk of contamination is still too high, and the native and migratory species' habitats are too fragile to support human incursion. Thus, in these spaces, natural systems are given priority and human intervention is often excluded, to the benefit of all. Landschaftspark Duisburg-Nord highlights the ways in which the regeneration of natural systems can satisfy both human and ecological interests.

A waterfront restoration can reveal the rich layers of cultural history at a site. Crissy Field, part of the Golden Gate National Recreation Area, represents the spectrum of its historical uses, from the days of the indigenous Ohlone people to its 20th-century use as an Army base (before, top, and after, bottom). *Hargreaves Associates*

Cultural Resources

Cultural resources come into existence when people first begin to leave their mark on waterfronts: they represent the palimpsest of human activity and influence on waterfront sites. Fill, landfill, remnant structures, and landforms: all bear testament to a site's history of human uses.

Waterfronts have attracted human settlement and activity since prehistoric times. Waterfront cities were founded at unique junctures of land, water, and culture that afforded opportunities for resource mining, trade, transportation, ceremony, life, growth, and development. The unique confluence of water, sanitation, food, salt and other minerals, fuel, building materials, and conveyance to other resources and markets provided the original impetus for the economies of many settlements.

Early settlements were tightly connected to waterfronts because their industries and activities were vitally water dependent. As the value of the resources in and around waterfronts grew, towns grew as well, and so did their dependency on their waterfronts. Typically, this growing dependency led to attempts to modify the wider environment (the flood control efforts discussed earlier are an example), but also resulted in site-specific physical modifications: harbors were filled in, and rivers dammed and channelized; bays became ports; streams became sewers; and forests were cleared for fuel and building materials. The environmental impacts of waterfront towns and cities began to appear in physical form.

Pointe-à-Callière, the waterfront Montreal Museum of Archaeology and History, is an excellent and moving example of the historic layering of cultural resources; through a variety of visual and interactive formats, the museum offers visitors both the opportunity to encounter physical remnants of the past and to explore attitudes toward the waterfront and the city's connection to it. The museum straddles the city's birthplace, at the confluence of the St. Lawrence River and a stream. Visitors can walk down into the basement, to the level that the city used to inhabit, and see how the stream became a drain and then a sewer, how the city was built and rebuilt, how fill was built on fill.

Crissy Field, part of the Golden Gate National Recreation Area on the San Francisco Bay, offers an example of how a contemporary waterfront restoration can not only reveal the rich and complex layers of cultural history at a site, but can also forge a conceptual and functional relationship between those layers. At Crissy Field, the restoration of the tidal marshes honors the early settlements of the Ohlone and other native peoples whose cultures depended on the marshes. Early Spanish and Mexican colonization of the site still makes its presence felt in the buildings, structures, archaeological ruins, and landscape features of the Presidio Campus, the former Army base,

Washington's Landing, a 42-acre (17-hectare) island on the Allegheny River, in Pittsburgh, rehabilitated a brownfield with a 200-year history of such water-dependent industrial uses as oil and paint refineries, and meat processing and rendering. Since its completion, in 2000, the development has added 90 residential units and 225,000 square feet (20,900 square meters) of office space. *Mark C. Schneider*

which were deliberately retained as a backdrop to the open space of Crissy Field itself. In the center of the site, a raised, 28-acre (11.3-hectare), kidney-shaped lawn recalls the Panama Pacific International Exposition Grand Prix race-track of 1915 and the World War I airbase, both of which were once sited here. At the eastern end of the site, constructed landforms, in dune shapes, filter out the noise and activity of the city and frame, at a human scale, an entrance to the majesty of the bay. At the site's west end, hunkered at the base of the Fort Point channel, earthen bunkers that recall military structures shelter picnic tables and amphitheater structures. A final major component of this national park is a promenade that crosses the site and connects all its elements, creating a continuous pedestrian and bicycle route along the bay and into the city.

To restore the tidal function of the saltwater marshes that had previously been cut off from salt water, it was necessary to remove a massive amount of fill and dismantle a concrete breakwall. While the salt marshes have not been restored to their full original extent, the 20-acre (eight-hectare) restoration is sufficiently ample to function as a marsh and has drawn native wildlife not seen at Crissy Field for over 50 years. The presence of wildlife is key to recalling the cultural landscape of the Ohlone and other native peoples: because of Crissy Field's rich natural resources, it was a site where food was gathered and processed. Thus, in addition to repairing a natural system and natural resources, the restoration of the salt marshes speaks to the relationship between local native cultures and the water.

The remaining, filled portion of the site is designed to recover and reexamine other historical cultural elements, including the grass landing strip where the first trans-Pacific test flights were launched and where important advances in aeronautical engineering were achieved. Input from the National Park Service and the public ensured that the airstrip would both provide an opportunity for historic veneration and interpretation and satisfy community requirements for a large, functional gathering space and for sports fields.

Finally, by recalling that dune and bunker structures were in earthworks, the design highlights both natural and cultural, site-specific forms associated with waterfront processes and purposes. These forms offer sheltered, evocative spaces for educational and small-group activities and also create a buffer between the urban edge and the recreational nature of the park. A sensitive placement of the promenade, which crosses all these areas—pointedly negotiating the interior spaces, the fragile water's edge, and the dune restorations—allows for contemporary appreciation and use of the site.

The example of Crissy Field highlights several important issues regarding cultural resources. First, Crissy Field strives to achieve a balance between the preservation of particular elements—such as structures listed on historic registers—and the conservation of wider concepts, such as cultural landscapes. (Such an approach has a parallel in the area of natural resources.) The design of Crissy Field is not based on blind adherence to regulatory requirements that demand the preservation of particular structural elements or the recreation of individual moments in the site's history. Instead, it strives to evoke a range of historical moments and cultural uses of the site. And so, rather than returning the site to a single moment in time, the design incorporates multiple eras, and even attempts—through programming and cross-functionality—to bring these eras into contemporary dialogue.

Contamination

As a result of cultural trends associated with industrial development; historical attitudes toward the ownership, use, and valuation of waterfront realty; and the necessities of transportation, power, and cooling (which often required industry to be sited along watercourses), many waterfronts are damaged—heir to a long history of pollution and neglect.

Through the combined effects of industrialization and zoning, waterfronts became not only places of specialized work but also the repositories of concentrated by-products. Materials brought from elsewhere were funneled through waterfront industries, processed, and sent to the next destination, leaving only waste behind. As time went on, waterfront uses and processes were not even necessarily water dependent. Instead, the value of the waterfront was reduced to, and equated with, its ability to serve as an expandable dumping site—an area that could be layered with additional waste and fill in order to create space for even more industry or for burgeoning urban infrastructure.

Even industries that were not water dependent have historically been sited at waterfronts to take advantage of water as a cleaning resource for industrial processes. Such uses brought with them a long history of spills, both intentional (dumping) and accidental, leaving chemicals and metals within the soil and groundwater. In addition, the traditional process of stabilizing waterfront sites and leveling natural slopes or eroded banks, to allow the construction of factories and warehouses, has added much toxic fill to site soil profiles.

Other potential contaminants prevalent at waterfront sites include the following: elevated levels of VOCs (volatile organic compounds), SVOCs (semi-volatile organic compounds) and PCBs (polychlorinated biphenyls), from leaking underground storage tanks or from petroleum spillage; cyanide and heavy metals, from shipbuilding processes and lumber mills; and slag, foundry sands, and general industrial fill. Even if these substances are removed or covered, remaining contamination—residing in the soil and even in the bricks of buildings—often continues to leach into the groundwater, and volatile residues in the soil can continue to affect the use of the site.

At the former site of the BP-Amoco refinery, on the North Platte River, in Casper, Wyoming, a 6,000-foot (1,829-meter) subsurface barrier was installed to counteract the plumes of petroleum contamination that still permeate the soil and migrate toward the waterway. The barrier is only a partial solution, however. Despite being contaminated, the groundwater is vital to the health and functioning of local ecologies and the river itself. Thus, the barrier has been paired with an aggressive program of inground groundwater recovery that relies on hydraulic well pumping, groundwater and soil flushing and cleaning via phytoremediation, and fresh groundwater recharge. Together, these measures ensure the full regeneration of the affected groundwater systems.

Programmatic elements of the reuse plan also contribute to the future health of the site: a golf course designed to complement a new business park includes wetlands and treatment ponds that collect and treat surface runoff and irrigation before they infiltrate the groundwater plume, and a whitewater and kayak course designed for this stretch of the North Platte actively supports the property's hydraulic containment system.

Once federal regulatory review is complete, remediation can take any of three approaches. Toxic materials may be excavated, contained, and moved off site to a specialized landfill, where they will be encapsulated or stabilized and buried. Alternatively, contaminated soils and fill may be covered with an impermeable cap of stable materials. Finally, in an approach gaining more currency in recent decades, contaminated materials can be subjected to a variety of both in situ and ex situ processes designed to reduce their toxic content or to at least stabilize the path of their chemical release and effect.

The first two alternatives—sometimes cynically dubbed "hog and haul" and "cap and cover," essentially perpetuate a culture of contamination. These approaches cover up the traces of an unsavory past, minimizing public awareness of industrial history and its physical effects by keeping contamination out of both physical reach and the public eye. In the third approach, remediation is regarded as an opportunity to incorporate regenerative processes as integral design elements and as part of the functional program of a site. At Landschaftspark Duisburg Nord, for example, remediation processes are embraced on three levels: as design elements, as a means of restoring natural systems, and as part of the programmatic structure. But this example is unusual: though a number of cutting-edge projects have adopted remediation as the core design element and focused on making reclamation visible to the public, not all remediation choices must be as radical to be either responsible or successful. Often, the most responsible approach includes the careful evaluation and selection of multiple remediation strategies: from capping and covering to hogging and hauling to strategic rezoning and land use planning.

The reclamation and redevelopment of HarborPark, in Kenosha, Wisconsin, illustrates the possible range of approaches to contamination: technological, policy oriented, market based, and zoning based. Here, on a site formerly occupied by a series of industries—a bedframe factory, a Chrysler assembly plant, a solid-waste disposal facility—a new, mixed-use development incorporates commercial facilities, recreational spaces, public transportation systems, new civic institutions, and a range of housing options.

Before handing the site over to the municipality, the Chrysler Corporation, working with environmental engineers, undertook remediation efforts. Remediation strategies included a combination of the three options described earlier: a large portion of the slag and foundry sands were removed from the site, other areas were capped, and some soils were treated to eliminate petrochemical residues. But because so much of the 69-acre (28-hectare) site was built on fill in Lake Michigan, the city had to take a lead role in its redevelopment, beginning with creative rezoning and the careful siting of housing and recreation. Housing was confined to the upper, nonfilled areas of the site, where hauling, capping, and remediation were combined to create the cleanest soils. Because private development is restricted on filled lakefront areas, the city took ownership and control of these parts of the site, reserving them

for major institutions, such as museums, and large-scale recreation, such as promenades and marinas.

The positive results—an integrated development containing housing, cultural institutions, commercial projects, and a recreational hub for the city—would not have been possible without strategic use of the full range of responses to contamination.

Approaches to the Issues

Sites affected by flooding, natural resources, cultural resources, and contamination—and few sites are not affected by all four—cannot be made usable without action on the developer's part. However, as is clear from the examples cited, the action that will be taken depends on one's view of the waterfront system and how it func-

HarborPark, in Kenosha, Wisconsin, is a 69-acre (28-hectare) redevelopment of a lakefront industrial site that incorporates commercial, recreational, civic, and residential facilities and new public transportation systems. *Kenosha Department of City Development*

tions. In each of examples cited so far, developers and designers have had to decide whether functional elements of systems should be addressed individually, as problems to be solved, or systematically, as design challenges to be embraced.

In the case of flooding, will on-site flooding be prevented mechanically, or will water-control and water-cleaning systems be incorporated into the site design—

work in concert with both urban and estuarial or marine systems at the local and regional scales?

Should cultural resources be peeled back to a particular valued point in time, or should a range of histories be recognized, affirmed, and skillfully woven together into a cohesive cultural and historical narrative?

What are the economic and cultural advantages and disadvantages of simply making contaminants invisible, versus allowing design to be informed by remediation processes?

What are the economic and cultural advantages and disadvantages of making contaminants invisible, versus displaying the remediation process in the design? At the Sydney Olympics site, greywater and stormwater runoff are treated and recycled in a water feature. *Hargreaves Associates*

which will, not incidentally, enhance the functioning of the larger regional water system?

In the case of natural systems, is success defined as restoring the landscape to conform to a particular image of what is "natural," or can the definition of success be expanded to include the design and support of functional systems of supporting adaptive environments that will

There are two possible attitudes that a developer can take toward environmental issues: a grudging sense of duty that results in a reactive strategy, or an active desire to address the issues through a proactive strategy.

Permits, Assessments, and Approvals Potentially Required for Waterfront Development

- Federal Emergency Management Act flood map approvals
- U.S. Army Corps of Engineers permits
- State water quality and pollution control approvals
- City land disturbance permits

- Environmental assessments or impact statements
- Cultural resource assessments
- Ecological assessments
- Coast Guard navigation approvals

Reactive Strategy

The reactive strategy generally relies on a conventional problem-solving methodology to ensure regulatory compliance or meet legal due diligence standards: identify the problem, then avoid, remove, or mitigate it. Under this approach, development is straightforward and is based on meeting a series of regulatory requirements. Environmental problems are essentially independent variables to be neutralized; they have discrete, linear solutions, and the end development ideal is a reversion of the site to some historical state, form, or function. Thus, the solutions put forward in this approach are often based on returning the site to a preexisting state: a degraded eelgrass habitat should be restored; registered historic structures should be retained; contamination should be removed.

At the heart of the reactive approach is the view that a natural or historic baseline still exists, to which a site can and should be returned. Also at the heart of this approach is a sharp dividing line between analysis and design: analysis is undertaken first, then design is developed *in reaction to* the analysis. Thus, broad (and potentially time-consuming and costly) research is conducted without any thought of an envisioned solution. Although it is true that, in general, the first major step in any redevelopment process is to assess existing conditions, the reactive process restricts this assessment to a set format based on regulatory requirements.

The required Phase 1 report provides a land use history and a graphic and surficial analysis of the site. If the results of the Phase 1 report trigger further analysis, a Phase 2 report, which requires a more intrusive analysis and evaluation of physical site conditions (soil, water, foreign material, and structures), will be undertaken. Since, in the United States, most waterfront developments require federal funding or permitting, an environmental assessment or an environmental impact statement will almost always be necessary. If property is to be transferred or subdivided, then a Phase 1 or Phase 2 environmental study is prudent. Any efforts to develop a waterfront site will trigger a full set of regulatory standards for research, decision making, design, and implementation.

In many cases, it is impractical or impossible to undertake direct experiments on environmental systems to understand how they work. Computer models, combined with suitable data-collection programs, can help deepen our understanding of waterfront systems and how they will react to various influences, human or otherwise. Scientific gathering and analysis of information is thus an invaluable tool for development. But whatever the results of such analyses, the choice of alternative actions ultimately depends on values—and, therefore, on subjective standards. It is essential to distinguish, in the decision-making process, between discussions about facts and discussions about values, and to explicitly acknowledge the values that are embedded in—or left out of—any debate.

The reactive approach is probably best suited to sites that are closer to pristine than not, and to cases in which there is likely to be agreement that the principal goals are to protect intact remnant systems and to limit any negative effects of development on these systems.

But what happens when developers, planners, and designers decide that the considerations driving a total development solution should not be limited to scientific factors alone, but should incorporate choices about which values will be given priority? It then becomes necessary to look beyond the structures provided by regulatory requirements, and to examine the opportunities for waterfront redevelopment in light of a more integrative approach: a proactive strategy.

Proactive Strategy

Most waterfront development opportunities do not occur in pristine physical environments or in cultural vacuums. Opportunities are usually found at sites that have been modified: used (and abused) sections of land and water where the existing environment may be the major environmental impact. Here, the development context is often highly charged, characterized by culturally derived beliefs about what a waterfront should be, and what development can bring to a site. These two central characteristics—the already altered or adaptive nature of waterfront environmental systems and the cultural values attached to redevelopment—together create an ideal situation for approaching environmental issues proactively with respect to planning and design.

In a proactive approach to waterfront development, environmental issues are viewed as opportunities for achieving better ecological function (if not form); the assumption is that a sensitive design can have positive effects not only on the site but on the regional environment. This type of design exhibits two key characteristics: it is forward-looking and integrative. It is forward-looking in that it gives weight to a newly appreciated, scientifically based view that an urban waterfront can never be returned

to a pristine, pre-settlement image or state. The larger ecological and cultural systems within which this original state existed have long since evolved and adapted, and restoring the site to an arbitrarily selected point in its history is generally unreasonable.

The integrative aspects of the proactive approach are manifold. Recognizing that a systems approach is most appropriate to working with complex environmental systems, the proactive methodology provides for the creation of a range of environmental strategies. It may, for example, entail modifying the regulatory requirements associated with the reactive approach to incorporate integrative research and design. The proactive approach also recognizes the importance of stakeholders' values, and takes them into account in decisions about the treatment of ecological systems and development priorities. The resulting design—a single, integrated solution—will combine consideration of all four major site issues: flooding, natural resources, cultural resources, and contamination. In this approach, analysis and design occur in parallel, and are linked in a constant feedback loop.

The nature of the ecological assessment is the major distinction between the proactive and reactive strategies. As intimated earlier, although an assessment may be couched in the objective language of science, its ultimate purpose is to lead to agreement on priorities—a goal that necessarily includes consideration of cultural values. The success or failure of an ecological assessment is likely to depend on how skillfully its managers balance science and values. To achieve such balance, it is necessary to consider two major factors: (1) the process of public involvement and stakeholder buy-in and (2) the overt inclusion of social values as a defining factor in the decision-making process.

Critics of the current use and formulation of ecological risk assessments are concerned that narrow, technical arguments can override debates over values. Instead of emerging from a single, technologically biased viewpoint, they argue, environmental debate often takes place on three levels.[1] At the base level, where complexity and conflict are lowest, technical expertise drives decisions. Discussion at the middle level focuses on trust: public confidence that institutions will be able to deal with environmental threats. The highest level of debate takes place over competing social and cultural values. Understood in this way, decision making requires consensus on the values under debate, and stakeholder involvement is crucial.

Sometimes, government and businesses attempt to reframe higher-level conflicts over trust and values into conflicts over facts and figures. By compelling citizens to use factual arguments to justify value-based concerns, experts effectively dismiss those concerns, which feeds citizen distrust of government and business.[2] In complex cases where conflict is high, stakeholder involvement is essential to forestall this outcome. In the planning stage, when the initial policy questions are first framed, debate needs to revolve around values, world views, and assumptions about how the benefits and costs of ecological decisions will be apportioned.[3] In essence, the questions are political: Which ecological changes are deemed undesirable? Which are deemed beneficial?[4]

Assessing the impact of human activities on the environment involves a purely technical analysis based on scientific data. But management decisions are based on values, and depend on effective communication between the technical people handling the assessment and the stakeholders who helped define the initial problem and who will be affected by its resolution.[5] Without attention to values, ecological assessment often becomes a battleground

for politicians, administrators, experts, and interest groups. As political scientist E.J. Woodhouse has observed, ecological assessments, instead of trying to resolve controversies through scientifically certain answers, may best be used to help political participants ask better questions and craft better strategies.[6]

Conclusion

Although the descriptions given in this chapter of the ecological and cultural import of waterfronts hold true in the abstract, the reality is that at most urban waterfront sites, historical development has obscured perceptible traces of many types of natural habitats and relationships. Continuous urban development, technological innovation, and economic change have reinforced an artificial edge between land and water and between urban and ecological conditions. In the current age of urban waterfront redevelopment, most of the original positive social and environmental characteristics of the water's edge have disappeared, and the negative aspects have become more apparent. However, at least in the ideological realm, the positive endures, and is being expressed in values that are creating the foundation for change.

The current desire to refocus on waterfronts is driven by community values. These values are what lead people to reexamine, and consequently remake, waterfronts. The desire to clean the waterfront, to live and work near the water, to interpret history, to spend leisure time on the water—all drive the contemporary interest in revaluing the potential of waterfronts. The key to discovering this potential lies in a better understanding of the environment of the waterfront: that particular juncture where land meets water, terrestrial meets aquatic.

Traditionally, as detailed in this chapter, environmental issues have been associated with constraints, problems, and regulations—in short, with reasons not to develop. But with current changes in community values, citizens are now looking at their forgotten waterfronts as natural and cultural resources and assets in the broadest possible sense, and are coming to believe that redevelopment can actually improve these environments. If this perspective is the new starting point for redeveloping waterfronts, then the process of looking at environmental issues has been transformed from a chore into a rewarding journey of discovery.

Waterfronts continue to embody interactions between cultural and natural systems. In prehistoric times, the environmental impacts of human influence on waterfront sites were more subtle, but nonetheless present. In more recent history, cultural processes have had a major impact on the environment, producing dilatory and unsustainable results. For the future, in order to reclaim these sites, the choices are (1) to go back—to return, by means of ecological restoration, to a previous, preindustrial condition; (2) to stay still—to maintain, by means of conservation practices, aspects of an existing condition; or (3) to move forward. Moving forward involves a postindustrial scenario in which adaptation is key: a proactive approach to waterfront environmental issues requires remediation, monitoring, and management of hybrid cultural and natural environments such as artificial wetlands, stormwater retention systems, and groundwater pumping technology.

Notes

1. O. Renn, T. Webler, and P. Wiedemann, eds., *Fairness and Competence in Citizen Participation: Evaluating Models for Environmental Discourse* (Boston: Kluwer Academic Publishers, 1995).
2. Renn, Webler, and Wiedemann, *Citizen Participation.*
3. Robert T. Lackey, "The Future of Ecological Risk Assessment," *Human and Ecological Risk Assessment* 1, no. 4 (1995): 339–43.
4. Robert T. Lackey, "If Ecological Risk Assessment Is the Answer, What Is the Question?" *Human and Ecological Risk Assessment* 3, no. 6 (1997): 921–28.
5. A. Fairbrother, L.A. Kapuska, B.A. Williams, and J. Glicken, "Risk Assessment in Practice: Success and Failure," *Human and Ecological Risk Assessment* 1, no. 4 (1995): 367–75.
6. E.J. Woodhouse, "Can Science Be More Useful in Politics? The Case of Ecological Risk Assessment," *Human and Ecological Risk Assessment* 1, no. 4 (1995): 395–406.

Chapter 5

Implementing Urban Waterfront Redevelopment

David L.A. Gordon

Waterfront projects are long-term affairs. Typically, the decline of port-related activities, combined with years of underinvestment in infrastructure, yields sites that are the image of isolation and decay. To turn a waterfront site around, redevelopment agencies must not only get things right during an inevitably difficult startup process, but must also successfully manage the process over the long term. Good implementation practice requires waterfront redevelopment agencies to manage three areas: politics, finance, and urban design.

Startup Politics

Starting an urban waterfront development project takes money, (available) land, power, and a compelling vision of the future. The government that initiates the project also needs patience: the startup period alone may last a decade, and the redevelopment of any significant portion of a port may take another ten to 15 years.

The startup phase is characterized by a struggle for control of the site and by debate about its future use. As centers of port activity, most large urban waterfront sites have a history of at least partial public ownership by port or harbor agencies. Apart from high-profile closures such as that of St. Katharine's Dock, in London (1968), or the Boston Naval Shipyard (1973), waterfront decline is often gradual and almost unnoticed. But once the wharves have clearly been abandoned and are deteriorating, the port's central location ensures that there will be other proposals for its use. Port authorities often try to hold on to the property, and sometimes propose new marine uses (for example, a superliner terminal in New York, or new general cargo facilities in London). But the port agencies in many cities are in the shipping business, and few are skilled at urban redevelopment.

Control of a project generally goes to the government that focuses the most political will and money on it. The London Docklands Development Corporation and Toronto's Harbourfront Corporation were founded by national governments; New York State controls the Battery Park City Authority (BPCA); and the former Greater London Council was the prime sponsor of the Docklands Joint Committee. Few municipal governments directly implement redevelopment, perhaps because of broad concerns about the fiscal and political capacity of local governments to carry out complex, long-term development projects.

(Boston does not quite fit into this taxonomy: the state-chartered and nominally independent Boston Redevelopment Authority is, in practice, controlled by the mayor's office.)

Because the local politics of urban development will dominate the startup process for a waterfront renewal project, a sponsoring government at the national, state, or regional level will require locally based control—including the establishment, early in the startup phase, of a local implementation organization and a local planning process. The principal objectives during the startup phase are to establish an implementation agency and to obtain regulatory approval for a workable plan. To achieve these goals, the sponsoring government will have to go into the consensus-building business. Critical to this effort is the creation of a broad-based development coalition that includes the major governments involved, private-sector umbrella organizations, and citizens' groups. While this limited consensus at startup is key, it is equally important for the sponsoring government to recognize that project implementation cannot depend on the agreements forged by the specific politicians involved in this early phase. Because both the initial broad coalition and the consensus on the need to revitalize the waterfront usually fracture over time, under normal urban development political pressures, it is essential for a waterfront agency to obtain, early in the startup process, the powers and independence that will be needed for long-term implementation. It is rare for the required powers to be added later in an agency's mandate.

There are several possible methods to separate a long-term, revenue-producing redevelopment project from the hurly-burly of local development politics:

Top: St. Katharine's Dock suffered appalling damage from bombings during World War II. Equally damaging was the opening of the container port at Tilbury in the late 1960s, which sealed St. Katharine's fate as a commercial port. Taylor Woodrow Properties subsequently redeveloped the area, starting in the early 1970s, as a successful mixed-use environment. *UKPix.com*

Bottom: The New York Department of Marine and Aviation attempted to retain control of the Battery Park City site with this 1962 proposal for apartments and parks built on the roof of cargo facilities. *David L.A. Gordon*

- Waterfront development councils;
- Special private, for-profit development corporations;
- Public/private development ventures;
- Port authorities;
- Quasi-public development corporations.

Slow progress by London's Docklands Joint Committee caused the Thatcher government to designate these lands as an enterprise zone, attracting Olympia & York's proposals for the Canary Wharf office node.

A waterfront development committee or council is often the simplest organization to set up and may be useful for debating initial plans. However, councils like London's Docklands Joint Committee and Toronto's Waterfront Regeneration Trust had little success in redeveloping complicated urban waterfronts where multiple stakeholders jealously guarded ownership and control of their waterfront. A council may be able to coordinate some planning or infrastructure projects, but urban redevelopment is difficult without land ownership and access to a portion of the resulting revenues.

A special private development corporation may be appropriate if the waterfront project is small, or if the municipality has little development expertise. If the waterfront site is small, it makes sense to develop a plan and to then issue a request for qualifications or a request for proposals for a private corporation to develop it in one or two phases.

In the case of larger waterfront projects with multiple sites, if the local development industry has little capacity and the public sector has little experience in redevelopment, a master developer strategy may be worth considering. It may be comforting to have a large, sophisticated,

and competent developer in charge of a major project (as is the case, for example, with Olympia & York, at London's Canary Wharf). But if the developer later decides to proceed slowly (as happened in Boston's Charlestown Navy Yard, in the 1980s), the municipality may regret the decision. During a boom, some master developers may only build one site at a time because of limited project management capacity or limited access to financing.

The public sector may have more say in the development if the project is set up as a public/private partnership. North American cities have had considerable experience over the past 25 years with public/private partnerships in downtown settings, including high-profile festival marketplaces. This method is also appropriate for a single waterfront project with a limited number of phases. The structures of public/private partnerships vary as widely as the projects, from arrangements in which the public sector is confined to donating land and infrastructure, to real estate joint ventures, to tax increment financing.

Large-scale British and Canadian waterfront redevelopment has been largely implemented by single-purpose public redevelopment agencies rather than by port authorities, which have traditionally focused on shipping concerns. In the United States, however, the port author-

An interjurisdictional port authority is often the only way to structure a government agency that can deal with waterfront development issues that straddle state boundaries. Above: The riverfronts of Philadelphia and its counterpart across the Delaware River, Camden, New Jersey (foreground).

ities of cities like Long Beach, New York, Los Angeles, San Francisco, and Seattle have been quite active in waterfront redevelopment. The World Trade Center was a high-profile project undertaken in the 1960s by the Port Authority of New York and New Jersey (although the redevelopment of the destroyed site is being planned by the Lower Manhattan Development Corporation, a special-purpose agency). Where waterfronts straddle state boundaries (as in Philadelphia, Pennsylvania, and Camden, New Jersey; or New York, New York, and Hoboken, New Jersey), a port authority may be the only existing agency that can deal with complex interjurisdictional development issues.

A quasi-public development corporation is a proven vehicle for the implementation of waterfront redevelopment projects. Because such an agency will need active, broad-based support to sustain its development coalition over the years, it is important for the sponsoring government to ensure at the outset that the development corporation has sufficient political insulation; in particular, the government should avoid the temptation to stack the authority's board of directors with either patronage appointments or purely partisan supporters of the sponsoring regime. The authority will need a broadly inclusive vision of the objectives for waterfront planning, especially during the startup

period. This vision could be generated by a large board—or, perhaps more effectively, by a large planning committee that reports to a powerful and well-connected board. If political conditions change, the board will need good connections to other parties and other levels of government; such links should be established early in the process.

Because consensus within the political coalition will be strongest at the beginning, the startup period is the sponsoring government's best chance to secure the authority's independence, freedom of action, and financing structure. The critical objectives are (1) ownership of the land, (2) a powerful and independent board of directors, (3) a streamlined development approval process, (4) access to startup capital, and (5) freedom from restrictive government personnel and budget policies.

The most effective agencies started with an active board and a small staff led by an entrepreneurial chief executive. They sometimes raided key staff from the local government—a tactic that effectively co-opted some early opposition from technical agencies like transportation and planning departments. It helps if the agency's managers have both entrepreneurial and consensus-building skills. Strong knowledge of local values and processes will also prove to be an asset.

In Boston, New York, London, and Toronto, it took between five and ten years just to achieve the political and planning consensus needed to start a major waterfront

The Barcelona waterfront industrial area was transformed into the 1992 Olympic Harbour in five years. Frank Gehry's fish sculpture stands atop the Vila Olimpica mixed-use complex at the gateway to the former Olympic Village. *C. Blam/Travel-Images.com*

project. The startup phase was considered complete when the waterfront redevelopment plan was approved. The most important factor affecting approval times was the complexity of the political environment. The fastest startup occurred in Boston, where only two parties negotiated: the city and the federal government. In Toronto, where four levels of government negotiated—the federal, provincial, metropolitan, and city governments—it took a decade to reach consensus. Surprisingly, project size does not appear to explain the varying startup times in these four cities. The sites in Boston, New York, and Toronto were all approximately 95 acres (38 hectares), but initial approval time varied from five to ten years. In contrast,

the first plan for the London Docklands took only eight years, even though the site, at over 5,200 acres (2,100 hectares) was far larger.

Private sector participation can play an important role. During the first attempt to redevelop the London Docklands, the sponsoring government created a committee to negotiate political agreement for a plan without significant private sector involvement its preparation. The 1976 London Docklands Strategic Plan had unrealistic development objectives, which later led to difficulties in attracting investment. Moreover, in the absence of private sector participation, the political consensus for waterfront redevelopment was also somewhat shallower than is the case, for example, for many public/private partnerships for downtown retail redevelopment, where the local government and the private sector are both directly engaged in the process and dependent on each other for success. In New York and Toronto, the private sector was initially involved in waterfront redevelopment through organizations such as the Downtown-Lower Manhattan Association and the Toronto Downtown Business Council. In these cities, local business leaders were often included on the board of the redevelopment agency.

Managing Political Change over the Long Term

Excellent long-term political management is required for implementation of waterfront redevelopment, except in rare cases such as the Barcelona Olympics or the Lisbon World's Fair, where absolute deadlines and national pride push a project forward in record time.

Unilateral action on the part of a higher-level government usually does not work, especially in the long term. In 1966, for example, when New York governor Nelson Rockefeller seized the initiative on Battery Park City, the resulting confrontation with Mayor John Lindsay's regime delayed the project for years, even though both men were members of the Republican Party.

A waterfront project can be delayed after the startup period if its political coalition falls apart. As time passes, it is inevitable that the elected officials who were members of the original coalition will retire, be defeated, or move on to other offices. For long-term stability, the implementation agency must manage the relationships with the level of government that appoints its board and has ultimate financial responsibility for its survival. Nevertheless, an election that produces a change in the sponsor's governing party can create difficulties for a waterfront agency if the change in regime is accompanied by a significant shift in ideology (such as occurred with the 1979 election of Mrs. Thatcher in Britain), especially if little redevelopment has been completed, or if large capital expenditures are required. A nimble agency can minimize delays during a change in regime if it has produced some results and already has a broadly based board of directors that includes representatives from the new party. Some readjustment in objectives and senior officials may then allow the project to continue. For example, when Mario Cuomo was elected governor of New York, the BPCA replaced its president and pursued social housing to accommodate Cuomo's objectives for the agency.

Finally, the waterfront agency must manage its relationship with local governments, which own or control the infrastructure needed for redevelopment. An intransigent municipal government can delay and frustrate implementation even if the agency owns the land and was granted complete planning and building authority, as was the case with the London Docklands Development Corporation in 1981. Through a combination of red tape and delay, local governments can often inflict "the death of a thousand cuts": even the LDDC was brought back to the negotiating table by the London Boroughs.

In contrast to a typical real estate project, where the developer focuses all its energy on a single vote, waterfront projects with multiple sites mean repeated trips back to the well. Thus, their success depends on cooperative strategies for maintaining good relations with local governments. Some elements in such a strategy include

- Recruiting local staff for key agency positions;
- Retaining trusted local consultants;
- Appointing local elected officials to the agency board;
- Offering public benefits and development charges;
- Maintaining good relations with local residents.

Startup Financial Strategy

It often takes a long time to find the startup capital for waterfront redevelopment. Large, early expenditures are required for land assembly, site clearance, environmental remediation, and new infrastructure. These costs make most projects unattractive to the private sector, since it may be years before land is ready for redevelopment. Substantial government grants are required for most waterfront projects, although in many countries the public funds available for urban redevelopment are declining.

Projects in Boston and Toronto were significantly undercapitalized, while the London Docklands faced delays when its demands for infrastructure funding skyrocketed, in the late 1980s. In New York, the BPCA issued long-term bonds to finance its infrastructure program. Although an optimistic repayment schedule almost caused this strategy to backfire, in the end, long-term capital requirements were matched with long-term financing. This approach allows an agency to reduce its cash demands on its sponsoring government and build high-quality infrastructure.

In Boston, New York, London, and Toronto, private investment started late, built slowly, and cycled with the local property market (see the cash flow chart in the accompanying figure). Initial private investments were small, since the big developers did not trust waterfront sites, and the flagship projects—such as the World Financial Center, in New York; Canary Wharf, in London; and Queen's Quay Terminal, in Toronto—all took well over a decade to arrive. In Boston, it took nine years for property revenue to exceed 25 percent of the annual project costs; in New York, it took 22 years.

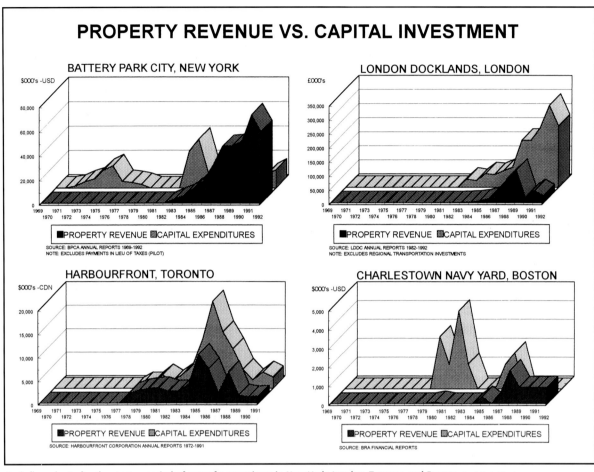

PROPERTY REVENUE VS. CAPITAL INVESTMENT

BATTERY PARK CITY, NEW YORK
$000's -USD

■ PROPERTY REVENUE ▨ CAPITAL EXPENDITURES

SOURCE: BPCA ANNUAL REPORTS 1989-1992
NOTE: EXCLUDES PAYMENTS IN LIEU OF TAXES (PILOT)

LONDON DOCKLANDS, LONDON
£000's

■ PROPERTY REVENUE ▨ CAPITAL EXPENDITURES

SOURCE: LDDC ANNUAL REPORTS 1982-1992
NOTE: EXCLUDES REGIONAL TRANSPORTATION INVESTMENTS

HARBOURFRONT, TORONTO
$000's -CDN

■ PROPERTY REVENUE ▨ CAPITAL EXPENDITURES

SOURCE: HARBOURFRONT CORPORATION ANNUAL REPORTS 1972-1991

CHARLESTOWN NAVY YARD, BOSTON
$000's -USD

■ PROPERTY REVENUE ▨ CAPITAL EXPENDITURES

SOURCE: BRA FINANCIAL REPORTS

Cash flow charts for the startup period of waterfront projects in New York, London, Toronto, and Boston. *David L.A. Gordon*

The lesson here is that the major deals were not made until the waterfront agency had demonstrated its credibility through site improvements, small developments, and other changes to the image of the waterfront. The projects also had to wait for a positive point in the real estate market cycle or risk going bankrupt, as Canary Wharf did (see feature box).

Managing a Changing Financial Environment

The flow of private investment can also be impeded if the agency's developer selection process is too slow or if the local development approval process is too cumbersome. In some cases, a streamlined development approval process can allow waterfront redevelopment agencies to react quickly to mar-

ket conditions, taking advantage of developer interest during the relatively brief boom periods in the local real estate cycle. With a less nimble agency or a slow approval process, the market window may be missed.

A six-month delay in the approval process, for example, can lead to years of frustration if the local economy moves into a recession in the meantime, and the designated developers refuse to build because they cannot obtain construction financing—which is just what happened, in the early 1980s, with many of the Boston Redevelopment Authority's projects in the Charlestown Navy Yard. Similarly, both the London Docklands Joint Committee and the BPCA discovered, in the late 1970s, that the combination of poor market conditions and a cumbersome approval process could be fatal for a waterfront project. The waterfront agencies in New York, London, and Toronto, in con-

Canary Wharf's Bankruptcy and Recovery

Canary Wharf, which had over 14 million square feet (1.3 million square meters) completed or in construction in 2004, is now the central business district of the London Docklands and the third office node of Greater London. As a result of the 1992 bankruptcy of Olympia & York, the world's largest office developer, the project was politically controversial and widely regarded as a planning disaster. Canary Wharf initially failed as a result of six factors: a recession in the London property market, competition from the city of London, poor transportation links, few British tenants, com-

plicated finances, and developer overconfidence.

By 1995, improved performance in many of these factors had allowed the project to emerge from bankruptcy and to become an important element in London's office market. Its previous developer, Paul Reichmann, assembled a syndicate of investors to buy the project back, then took the company public in 1999, after leasing the vacant space. Canary Wharf Limited then leased all the remaining building sites and got them into construction by 2002, completing one of the most remarkable real estate turnarounds in modern history.

---

trast, were able to adjust to market conditions and get projects into construction quickly during the late 1980s and early 1990s, which was a major financial advantage.

The developer selection process is largely within the redevelopment agency's control, but streamlining the public approval process requires the cooperation of the local government. The best time to negotiate a new, streamlined process is during the warm glow of success immediately after the approval of the waterfront plan. The city may be willing to streamline the process for the early phases of the project: New York City, for example, exempted the first phase of the World Financial Center from its cumbersome Uniform Land Use Review Procedure, provided that the project conformed to density and height limits and to the BPCA's new urban design guidelines.

However, municipalities are usually loath to give up their approval power over the long term, largely because they are concerned about the future actions of parties who were not involved in the early development consensus. No legal agreement will force a municipality to fast-track a project that it despises, and a determined local government can eventually stall projects even if a higher-level government removes its approval power, as happened in the London Docklands in the 1980s.

The most effective agencies also recognized that recessions are a normal part of the economic cycle. They had plans for parks, infrastructure, and social housing in hand, so that they could respond quickly, with the usual public works programs, to create employment in a recession. These projects continued the momentum for waterfront redevelopment and positioned the agencies for rapid growth during the next up-cycle.

Finally, most developers and implementation agencies want flexible plans for long-term projects. The best urban design plans now provide for changing uses within the same building types and envelopes. At the same time, too much flexibility can also be a problem. For example, when Toronto's Harbourfront Corporation changed from mid-rise to high-rise building types, the political consequences were disastrous (see the feature box on the following page). In London, the Canary Wharf project was designated as an Enterprise Zone, and therefore had essentially no planning controls. This arrangement was acceptable for the initial small-scale industrial parks but did not support the site's transition to a high-quality corporate headquarters precinct. The private developers recognized that the lack of planning controls was a problem and commissioned urban design

What Happened on the Toronto Waterfront?

The Harbourfront Corporation was established in 1976 to implement a new plan for the redevelopment of part of Toronto's central waterfront. The federal government had bungled the startup of the project in 1972, but the new agency made rapid progress in establishing political consensus, designing an award-winning plan, and attracting people to the site with public programming. In the early 1980s, the project was widely cited as an example of good planning practice. However, the redevelopment agency was disassembled in 1990, after a public furor.

How did the Harbourfront Corporation go from being a model for urban waterfront redevelopment to being dismantled, with a half-finished project, 25 years after it was formed? Two incorrect explanations are commonly put forward for the agency's fall from grace. The first concerns the plan to replace the initial proposal for a large waterfront park and medium-rise buildings with a "concrete curtain" of high-rise buildings. The response of the city of Toronto to the loss of parkland was to freeze all private development. The second conjecture was that the financial demands of the cultural program pushed the agency away from its broader public objectives. A proposed solution was to provide the program agency with independent funding and close the development agency.

In fact, the vast waterfront park was abandoned early in the planning process, partly at the behest of the city of Toronto itself. The unpopular change from a medium-rise to a high-rise built form was largely forced by the demands of other public agencies, who wanted additional waterfront land. Two federal inquiries and a royal commission found no evidence that private developers had manipulated the Harbourfront Corporation. However, freezing all private development proved to be an excellent negotiating tactic for the city of Toronto: it forced the agency back to the table to develop a new plan that involved the significant transfer of land and payments to the city.

The Harbourfront Corporation ran into financial trouble not because of programming expenditures but because it attempted to fund long-term capital costs with short-term grants and cyclical private development revenue. The public program expenditures were relatively modest compared with the enormous capital costs involved in redeveloping the site. Although the corporation was perhaps too eager to attract private investment after the recession of the early 1980s, cultural programming expenditures threatened the organization's solvency only after development had been frozen and the redevelopment arm disbanded. Although the Harbourfront

Corporation's land and financial assets were seized in 1990, the planned endowment fund for the program agency was never established.

The Harbourfront story is a cautionary tale. The demise of the redevelopment agency demonstrates that implementation is far more difficult than planning. The project's financial implementation was flawed by a fundamental mismatch of long-term obligations and short-term revenues. Unlike the Battery Park City Authority (BPCA), for example, which had issued long-term bonds to finance its infrastructure, the Harbourfront Corporation was not allowed to borrow against its assets. So, while the BPCA was able to sustain its projects during New York City's fiscal crisis and to put in place the parks and water's edge promenade early in the project, the Harbourfront Corporation was unable to follow the BPCA's example.

Urban Strategies Inc

guidelines for the vacant site that provided both context for the many future architects and quality assurance for prospective tenants and building owners.

Urban Design and Planning for Implementation

Urban design for waterfront redevelopment should facilitate implementation over several decades. A successful long-term implementation plan has the following characteristics: small development increments; tight phasing; simple infrastructure (that can be phased); the adaptive use of existing infrastructure and buildings; and continuous public access to the water's edge.

Comprehensive schemes designed by a single architect were discredited by early urban renewal projects. The 1979 plan for New York's Battery Park City was influential for its approach and urban design guidelines. The plan's extension of the Manhattan street grid allowed small development increments, simple infrastructure, easy phasing, and flexibility. The BPCA's commitment to the idea of creating high-quality public space before beginning development made it a leader in urban waterfront design (see the feature box on page 90).

Nevertheless, the development of Battery Park City was not without problems. A unilateral initial announcement of the project and clumsy early moves on the part of the state government botched the startup politics of the project. And except during the period from 1977 to 1985, the project was also plagued by poor relations with the local government. In contrast, the Harbourfront Corporation managed its relationship with its federal boss fairly well during its early years. At the end, however, its partisan board of directors was unable to rebuild

consensus within the Toronto political environment, which splintered after 1985. The agency never developed a good relationship with the waterfront's new residents, who worked hard to undermine its political support at all levels.

Harbourfront's planning showed great promise after the original political problems were resolved. The development framework was a strong urban design plan, and the early parks and programming were successful by any measure. The initial development projects included innovative examples of the adaptive use of industrial buildings. Handsome mid-rise buildings were built at Spadina Quay, and Bathurst Quay was the largest social housing neighborhood built in Toronto during the 1980s. Once again, however, implementation errors ruined a good start. The phasing plan scattered development across the site. Public spaces arrived late and were disconnected. The flexible zoning actually worked against the Harbourfront Corporation, as other public agencies exploited it to demand more land while stacking the permitted development ever higher on the

remaining parcels. The cure was perhaps as bad as the disease. Three waterfront parcels, totaling 2.5 acres (one hectare), were saved from development to become parks, although they remained as parking lots for a decade. The development freeze left the project half-completed, in a state that was neither a park nor an urban waterfront. Nor was there an agency—or sufficient funds—left to complete it.

Despite this sorry tale, the waterfront site was sufficiently attractive that the parcels owned by private developers were redeveloped when market conditions improved, in the mid-1990s. While some local firms were driven away by the freeze and the real estate collapse, international investment has been attracted to the site and to the adjacent railway yards.

A new redevelopment agency, the Toronto Waterfront Revitalization Corporation (TWRC), was established in 2003, after four years of negotiation between the federal, provincial, and city governments. This new, tripartite (federal/provincial/municipal) agency is responsible for the entire city waterfront, although its initial plans were for the downtown area. The TWRC's implementation powers are quite different from those of the former Harbourfront Corporation. It is subject to close political control by its three sponsors and was not given ownership of the land held by other waterfront agencies.

Changing the image of the waterfront is one of the first tasks of most redevelopment agencies, which usually use two strategies: historic preservation and improved public access. The London Docklands Development Authority and the Boston Redevelopment Authority, for example, placed strong emphasis on preservation, taking advantage of the resources of their sites. In London, historic warehouses were rehabilitated as apartments, offices, and retail at the Shad Thames, Tobacco Dock, and Limehouse. Under the BRA's sponsorship, historic Charlestown Navy

Yard buildings were renovated as offices, housing for seniors, and a YMCA. Other warehouses were transformed into biotech research labs and a parking garage.

The BPCA focused its initial efforts on building high-quality public spaces to provide access to the waterfront, including a fine waterfront esplanade, first-rate parks in the residential neighborhoods, and a large public wintergarden in the office node of the project. By building

Battery Park City: Urban Design for Implementation

oor planning and urban design can delay a waterfront redevelopment project. For example, rigid master plans that require large and early infrastructure investments can make implementation difficult. A comparison of the 1969 and 1979 plans for Battery Park City illustrates the impact—for good and for ill—of urban design on implementation.

Each plan called for 14,000 units of housing and 6 million square feet (557,420 square meters) of office space. The 1969 plan is a megastructure that looks a bit like a spaceship moored to the Manhattan waterfront (see figure). A seven-story circulation spine, over one mile (1.6 kilometers) long, needed to be built before huge pods of development were plugged into the top. The BPCA could not afford to build the spine, and no developer wanted to start construction without infrastructure. Moreover, the city government hated the plan because it blocked the street views of the water. Nothing was built for a decade.

In contrast, the 1979 plan was based on a limited extension of the Manhattan grid to create streets, blocks, and parks. This plan permitted smaller buildings and more development increments: 36 blocks, rather than seven pods. In addition to yielding a finer-grained urban fabric, an attribute that is now appreciated, the smaller sites allowed the BPCA to involve many types of developers rather than the few enormous firms capable of building a pod.

Streets, blocks, and parks are cheaper to build and maintain than a spine, and are easier to implement through traditional building regulations. While it is perhaps too easy to criticize the megastructure in hindsight, the comparison does illustrate the characteristics of urban design that facilitate implementation: flexibility, easy phasing, small increments, and simple infrastructure. The open web of the grid plan also allowed many waterfront views and permitted the project to be integrated into the existing city, which reduced local political tensions. The preliminary redevelopment plans for the adjacent World Trade Center site attempt to knit the Battery Park City blocks back into lower Manhattan, but the highway separating the two sites has proved to be a formidable barrier.

Implementation Comparison: 1969 and 1979 Plans for Battery Park City

1969 Development Plan	1979 Master Plan
Physical Design Concept	
Megastructure	Extension of Manhattan street grid
Public circulation spine	Streets
Seven pods	36 blocks
Open-space decks	Public parks

1969 Development Plan	1979 Master Plan
Planning Controls	
City ownership	Battery Park City Authority (BPCA) ownership
Master lease	City repurchase option
Master development plan	Master plan
Special district zoning	Urban design guidelines

Site Improvement Cost Estimates ($ millions)

	1973	1979[a]		1979
Utilities	14.1	25.2	Utilities	8.5
Civic facilities	41.1	73.6	Civic facilities	3.0
Streets, spine	58.3	104.4	Streets	13.7
Foundations	19.2	34.4	Foundations	Not applicable
Architecture and engineering	26.0	46.5	Architecture and engineering	Included
Contingencies	15.8	28.3	Contingencies	Included
Total	174.5	312.4	Total	53.2

Implementation Process

1969 Development Plan	1979 Master Plan
1. BPCA designs service spine	1. BPCA prepares design guidelines
2. Port Authority Review Board (PARB) reviews spine design	2. BPCA designs streets and parks
3. City Planning Commission (CPC) amendments	3. BPCA selects developer(s)
4. Board of Estimate amendments	4. Developer designs buildings
5. BPCA starts spine construction	5. BPCA reviews designs
6. BPCA selects pod developer	6. BPCA builds streets and parks
7. Developer designs pod platform	7. Developer builds buildings
8. BPCA reviews pod/spine connection	
9. Developer designs towers	
10. BPCA approves tower design	
11. PARB reviews pod design	
12. CPC amends master development plan (if required)	
13. Board of Estimate amends master development plan (if required)	
14. Developer builds pod platform	
15. Developer builds first building	

Source: *Economic Report of the President,* 1987.

a. 1973 figures adjusted for inflation using the consumer price index to provide costs in 1979 dollars (1973 = 128.4; 1979 = 230.1).

1969

1979

a new park and a water's edge promenade in the part of the site closest to downtown, Toronto's Harbourfront Corporation also attempted to use public spaces to modify the image of the site. In addition, the corporation animated the indoor and outdoor spaces with innovative public programming, which introduced potential residents to the isolated site before development began.

Images of abandoned waterfront buildings and derelict sites are often used to build political support for redevelopment during the startup phase. Redevelopment agencies typically use the initial rehabilitation and open-space projects as symbols of the rejuvenation of the waterfront. To give evidence of early success and make the site more attractive for redevelopment, most media releases include dramatic "before and after" photos. Images of new parks and restored buildings appear to have considerable power, and can be regarded as important tools in the politics of redevelopment.

Planning for Change

Controlling the aesthetic quality of the physical environment during the redevelopment of an urban waterfront is a long-term proposition. Most agencies have architects on staff for design review and coordination, but the best long-term results appear to come from a systematic approach to facilitating good design, rather than from the benevolent dictatorship of an in-house architect. Senior administrators who appreciate good urbanism and are willing to listen to, and take the advice of, talented consultants appear to be more important than the presence of a design wizard on the staff, perhaps because it is difficult to get the best designers to leave their independent practices to administer a long-term project.

Redevelopment agencies can take a number of steps to control the site's overall appearance during various phases of the process. A well-conceived phasing plan, for example, can not only improve the image of the site during implementation but also reduce costs. Proper phasing allows for infrastructure to be extended incrementally, and for each neighborhood to be completely finished before the next is begun, minimizing the "construction site" effect.

In an attempt to open up as much of its waterfront site as possible, the Toronto Harbourfront Corporation tried to "get something going" on each of its quays. Although this approach allowed the agency to get the easiest sites started first, in hindsight it may have been a political mistake. The entire site was in construction for a decade; and, since landscaping is often done last in a construction project, little of the public open space was available for use in the early period. The public grew restless at the lack of parks, and the city council froze all further development until the agency agreed to double the amount of open space.

The Battery Park City Authority, in contrast, had few constraints, since the project was sited on landfill. The BPCA's plan was perfectly phased during implementation. The first area developed was adjacent to the subway station that served the World Trade Center. After the public spaces were completely finished and most of the buildings were complete, the second and third phases were built on adjacent sites (see figure on previous page). Although the entire site was not open from the beginning, the public benefits were immediately visible to public officials, investors, users, and visitors. The citizens had no reason to doubt that the public benefits would continue as the project moved toward completion.

Urban designers appreciate a smaller grain size within the urban fabric, and limiting the size of parcels and increasing the number of developers can moderate the monolithic appearance of urban revitalization projects. Such an approach also gives the agency the option of distributing the parcels to many small developers (and architects) or giving several parcels to larger organizations, as occurred in the World Financial Center at Battery Park City.

Building high-quality public spaces is an opportunity for joint gains for most waterfront redevelopment agencies and their developers. In several cities, waterfront parks have created high-profile public benefits that built political capital. First-rate streets, sidewalks, and parks can improve the value of adjacent parcels by increasing the quality of local amenities and signaling that the agency is serious about creating a high-quality environment. A generous water's edge promenade and other connections to the surrounding urban fabric can help change the isolated image of the abandoned harbor. As Battery Park City and the Charlestown Navy Yard demonstrated, the design for the initial public spaces can be particularly influential. On the other hand, when an agency's first projects are somewhat slapdash in appearance, as in the London Docklands, it can be difficult to gain a reputation for high-quality development later.

The developer selection process is another opportunity for the redevelopment agency to influence overall project quality. Experience has revealed two best practices concerning this process: first, to give the developer context, requests for proposals should include both design guidelines and plans for the surrounding area; second, it is preferable to use a two-stage process that separates financial issues from design.

In a one-stage request for proposals (RFP) process, the best designs are often coupled to the weakest financial proposals, and the most appealing financial proposals to the weakest designs. It is difficult for a public agency to reject the highest financial bid without creating the appearance of corruption. Moreover, the architects and developers who are not selected (and who are often not fully paid for RFP work) often complain bitterly and publicly. Delaying the design evaluation until the second phase of the RFP process avoids both of these problems.

The advantages of the two-stage process offset the complexity and time involved. For example, Olympia & York won the RFP for the office node at Battery Park City on the basis of its superior financial bid. The firm then held a limited design competition for the project, using the public agency's design guidelines. The winning proposal, from architect Cesar Pelli, was immediately hailed by *New York Times* critic Ada Louise Huxtable as "the next Rockefeller Center." The project was critically admired, got good press, leased quickly, and was financially successful for the developer and the agency. Pelli, then a relatively obscure professor at Yale, had become a star skyscraper designer by the 1990s, most recently winning renown for the world's tallest buildings, the twin Petronas Towers, in Malaysia.

The World Financial Center at Battery Park City, completed in 1985, was designed by Cesar Pelli, who won a design competition conducted by the development rights holder, Olympia & York.
Cesar Pelli & Associates

Because a single design cannot anticipate every political and economic change that lies ahead during a waterfront redevelopment spanning several decades, planning for these projects creates conflicts between agencies, which want to preserve the flexibility to respond to changing conditions, and the local government, which wants upfront guarantees of public benefits. One way to accommodate both objectives is through an incremental urban design approach, which includes general guidelines for building sites and focuses on the quality of public space. Thus, within the overall envelope approved in the master plan, the agency can reallocate uses; at the same time, the local government gains some certainty about the quality and extent of the public realm.

The incremental approach, which has widely replaced large-scale master planning for urban waterfront projects, is practical, allows many small builders to get involved in the project, and is also politically savvy, not only because it allows the work to be spread around but also because it creates many opportunities for elected officials to demonstrate their accomplishments. Unfortunately, the approach was not widely adopted until the early 1980s—too late to have an effect on the first efforts of most waterfront redevelopment agencies.

Risks of Waterfront Redevelopment

Urban waterfront development is a difficult, long-term task with limited political or financial rewards for the public sector. Any jurisdiction considering waterfront redevelopment should carefully consider the potential pitfalls. For example, a government should avoid sponsoring such a project if it needs quick political results, if it has no access to financial resources, or if the site is heavily polluted. Nor should a sponsoring government promise that redevelopment will restore the jobs of workers who were displaced by the relocation of port industries. Heeding the lessons from past experience can help a sponsoring government avoid recognized pitfalls.

Do Not Be in a Hurry for Results

Large-scale urban waterfront redevelopment does not fit the electoral cycle, and no sponsoring government will see any substantial results within its tenure. The only short-term political credit to be gained in starting this type of project is in "the politics of announcement." Even then, interjurisdictional rivalries make it likely that a local government will object—as New York, London, and Toronto did—to a higher-level government's generous offer to redevelop its waterfront.

Although a sponsoring government may be able to demonstrate symbolic progress by breaking ground, clearing the site, or unveiling models, it is equally likely to be abused for lack of progress on plans unveiled earlier. Unless the original regime lasts for over a decade, it is likely that one of its successors will get to claim credit for the results.

Governments Should Not Expect a Financial Benefit

Large-scale urban waterfront revitalization requires substantial startup funding from the public sector—and, by conventional measures, rarely generates a positive return on investment to the government. The large upfront cost of infrastructure and the need to provide working capital until private investment begins to trickle in reduce net present value. Although port facilities are often quite close to the downtown, political controversy during the startup phase and the ebbs and flows of the real estate market may mean that over a decade will pass before any significant private sector revenue is generated. Large developers that have other investment opportunities often wait until the market potential of a risky site is proven by small-scale projects completed by local entrepreneurs. Thus, a government should not expect startup costs for waterfront redevelopment to be privately funded, and must be prepared to commit its own tax revenue, grant income, or borrowing power to the project.

On the other hand, waterfront redevelopment does offer the opportunity to generate some private revenues, which can be used to offset capital and operating costs. A sponsoring government might reduce its cash contribution to the project by borrowing against the future revenue stream from property development. This strategy might be attractive if the sponsoring government is constrained by limitations on increases in the tax rate. Redevelopment agencies like the BPCA have secured private capital from the municipal bond market—but to be marketable, the bonds required a government guarantee and a tax exemption. Similarly, property tax exemptions or tax increment financing have been used to attract private developers without the type of capital investment that might trigger referenda or taxpayer resistance. A fiscally responsible government ought to incorporate the cost of these "off-the-balance-sheet" financial techniques into its decision-making processes, but few actually do so.

Do Not Expect to Solve Waterfront Unemployment Problems

Waterfront redevelopment is a poor employment program for the people who lost their jobs when port industries closed or moved. In practical terms, the long startup period means that new jobs will not arrive in time to help displaced workers. Also, the new jobs are likely to require different skills, since most attempts to attract high-wage manufacturing firms to the waterfront have foundered because of broad overall trends, including deindustrialization and the migration of plants to larger suburban sites.

While the crisis atmosphere surrounding the closure of a naval base or port may tempt elected officials to announce that the site will be redeveloped to benefit the newly unemployed, such promises will likely lead to frustration and bitterness over the slow progress and the sparse number of jobs available for local workers. Perhaps the best bet in the medium term is to retrain workers for construction jobs and to impose hiring quotas requiring the use of local workers for site clearance, infrastructure, and redevelopment contracts.

Waterfront redevelopment can result in a long-term increase in employment, but the jobs will probably be in service industries. Some retail projects have incorporated local training and hiring programs, such as the developer-sponsored training programs that trained Isle of Dogs residents to work in Canary Wharf offices. If sponsoring governments wish to ensure that these programs survive the term of the original developer, they must ensure that the programs are incorporated into the project agreements.

The Risks of Environmental Damage

Many of the currently undeveloped waterfront sites require major soil and groundwater cleanups because of the past presence of heavy industrial uses such as gasworks, power stations, coal-tar plants, and petrochemical refineries. Such waterfront sites can paralyze the current environmental decision-making process, which has a history of expertly identifying the impacts of urban redevelopment but of being uncertain about the techniques and benefits of remediation. During the 1970s, public authorities drained marshes, removed piers, filled docks, and extended shorelines. Many of the practices common to older developments, such as destroying wetlands, would be prohibited today.

New environmental mitigation techniques will be the starting point for the redevelopment of important waterfront sites such as the former British Gas works in Greenwich and the port industrial district in Toronto. The costs of such cleanups can be enormous, and some of the remediation techniques needed for polluted soils do not yet exist or are still prohibitively expensive. Major public subsidies, like the U.S. Environmental Protection Agency's Superfund, are required to clean up the most heavily polluted sites.

In the future, the need for environmental planning will require a reassessment of the "public authority" model of project implementation. Ecosystem planning demands a focus on the entire watershed, but the best waterfront redevelopment agencies are often narrowly focused on parcels that are only a portion of the former harbor. New implementation models may be needed to combine the public entrepreneurship of redevelopment agencies with the wider vision of conservation authorities, which operate on a natural systems basis.

Rewards of Waterfront Redevelopment

Despite the potential risks, waterfront redevelopment can offer many rewards. Individual building projects may be profitable for a private developer. Old harbor sites can be convenient places to expand the downtown core or diversify its uses. Some spectacular parks have been built on the water's edge, and rehabilitated waterfronts often become popular new residential neighborhoods. Finally, redeveloping a decaying and abandoned waterfront can be a powerful symbol of the rejuvenation of the inner city.

Expanding Downtown

If a city's central business district needs room to grow, expanding into the waterfront may be a more attractive option than destroying the existing fabric of the downtown, especially if the downtown has historic value. Lower Manhattan expanded in the direction of the waterfront for centuries, and London added a third business center at Canary Wharf. Waterfront redevelopment may also be preferable to expansion into adjacent residential neighborhoods or environmentally sensitive areas. Toronto's Central Area Plan directs downtown growth south, toward the waterfront, rather than east or west into gentrified neighborhoods or older warehouse zones that were being converted into arts and communications districts.

Developers considering downtown expansion on the waterfront should carefully check the pattern and capacity of existing infrastructure (especially transportation) for redevelopment potential. Projects that take advantage of existing capacity are likely to have the best chances of early success, as was the case with the World Financial Center, linked to the PATH (Port Authority Trans-Hudson) subway; and St. Katharine's Dock, located near the London Underground. To achieve long-term success, isolated projects like Canary Wharf and the Charlestown Navy Yard are likely to need investment in expensive new public transportation services.

The Public Interest in the Waterfront

The Public Trust Doctrine

The significance of the Public Trust Doctrine, which establishes public ownership rights to water and to land touched by water, cannot be overstated. The doctrine has been described as "one of the most important and far-reaching doctrines of American property law."[1] Ironically, although the doctrine defines one of the most important meanings of "the public interest" with regard to the waterfront, that meaning is little known and little understood by the public.

According to the Public Trust Doctrine, tidelands, freshwater shore lands, the land beneath the water, and the living resources they contain are, generally speaking, owned by the public and held in trust by the state for the public benefit. The doctrine establishes that the public has the right to fully enjoy and use these "public trust lands." Most important, the public's right to these lands is a property right that cannot be conveyed to private ownership even when public trust lands are privately owned. Thus, the private property rights to own and use public trust lands are subject to the dominant public interest.

The protected public uses of public trust lands originally included navigation, commerce, and fishing—important uses of the water in early times. But a key aspect of these protected uses is that they are flexibly interpreted to extend to those "related to the natural uses peculiar to the resource," as those uses change with time. Thus, the list of protected uses now often includes strolling, swimming, sunbathing, and recreational as well as commercial navigation; even broader rights that may be included are the protection of the environment and of aesthetic appearance. When public trust lands are under private ownership, the applicable collective public rights, while remaining dominant, are usually diminished, though whether and how they are diminished varies tremendously by state.

The Public Trust Doctrine is not a new law, is not limited to the United States, and is not a single law with a single interpretation. The doctrine has its roots in Roman civil law, and remained applicable for the duration of Rome's imperial power. After the fall of Rome, the doctrine reemerged, appearing in a variety of forms in the common law of states that had once been part of the Roman Empire. Transplanted to the American colonies by the kings of England, France, and Spain, it became common law and was preserved as such when the colonies achieved independence.

The doctrine is thus a body of law that is subject to different interpretations and applications in different places. Nevertheless, it is based on a common set of principles. The particular power of the Public Trust Doctrine stems from the fact that it establishes an ongoing public property interest in public trust lands. Through it, the state can manage these lands as a property owner, without recourse to its police powers, regulatory powers, or power of eminent domain.

The Public Trust Doctrine Applied

A look at how the Public Trust Doctrine can be applied will demonstrate the strength of this tool. In Massachusetts, for example, the Public Trust Doctrine has been used to impose public access requirements on private waterfront development.

The Public Trust Doctrine is codified and implemented through the state's waterways regulations. By basing the regulations on the doctrine, Massachusetts has not only avoided vulnerability to "takings" claims, but has also been able to ensure continuous public access to the waterfront through regulatory means—that is, without having to rely on the purchase of large amounts of expensive waterfront property.

According to the regulations, the doctrine's jurisdiction includes all tidelands (that is, areas now or previously underwater but currently filled with land, and tidal flats between the high-water mark and the seaward limit of state jurisdiction). For the most part, the landward limit of filled tidelands is up to the first public way or within 250 feet (76 meters) landward of the high-water mark.[2]

Tidelands are classified as either private or commonwealth. Generally, private tidelands are privately owned and landward of the historic low-water mark. They are subject to public rights to fish, fowl, navigation, and passing freely over and through water, Massachusetts being one of the very few states in which such public rights are so narrowly defined. Commonwealth tidelands are seaward of the historic low-water mark and are either publicly owned, or privately owned and subject to the implied condition that they be used for public purposes.

The regulations give priority to water-dependent uses: any use of public trust lands that is not dependent on a waterfront location must (1) serve a proper public purpose and (2) provide a greater benefit than detriment to the rights of the public as they apply to these lands. To meet

the public-purpose test, non-water-dependent uses in areas within the law's jurisdiction must meet broad public access requirements. The combination of this preferential treatment of uses and its application to filled tidelands makes the regulations particularly significant in impact. In Boston and other urban coastal communities where there are extensive filled tidelands, the jurisdiction of the doctrine encompasses some of the most important waterfront areas, and private development in these areas is therefore subject to requirements for public access. (The regulations do allow, however, the use of innovative measures to meet these requirements.)

For a non-water-dependent project on public trust lands, the state's public access requirements include the following:

■ Provision of a zone along the shoreline, and along the edges of the piers and wharves in a project, where nothing is permitted except water-dependent uses. The required overall width of the zone varies with the dimensions of the property and the piers, and with the location of the high-water mark.

■ Provision of a public walkway that is at least ten feet (three meters) wide, that runs along the edge of the zone reserved for water-dependent uses, and that connects to the street.

■ Provision of open space located off piers and wharves. The total amount of open space must equal the footprint of all non-water-dependent uses on the project site combined.

■ A prohibition on residential, office, and other such private uses on structures built over the water or at ground level within 100 feet (31 meters) of the shoreline.

A project on commonwealth tidelands requires (1) provision of exterior space for public recreation and (2) interior space for uses that will both accommodate and attract a broad cross-section of the public and that will enhance the destination value of the waterfront.

By obtaining state approval for a harbor plan, communities can modify these and other requirements to better meet local circumstances. For the modifications to be approved, the harbor plan must reflect the underlying principles of the regulations and meet the goals of the regulations with equal or greater effectiveness. Boston is one of several communities that have taken advantage of the flexibility afforded through a state-approved plan.

In addition to the state regulations, some Massachusetts communities have regulations of their own that rely of the Public Trust Doctrine. Boston is one such case. Its waterfront zoning ordinance is founded on a state requirement, according to which a local community must determine whether a project meets the public-purpose test. Boston's ordinance mandates that this determination be based on a number of provisions, including

the extent to which the project reasonably and appropriately preserves and enhances the public's rights in Tidelands including, without limitation, the public's:

■ *Visual access to the water . . .*
■ *Rights to fishing, fowling, and navigation and the natural derivatives thereof . . .*
■ *Physical access to and along the water's edge for recreation, commerce, and other lawful purposes, and interest in public recreational opportunities at the water's edge and open space for public use and enjoyment . . .*
■ *Interest in the preservation of the historic character of the project's site.*
■ *Interest in industrial and commercial waterborne transportation of goods and persons.*
■ *Interest in repair and rehabilitation of dilapidated piers that blight the Harborpark District and limit public access.*
■ *Interest in safe and convenient navigation in Boston Harbor.*

Boston's implementation of the Public Trust Doctrine has played a significant role in the development of public access along more than 40 miles (64 kilometers) of the city's waterfront. Appropriately, Harborpark is the name of both the major zoning district of the waterfront and of the city's overall harbor plan.

Outside the Reach of the Public Trust Doctrine

Outside the reach of the Public Trust Doctrine—that is, where neither Roman law, Napoleonic civil law, nor American or British common law applies—the public rights to the waterfront vary according to systems of property ownership, which generally fall into two main groups.

In one system, which is in place in areas such as the former Soviet Union—in the Ukraine, for example—state and private ownership are a matter of interrelated rights and responsibilities. Thus, obligations are considered inherent in the concept of ownership. The balance between private rights and the public interest varies with the

legal categories into which all land is divided. For example, for the category of housing, private rights are the highest, and the public interest is the lowest; for the use category that applies to waterfronts and water areas, the public interest is the highest and private rights are the lowest.

A second system of property ownership applies in traditional societies, such as those of certain African tribes and the Indians of North America. In these societies, ownership of both land and water rests with ancestors and with future descendants; all property rights are thus those of the state.

Integrated Coastal Management and Public Rights to the Waterfront

Support for public rights to waterfront areas, particularly the right to public access, is increasing. Integrated coastal management (ICM), which has as one of its principal goals the improvement of public access, is a significant source of support. Twenty-nine coastal states and five island territories of the United States have ICM programs; and, according to a survey undertaken by the U.S. National Oceanic and Atmospheric Administration, the majority of these programs include the regulation of public access to coastal and marine areas.[3] Many of the world's coastal nations also participate in ICM, and full participation is encouraged by leading global organizations such as UNESCO (the United Nations Educational, Scientific, and Cultural Organization) and the World Bank.

Under the auspices of the United Nations (U.N.), participation in ICM is extending to Eastern Asia. In 1994, the U.N. spearheaded the Regional Program for the Prevention and Management of Marine Pollution in the East Asian Seas; the effort included a demonstration project in Xiamen, China, that was designed to build up the ICM program in that community. The project led to the enactment of a zoning scheme under which water uses and waterfront uses require permits. For example, in areas where tourism (including the public access and enjoyment of the waterfront that this use entails) is designated as the dominant use, permit enforcement is being used to protect tourism and to prohibit conflicting activities.

Under another U.N.-sponsored effort, Urban 21—a global conference on the urban future—a principle addressing the importance of public access to the waterfront was one of ten principles of sustainable urban waterfront development that

was endorsed: "Principle 5: Public access is a prerequisite. Waterfronts should be both physically and visually accessible for locals and tourists of all ages and income."

Other Meanings of the Public Interest in the Waterfront

The public interest in the waterfront has another meaning that is connected to and overlaps with, but goes beyond, the issue of property rights. This public interest concerns the broader role of the waterfront in relation to the surrounding community and region.

The waterfront resource is an important asset that can be marshaled to meet different objectives. Over time, these objectives have expanded in number and changed in kind. The current trend is toward seeing the waterfront as a new type of community resource—one that has a central role in not only in enhancing a community's image and identity but also in strengthening its competitive advantage. Viewed as a public asset whose character and function must be protected, the waterfront is properly the subject of open and public planning processes. But although such planning processes ultimately have the potential to create a shared vision of the waterfront, there is likely to be significant conflict along the way about just what the character and functions of the waterfront should be.

Differences are to be expected between waterfront residents, commercial fishermen, terminal operators, industry, property owners, real estate developers, recreational users, tourists, and environmental and civic groups. Resolving these differences is one of the main challenges that a city will confront when it takes on the task of remaking the waterfront. One of the consistent lessons of past experience is the critical importance of ensuring that representatives of all interests, including the public at large, are party to the decision-making process.

The Public Trust Doctrine and analogous systems codify the value placed on—that is, the public interest in—the limited and precious resource of the waterfront. As consideration is given to the transformation of a waterfront, consideration also needs to be given to the public interest issues involved in addressing this unique resource.—**Laurel Rafferty**

Notes
1. See www.olemiss.edu/orgs/SGLC/6publictrust.html.
2. These limits do not apply to areas designated by the state for the preservation of port uses.
3. See http://icm.noaa.gov.

Parks and Public Access

If, for the past century, most of the downtown shoreline has been devoted to industry, port uses, and transportation routes, public access may be a particularly compelling rationale for waterfront redevelopment. Good waterfront public spaces are relatively inexpensive compared to other forms of redevelopment—and, since they are open to all, provide a democratic benefit. Indeed, the value of public access is demonstrated by the popular pressure to preserve it. Once the public gets access to the waterfront, the area often becomes so popular that sponsoring governments risk severe criticism if they do not preserve the entire water's edge for public use.

New Housing

The long-distance views and other characteristics that make waterfront parks special also make the area attractive for residential uses. While the city may have historically turned its back on the noise and odor of the working waterfront, old harbor areas often prove to be popular new neighborhoods once the industries relocate or close down. In Boston, London, and Toronto, some downtown employees became hardy urban pioneers, moving into the waterfront before site clearance was complete. In the early years of redevelopment, the waterfront can also be a "NIMBY-free" zone, allowing for the construction of mixed-income housing without the usual neighborhood backlash.

However, even if residents start out with a pioneering spirit, sponsoring governments should expect eventual demands for schools and other social services. Community services, such as schools, are particularly important if housing for low- and moderate-income families is being developed. New York City initially encouraged Battery Park City to become a middle-income and luxury development so that limited funds for community facilities and housing subsidies could be used elsewhere. Despite the city's early policy and the presence of many wealthy residents, however, the project eventually had to change its plan and add a local high school, elementary school, and neighborhood recreation facilities.

Residential development may not be desirable if the waterfront is highly contaminated or if the city wishes to protect its remaining waterfront industries, such as fishing, food processing, and marine repair. New residents often make the local political climate more hostile for industrial operations by complaining about noise, truck traffic, and the appearance of plants. Because housing drives up property values beyond the reach of most industrial uses, some jurisdictions have passed regulations to ensure that industrial activities that require access to the water's edge are not crowded out.

Projects that take advantage of existing infrastructure capacity, like Thames Court, in London, have the best chances of early success. Completed in 1998, the Class A office building replaced a Victorian-era warehouse near the Mansion House stop on the London Underground. *Kohn Pedersen Fox Associates PC*

Symbolic Transformation

Redevelopment of the waterfront can be planned to send powerful symbolic messages about the regeneration of the inner city. While physical redevelopment is complex and expensive, it is relatively straightforward (faster, and more predictable in terms of results) when compared with the more difficult task of social renewal. As demonstrated by Baltimore's Inner Harbor, in the 1970s, simple waterfront projects may be fertile ground for a symbolic "quick fix" for the inner city.

Governments that are contemplating waterfront redevelopment should consider the symbolic consequences of

Baltimore's Inner Harbor is an example of a symbolic "quick fix" that has contributed to the regeneration of an entire downtown.

their actions quite carefully, since the social benefits of waterfront redevelopment are hard to estimate. It may be possible to assign a monetary value to financial subsidies, infrastructure, and design amenities made of bricks and mortar, but how does one assign a value to the views from a waterfront park, or to a peaceful stroll along an esplanade? In London and Toronto, the agency officials who used rational decision-making techniques to account for the value of these public benefits significantly underestimated their worth in terms of symbolic importance.

Conclusions: Lessons for Faster Implementation

The experience of four decades of waterfront development shows that the agencies that possessed certain characteristics and followed best practices achieved faster project implementation.

■ Political characteristics and policies
  • Good relations with, and no surprises for, the sponsoring government;
  • Boards of directors whose members are well connected to all levels of government;
  • Strong links to local government at staff and board levels;
  • Good relations with local residents;
  • The ability to link private development with public benefits, especially waterfront parks.
■ Financial characteristics and policies
  • Land ownership

  • Access to long-term funding for infrastructure;
  • A streamlined process for the selection of developers;
  • A streamlined municipal approval process;
  • Plans for recessions, including infrastructure and social housing.
■ Planning and urban design characteristics and policies
  • Small development increments;
  • Tight phasing plans;
  • Simple infrastructure that can be phased;
  • The adoption of existing infrastructure and buildings for other uses;
  • A plan that calls for continuous public access to the water's edge.

Today, many of these recommendations appear to be simple common sense, but this group of best practices was not arrived at until redevelopment authorities had succeeded in "unlearning" the urban renewal methods of the 1950s and 1960s. Perhaps the most illuminating case was the transformation of New York's Battery Park City Authority, which was near bankruptcy in the 1970s and had become, within a decade, a highly effective implementation agency and a leader in the new political, financial, and design practices. However, it is likely that in the coming years, other new implementation techniques will be needed, as public sector budgets continue to shrink and the role of private developers continues to grow, as has been the case in projects like San Francisco's Mission Bay, Vancouver's False Creek, and Manhattan's Riverside South.

Laganside

Belfast, Northern Ireland

Virginia Sorrells and Leslie Holst

Belfast's waterfront development, on the banks of the Lagan River, has been a work in progress for the past 13 years. Known as Laganside, the project consists of a series of linked development areas that maximize the benefits of their waterfront locations and telecommunications capabilities. Belfast's history as an industrial region—and its 25 years of sectarian violence—have played a strong role in the way the area was developed.

Laganside Corporation is a government entity that manages the waterfront development area, acts as a facilitator for private investment, and encourages community linkages. The corporation seeks ways to connect residents to the waterfront, to connect the city center to Laganside, to provide employment training assistance, and to support the arts community.

A Troubled History

Belfast, Northern Ireland's capital city, was founded in the 12th century. Over the years, while Dublin became Ireland's cultural and administrative capital, Belfast found its niche as the island's industrial hub. During the 19th-century industrial boom, Belfast became the regional center for textile manufacturing, shipbuilding, engineering, and service industries, all of which lined the Lagan River and used its waters to power production. It was here, in the Harland and Wolff Shipyard, where the Lagan River meets Belfast Lough and the Irish Sea beyond, that the HMS *Titanic* was built.

Belfast's population peaked in 1911, at 386,000, during the city's industrial heyday. The depression of the 1930s took its toll on the city's key export industries, starting a decades-long decline in the city's fortunes that was exacerbated by population loss (at times as much as 10,000 people per year), large-scale unemployment, and the advent of the "the Troubles," the 25-year war for civil rights in Northern Ireland.

As a target in the bombing campaign of the Irish Republican Army, the city center was in a virtual state of siege, with a "ring of steel" security barrier surrounding the downtown. Shoppers parked their cars outside the ring and were frisked before entering stores. No one went downtown in the evenings. The Troubles even influenced urban design and architecture: buildings were designed not only for aesthetics but also for their ability to resist the impact of high-powered explosives.

Once a run-down and neglected area adjacent to the river—and best known for its cattle market—Lanyon Place has been transformed into one of Belfast's premier business locations.

Even during the height of the Troubles, however, investment in central Belfast continued, although mostly by government entities; private sector companies became less and less interested in center-city locations. The Grand Opera House, for example, located on the Golden Mile, in Belfast city center, was refurbished by the government in the 1970s as an "act of faith in troubled times," according to a Grand Opera House spokesperson. (The Europa Hotel, next door, was known as the most frequently bombed hotel in the world.) In the southern part of the city, the Castle Court shopping center was the city's main development initiative during the 1980s and 1990s. The land along the Lagan River is now the focus of regeneration for the eastern side of the city.

Manufacturing employment continued to decline during the 1980s, resulting in the loss of some 13,000 jobs. As the shipping industry shifted to containerization, the ports were moved to deeper water leaving vacant land along the river and creating more unemployment. And as employment continued to decline, the public and service sectors took on even greater importance. By 2000, it was estimated that 45 percent of Belfast's population was employed in the public sector; with the shifts in the employment base that have occurred during the past decade, 67 percent of all new jobs are now in the service sector.

A Stagnant Market

For the ten years prior to the 1998 peace accords between the Protestants and the Catholics, the office market in Belfast was stagnant. Government departments were the major users of office space, which was concentrated in seven- and eight-story buildings. Largely because of the low rents (£10 per square foot; £108 per square meter), no office

The motto of the Public Art Program is "Connecting people, places, and art." By establishing links between art and its audiences, places and people, public and private interest, Laganside aims to bring to the area unique and distinctive works of art for the benefit of Belfast's citizens and all who visit the city. *Starboard 2001* is embedded in the walkway along Greg's Quay.

buildings were built on spec; all construction was "pre-let." Even today, rents hover around £13 per square foot (£140 per square meter) for prime office space.

The tradition of long lease terms has also hampered the office development market. Property owners are reluctant to lease space for fewer than 15 years—a particular concern for information technology firms, which generally seek shorter lease terms. As some businesses have moved from the city center to Laganside, seeking more modern and flexible space, secondary space is now becoming available in the city center. But not all development is going to Laganside: Ulster Bank recently built a new, 120,000-square-foot (11,150-square-meter) headquarters next to city hall.

Apartment development is also booming in the city center, especially in some of the former office districts around city hall. Many units are being sold on the basis of floor plans alone; the market is being driven by buyers from the Republic of Ireland who are seeking better-priced investment than can be had in Dublin. However, because these high-priced units are beyond the reach of many local residents, many of them are unoccupied—which undermines the lively character the city was attempting to create. Another drawback to city-center living is that service retailing has not caught up with the expansion in the downtown population.

On the retail front, many United Kingdom–based clothing retailers are consolidating, freeing up space that is no longer modern enough for current retail standards. Castle Court, which opened in 1989, is the main covered mall, and is built around anchor stores and new retailers. Plans are under review for Victoria Square, a 807,300-square-foot (75,000-square-meter) mixed-use retail, entertainment, hotel, and apartment complex that will provide a vital connection between Laganside and the city center. The goal for Victoria Square is to complement Castle Court, creating a "dumbbell effect": two large malls anchoring the outer reaches of the shopping district.

Opportunity from Blight

As industry moved from the banks of the Lagan, Belfast was left with a blight that could be turned into an opportunity. Large tracts of land became available for new types of development that could expand and complement the adjacent city center. The city decided to focus its efforts on a mixed-use redevelopment plan that would yield a 24-hour, seven-day-a-week environment. To this end, in 1997 the city adopted the Laganside Concept Plan, which was a blueprint for the future of the river and its adjacent lands.

The plan identified an initial 346-acre (140-hectare) project area along a three-mile (five-kilometer) stretch of river; a later extension brought the total project area to 500 acres (202 hectares). Since this was the largest regeneration site in Northern Ireland, a new institution was needed to manage it. However, there was an institutional vacuum at the local government level. Because of sectarian political problems, the Department of the Environment for Northern Ireland (DOE)—which despite its name, focuses almost entirely on social issues—had captured the planning powers of the local planning authority. Sectarian conflicts also meant that political roles and power were diffuse: there was no one group that could take charge of this politically neutral part of the city. An interim organization, the Laganside Limited Company, was chartered while the city organized Northern Ireland's first urban development corporation.

Laganside Corporation

Laganside Corporation (Laganside) was formed from the interim organization in 1989. Its original mission, according to its mission statement, was to "tackle the economic regeneration of the identified area of land along the banks of the Lagan using public investment as a catalyst to secure private development capital." The corporation was expected to complement the DOE: just as the DOE emphasized social regeneration, Laganside would focus on physical regeneration.

In order to keep the corporation's mission clear, the surrounding residential areas were initially excluded from the Laganside project area. Later, however, Laganside expanded both the project area and the corporation's focus to include social and community issues and encouraged the involvement of the surrounding community in the corporation's plans. Laganside now facilitates public access to the waterfront and supports the local arts community. It has also teamed up with other government organizations and private corporations to provide local residents with employment training and job placement assistance.

Despite the environmental challenges presented by a working port, the project area had an advantage: because parcels tended to be large and under single (often public) ownership, site assembly was relatively easy. And, since most harbor commission activities had moved to deeper water, the commission rarely used the land. Market interest in the area was limited, however, and although the government was willing to subsidize development it did not want to make direct contributions to developers. Instead, Laganside decided to focus on environmental improvements that would spark the interest of private developers and foster mixed-use development.

The river was the obvious place to begin public investment. Because the Lagan is a tidal river, its foul-smelling mudflats were exposed when the tide was out, making the surrounding land less desirable for new development. Laganside's first task was to build a weir to keep

Laganside actively sponsors local events, festivals, and exhibitions, such as this ten-kilometer race along the waterfront.

the river's water level constant. The weir, which glows a brilliant blue at night and features a lookout point and a visitors' center, became a tourist attraction in itself.

Once the weir was completed, in 1994, Laganside could turn its attention to the surrounding contaminated land. Grants from the European Union (EU) provided approximately £20 million of the £30 million in costs for remediating the site and building the weir; the DOE provided the remaining £10 million.

With the signing of the Good Friday peace accords, in 1998, Belfast began to attract investors who had been wary of locating in a war zone. Business investment in the area increased, particularly as investment in red-hot Dublin, a little over an hour to the south, spilled over into Belfast. Although Belfast's economy is clearly on the upswing, the communities lining the Laganside development area are still beset by high unemployment. While the national unemployment rate is hovering around 6 percent, pockets of 40 to 60 percent unemployment still exist in some neighborhoods;

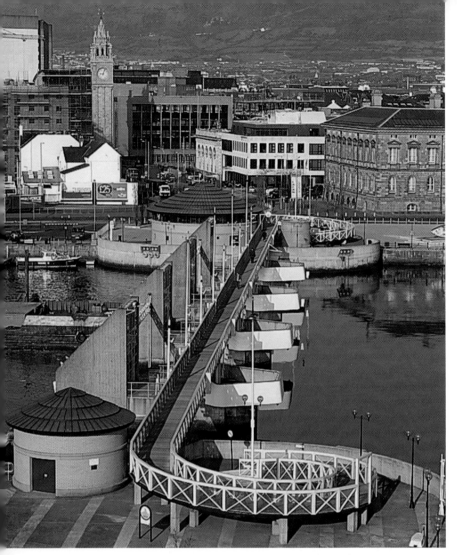

The Laganside weir boardwalk, which glows a brilliant blue at night and features a lookout point and a visitors' center, has became a tourist attraction in itself.

and in some households, no one has held a job for generations. Of the 32 wards in Belfast, 14 are adjacent to the Laganside development area; of those, ten have been designated (on the basis of poverty levels and other demographic characteristics) as "targeting social needs" areas, which means that residents are eligible for special employment training assistance from the central government.

Laganside Development Areas

There are currently nine mixed-use development sites in the Laganside project area.

Lanyon Place and Waterfront Hall

History was made in May 1998, when Unionist leader David Trimble and Nationalist leader John Hume shook hands on the stage of Laganside's Waterfront Hall as a show of unity and support for the Good Friday peace accords.

With that gesture, the building's position as a national symbol of unity was secured. The hall itself is the focal point of Lanyon Place, Laganside's flagship development site.

Although designated for an arts and conference center in the 1960s Urban Area Plan, the 15-acre (six-hectare) site that would become Lanyon Place was home to sheep and cattle markets for another 20 years. Now, Lanyon Place is a premier business location serving leisure, convention, and office markets.

Since it was the first—and hence the riskiest—area of Laganside to develop, there was "a wee bit of bluff" in the early days, as there was no great certainty that the Laganside plans were going to work. Six development companies responded to the request for qualifications issued by Laganside; Enterprise, a subsidiary of the Rouse Company, was selected. The proposed site plan called for an 80,000-square-foot (7,430-square-meter) festival marketplace that would feature an inlet of water running through the site. The development team wanted the city to pay for the inlet, however; when the city declined, citing high infrastructure costs, Dunloe Ewart took over the project, and Waterfront Hall was constructed on Lanyon Place.

The music hall, which is owned by the Belfast City Council, features a 24,100-square-foot (2,240-square-meter) auditorium, a 4,100-square-foot (380-square-meter) studio, 16 meeting rooms, exhibition space, a restaurant and bar, and structured parking. The building's circular form provides the interior public spaces with extensive views of the city, and the flexible space in the main hall is designed to accommodate a broad range of events and performances. Adjacent to Waterfront Hall is the 195-room Hilton Belfast Hotel. The hotel's 12-story tower sits upon a podium, and the gently sloping aluminum roof of the tower appears to float over the flat concrete roof of the podium. The Hilton Hotel Group had such faith in the Belfast market that it invested 75 percent equity in the project.

British Telecom (BT) consolidated a staff of 1,200 from five other offices into Riverside Towers, its new building at Lanyon Place. The building, which houses BT's regional headquarters for Northern Ireland as well as its software engineering center, features 116,110 square feet (10,790 square meters) of floor space and was constructed for £35 million.

Number 9 Lanyon Place offers 150,700 square feet (14,000 square meters) of office space built on spec by Dunloe Ewart. Fujitsu occupies three floors at £13.50 per square foot (£145 per square meter), and Northrope Technology occupies 17,000 square feet (1,580 square meters) at £15 per square foot (£161 per square meter). More development is expected: plans are already underway for a retail and entertainment area with terraced public spaces that would overlook the river and help focus activity on the waterfront.

The Gasworks

Established by the city's founding fathers over 150 years ago and closed in 1988, the Gasworks, a landmark 22-acre (nine-hectare) site strategically located between the waterfront and the city center, is ideal for a mix of commercial and entertainment uses. It was also the most polluted site in Northern Ireland: about seven feet (two meters) of contaminated material from the area around the gas tanks had to be removed, and to protect the inhabitants from possible fumes, gas-impermeable membranes had to be installed on each floor of every building. The Gasworks was developed as a partnership between Laganside and the Belfast City Council; the council had responsibility for on-site environmental reclamation and public infrastructure improvements, but the required £8 million was largely funded through grants from the EU.

Belfast is well known for its high-bandwidth communications infrastructure, which made the historic Gasworks site attractive to e-commerce and global telecommunications businesses as well as to customer care centers. The 150,700-square-foot (14,000-square-meter) call center built in 2001 by Halifax Direct is, in terms of employment opportunities, "possibly the most significant investment ever in Northern Ireland": when fully staffed, it will create an estimated 1,800 jobs. Other companies located at the Gasworks include Nevada tele.com and BBC Resources, which together occupy a 20,000-square-foot (1,860-square-meter) spec building. In addition to large offices, there are ten "own door" office suites of 5,000 to 6,000 square feet (465 to 560 square meters) for startup businesses, and 28 units designated for small, local, or new businesses.

The Odyssey

The Odyssey entertainment complex is one of Northern Ireland's major visitor attractions. Built on a 25-acre (ten-hectare) docklands site, the Odyssey offers a 10,000-seat "indoor area" for the Belfast Giants hockey team; a science, engineering, and technology museum; an IMAX theater; a cinema; and an attractive, "European-style" pavilion with shops, bars, and restaurants, featuring a Hard Rock Café. In one of its largest single investments, Laganside Corporation contributed £9 million to the £100 million project. The Odyssey has created approximately 600 full- and part-time jobs.

Clarendon Dock

Laganside Corporation and the Belfast Harbour Commissioners own Clarendon Dock, a 30-acre (12-hectare) business and entertainment park, in partnership. Businesses are drawn to Clarendon Dock by the city's relatively young, untapped, and well-educated labor pool, and by the superior telecommunications infrastructure. Clarendon Dock is home to many national and international companies, including Prudential Assurance Society, Phoenix Natural Gas, Tesco, and Regus Office Services. Government agencies have relocated from the city center into two office buildings on Clarendon Dock. Each building features two floors of offices with five floors of apartments above.

The area stretching between Waterfront Hall and Waterfront Plaza encompasses the £110 million Odyssey building, which is the permanent home of the Belfast Giants ice hockey team. Also pictured is the five-star, 195-room Hilton Belfast Hotel.

Clarendon Dock is also known for its entertainment venues and weekend music festivals. The site's business and entertainment uses are complemented by recent apartment, retail, and restaurant construction.

Mays Meadow and East Bank

While continuing Laganside's mixed-use focus, Mays Meadow and East Bank will incorporate more housing options than other development areas. Mays Meadow is a five-acre (two-hectare) site that currently offers 140 market-rate and 48 social-housing apartments. Pricewaterhouse-Coopers occupies 107,600 square feet (9,995 square meters) of office space in Mays Meadow, and the Abbey National Call Center and a local bar and grill round out the area.

Winding streets, cobbled lanes, and a mix of historic architectural styles give Cathedral Quarter, one of the oldest areas in Belfast, its distinctive character. The neighborhood is a haven for writers and artists, who gather for the Cathedral Quarter Arts Festival, shown here.

East Bank's 105 acres (43 hectares) are still in the planning stages. Over the next ten years, development on the site will feature commercial space and an environmentally sustainable housing community. Other project components include the development of public space along the waterfront and the creation of linkages to other communities.

Laganside introduced Belfast residents to apartment living, and Quay Gate, developed by Malone Enterprises, is an example of a new apartment project. The first 75 of the 118 units were sold from the plans, sight unseen. The smooth-fronted red brick building reflects the area's Victorian architecture, and each floor has views of the Lagan River. Buyers, a mix of young professionals and corporations (who buy apartments for employees who regularly visit Belfast on business), are attracted to the river views and to the location in Laganside, which is close to the city center and the soon-to-be-completed Victoria Square retail complex; local buyers are also drawn by the proximity of employment opportunities. A one-bedroom unit with 500 square feet (45 square meters) sells for £86,950; most units are two-bedroom, however, offering between 750 and 1,000 square feet (between 70 and 93 square meters) and selling for between £94,950 and £139, 950.

Cathedral Quarter

A five-minute walk from city hall, Cathedral Quarter is a 30-acre (12-hectare) neighborhood that houses artists and organizations as well as private residences and links the original Laganside project area to the city center. CUSP Ltd developers and the Belfast Education and Library Board jointly own the land with Laganside, and CUSP will serve as the master developer for a central portion of the project area.

The Cathedral Quarter development area will be different from other Laganside projects: the master plan emphasizes physical, social, and economic revitalization, and development will highlight the community's focus on organizations and the arts. The University of Ulster Arts College is engaged in its own £40 million redevelopment in conjunction with the regeneration of Cathedral Quarter.

Three dilapidated buildings have been restored, yielding 43,500 square feet (4,040 square meters) of managed workspace for artists and community businesses that is "designed to attract the energy and creativity of small arts and community organizations into the heart of Cathedral Quarter." Also in the works is the Four Corners project. Developed by the Merrion Property Group, the 14,488-square-foot (1,345-square-meter) building will be partially constructed behind a restored 1867 facade. The mixed-use development will feature an 8,270-square-foot (770-square-meter) bar and restaurant, a 50-bed boutique hotel, and 30 upscale apartments with 31 underground parking spaces. The project will reflect the area's historic character and is expected to begin construction in early 2003.

Titanic Quarter and Donegall Quay

Titanic Quarter and Donegall Quay are the next large areas slated for development. Titanic Quarter, which consists of 185 acres (75 hectares) in the former Hartland and Wolff Shipyard, is planned as a mixed-use commercial, retail, entertainment, and residential area that will include the 25-acre (ten-hectare) Northern Ireland Science Park. The Titanic Interpretive Center, designed by Murray O'Laoire Architects, will be housed in the original dry dock. By leveraging £200 million in public investment, the development has obtained £200 million in private investment—and is expected to provide 10,000 job opportunities over the next 15 years. Infrastructure construction is set to begin in 2003.

Plans for the £30 million mixed-use development at Donegall Quay were recently announced. This half-acre (0.20-hectare) site will feature a seven-story building linked to an 18-story tower and offer 250,000 square feet (23,225 square meters) of floor space for a four-star hotel, 130 apartments, specialty retail, and office space.

Community Support

The city of Belfast has programs in place to support community services, the arts community, and new industries. The goal of Investment Belfast, a public/private partnership designed to support economic development, is to develop and support a knowledge economy through infrastructure, innovation and entrepreneurship, the commercialization of university research, and international marketing and trade. In its efforts to promote the city to private sector investors, Investment Belfast highlights Belfast's high-tech advantages, including

■ A young, highly skilled workforce that includes approximately 3,000 information technology graduates each year;

■ Affordable land and labor costs (Belfast is the eighth-least-expensive city for business out of 46 ranked in a 2001 study by Insignia);

■ Three competing broadband networks: BT, NTL, and Eirecomm.

Investment Belfast is leading the city's bid for European City of Culture status, a designation granted by the European Union, and plans to be ready for nomination in 2008. Development plans to expand the Cathedral Quarter into an arts and culture zone, which would include a theater, are central to the application. (Liverpool, England, was recently chosen to win this designation.)

The Belfast Gasworks Employee Matching Service (GEMS) provides job training and placement assistance to Belfast residents interested in working for businesses located on the Gasworks site. Formed as a partnership with key local community and statutory agencies, GEMS focuses on support services for the long-term unemployed as they return to work.

Laganside Corporation gives grants to local community organizations that hold events in Laganside. Sponsored events might include those held by the Docker's Club, a "cross-community" club for boxing; the Sailortown Ex-Residents' Society; the Half-Bap Community Association; and the Little Italy Association, which has applied for grants for a summer festival. Grants typically range from £250 to £1,000, and about 100 are made each year for football matches, floats for the Lord Mayor's parade, and boat rides for kids.

Laganlines, Laganside Corporation's quarterly community newsletter, is distributed to 180,000 households and provides updates on the corporation and the development sites, and notifies residents of community events.

To support community artists, Laganside developed an arts trail along the river. At Lanyon Place, a "sheep in the road" sculpture commemorates the land's former role as a livestock market. Arts projects at Laganside are funded through a "percent for art" program that requires developers to submit, as part of their development proposals, an arts project that encompasses no more than 1 percent of the project's total costs.

Project Data: **Laganside**

Land Use Information

Total site area, Laganside
(acres/hectares)   500/202

Development Area	Size of Site (Acres/Hectares)	Project or Type of Use	Project Area (Square Feet/ Square Meters, Unless Otherwise Noted)
Lanyon Place	15/6	Waterfront Hall	28,200/2,620
		Riverside Towers (British Telecom headquarters)	160,110/14,875
		Number 9 Lanyon Place	150,700/14,000
		Hilton Belfast Hotel	195 rooms
Gasworks	22/9	Halifax Direct call center	150,700/14,000
		Nevada tele.com/BBC Resources	20,000/1,860
		"Own-door" offices	5,000–6,000/465–560
Odyssey	25/10	Entertainment complex	
Clarendon Dock	30/12	Business/entertainment park	
East Bank	105/43	Mixed-use development	
Mays Meadow	5/2	Mixed-use development	
		Apartments	188 units
		PricewaterhouseCoopers	107,600/9,995
Cathedral Quarter	30/12	Managed workspaces	43,500/4,040
		Four Corners project	14,488/1,345
		• Bar and restaurant	8,270/770
		• Hotel	6,240/580 (lobby only)
Titanic Quarter	185/75	Northern Ireland Science Park	25 acres/10 hectares
Donegall Quay	0.5/0.20	Mixed-use development	250,000/23,225

Measuring Success

As of October 2002, total investment in Laganside had reached £730 million, including £120 million from the public sector, and created 10,000 permanent jobs. Laganside is home to some of Belfast's most prestigious buildings, including the Odyssey and Waterfront Hall. Over the years, approximately 500 apartments have been built in the area, along with 4.5 miles (7.2 kilometers) of walkways along the waterfront.

Laganside works by forging strategic partnerships with city agencies, investing in public infrastructure, and marketing the area's opportunities to private companies and developers. Laganside leverages its own monies at a rate of £1 for every £5 of noncorporation funding.

The key to Laganside's success was its initial focus on environmental remediation as a means of attracting private development. As the need for physical and economic infrastructure has diminished, Laganside Corporation is in transition and is now forming alliances and partnerships with other entities to develop project areas. It is also turning its focus to social and community issues, such as supporting the local arts community and providing economic opportunities for local residents.

Lessons Learned

Laganside provides a model for public/private partnerships engaged in urban regeneration.

Success depends on getting developers into a comfortable state of mind. Instead of passing along benefits to developers, public entities should use public funds to

Residential Information, Quay Gate

Unit Type	Unit Size (Square Feet/Square Meters)	Range of Initial Sales Prices
One-bedroom	500/45	£86,950
Two-bedroom	750/70	£94,950–£129,950
Two-bedroom with study	1,000/93	£118,950–£139,950

Major Project Participants

Laganside Corporation
Clarendon Building
15 Clarendon Road
Belfast BT1 3BG
Northern Ireland
+44 (028) 9032 8507

Department of the Environment
Clarence Court
10-18 Adelaide Street
Belfast BT1 2GB
Northern Ireland
+44 (028) 9054 0540

Belfast City Council
City Hall
Belfast BT1 5GS
Northern Ireland
+44 (028) 9032 0202

Belfast Waterfront Hall
2 Lanyon Place
Belfast BT1 3WH
Northern Ireland
+44 (028) 9033 4400

Dunloe Ewart plc
9 Fitzwilliam Square
Dublin 2
Ireland
+353 1 661 4344

Odyssey
2 Queens Quay
Belfast BT3 9QQ
Northern Ireland
+44 (028) 9045 1055

Belfast Harbour Commissioners
+44 (028) 9055 4422

Murray O'Laoire Architects
Fumbally Court
Fumbally Lane
Dublin 8
Ireland
+353 1 453 7300
Web site: www.murrayolaoire.com

CUSP Ltd
10a Clarendon Road
Belfast BT1 3BG
Northern Ireland
+44 (028) 9083 8322

Harland and Wolff Group plc
+44 (028) 9053 4102

Investment Belfast
40 Linenhall Street, Fifth Floor
Belfast BT2 8BA
Northern Ireland
+44 (028) 9033 1136
Web site: www.investment-belfast.co.uk/

improve the value of the land and to make it attractive to residents and new businesses. Dublin had tax incentives to attract new development, but it still took a while for things to heat up. Laganside laid out its entire infrastructure first, so that it would be ready when the developers were.

The decision to place a major public building at Laganside—Waterfront Hall—made a very strong statement about the general commitment to the area. It was also important that, unlike the Millennium Dome (built on the meridian line in Greenwich, England, in celebration of the millennium) and other splashy projects, Laganside was sustainable.

The "branding" of Laganside was very important. There are now about 100 organizations in the telephone book with "Laganside" in their names: ten years ago, no such place existed.

Area-based planning should be done in partnership with the landowners: it is not necessary to own the development sites in order to promote them or plan for them.

Planning for one area may help to alleviate a problem for another. In Laganside, for example, the development of own-entrance offices succeeded in luring businesses away from residential neighborhoods.

On the residential front: if you build it, they might come, but there is no guarantee they will stay. More sensitive pricing or even a larger number of rental units might have better accomplished Laganside's goal of using residential development to promote a round-the-clock ambience.

Brindleyplace

Birmingham, England

Virginia Sorrells

The largest mixed-use project ever attempted in the United Kingdom (U.K.), Brindleyplace is a master-planned development situated between the Birmingham and Brindley Loop canals in Birmingham, England, approximately 115 miles (185 kilometers) northwest of London. This 17-acre (seven-hectare) project features office, retail, residential, and cultural uses surrounding two public squares.

Centered around Canals

In the early 1980s, Birmingham was forced, like many other industrial cities around the world, to search for new strategies to revive its flagging economy. The city chose to use its canal system as a catalyst for urban revitalization.

For nearly 300 years, Birmingham's economic life had centered on its canals. During the early years of the industrial revolution, over 200 miles (322 kilometers) of canals were built to connect Birmingham to the larger region and to the rest of England, placing the city at the heart of the national canal network. Although the canals are all connected, those in Birmingham and in the surrounding Black Country were built in stages, by different companies, between 1768 and 1799. James Brindley, a pioneering canal engineer, built the Birmingham canal in 1768; it was one of several canals used to transport coal, ore, and finished products for the metals industry. As the canal system grew, so did the city's manufacturing base. The Birmingham and Fazeley Canal, which runs through the heart of the Brindleyplace development, was completed in 1789, providing the link to the Coventry Canal and to the waterways east of the city. Although many of the canals have been filled in over time, over 50 navigable miles (80 kilometers) remain within the city itself.

The city's industrial economy, long based on metals manufacturing, was in decline by the 1930s. And as industry began to abandon Birmingham, the city began to abandon its canals. The towpaths became derelict and the channels became filled with silt. Heavy bombing during World War II destroyed much of the remaining industry. As part of the post–World War II nationalization of the railroads, the British Transport Commission, which had been established in 1948, acquired all rail and canal routes. In 1958, management of the canals was placed under the control of British Waterways, which is still responsible today for overseeing mooring practices, maintaining towpaths, and ensuring water quality and supply.

A Plan to Revitalize Birmingham

Like many cities, Birmingham attempted to design its way out of decline in the 1960s. And like many cities, it chose to invest in a highway megaproject, the Inner Ring Road, which circled the center of the city and effectively cut it off from surrounding neighborhoods. Many historic buildings were demolished to make way for this "concrete collar"; 20 years later, planners would encounter a major challenge in attempting to mitigate its effects. The 1960s also saw the development of Cambrian Wharf, a high-rise, mixed-use development along the canal, north of the city center, that was the city's first attempt at an inner-city revitalization project.

By the 1970s the city had decided to focus its economic redevelopment strategy on business tourism; plans for the National Exhibition Centre (NEC) were undertaken in 1975. At that time, there were no purpose-built convention centers in the U.K. The plan was to capitalize on the city's location at a "crossroads of opportunity"—the meeting place of not just the national canal system but major rail and motorway routes as well. Debate ensued over whether to build the NEC near the city center or on a greenfield site on the perimeter. The choice of a city-center location—a 40-acre (16-hectare) site along the canal, just outside the Inner Ring Road—would be key to the city's future redevelopment.

In 1988 Birmingham hosted the Highbury Initiative, an intensive, 48-hour "urban regeneration brainstorming session" that became the basis for a 13-year implementation strategy. Two recurring themes emerged at Highbury. First, the city had no clear visual identity: it was impossible to draw a map of its center from memory. Second, the Inner Ring Road had strangled the center, separating it from the surrounding historic districts. In response to these findings, the city decided to develop a pedestrian-friendly concept for the city center—and, as part of that concept, to downgrade the Inner Ring Road. The Birmingham Urban Design Strategy (BUDS) was a result of the Highbury Initiative. As part of the BUDS, the city commissioned a city-center plan that would give the center a clearer identity.

The city council hired consultants Tibbalds, Colbourne, Karski, and Williams to design the plan. Their goals were to

■ Relate the buildings to the streets;

■ Create "people-friendly city centers" for the commercial, sports, and convention areas;

■ Make better use of the area's natural topography;

Brindleyplace Square was designed both to relate to the surrounding buildings and to be a distinctive "address" at the heart of the development. The café, designed by Piers Gough, is the principal focus of the square. The water feature captures and reflects the light throughout the day; the Miles Davies sculpture symbolizes Brindleyplace's historic past. *Argent Group plc*

Oozells Square was designed to have a strong identity that would complement, but not compete with, the main square. A rill runs diagonally across Oozells Square, leading the eye to the tower of the Ikon Gallery. *Argent Group plc*

mitigation to make the canals navigable once again: towpaths were restored and canal walls shored up. The city's decision to open a Brussels office to lobby the EU for redevelopment funds proved to be a good one: in the course of the 1990s, Birmingham received approximately £25 million in EU funds for environmental cleanup and infrastructure improvements. Much of the EU money was used for remediation of the site of the former brass foundries, as were "derelict land grants" from the central U.K. government.

■ Encourage development in distinctive quarters;

■ Foster the development of new landmarks and open space.

The canals became the backdrop for this plan, knitting together a total development area that now amounts to 2,000 acres (810 hectares). The city decided to abandon the 1960s-era U.S. planning model of inward-looking malls and other developments, which had universally fallen out of favor. Instead, the plans emphasized permeability and were designed so that new construction would create a "necklace of places" within the center city.

But before development along the canals could proceed, the city needed to address the problems left behind by their former users. The sediments within the canals and the land alongside them were contaminated by cadmium, zinc, and other heavy-metal residues and would need to be dredged; the cost of £2.2 million was largely covered by the European Union's (EU's) Project Aquarius.

Fish had vanished from the waterways long ago—but, over the years, reed beds had sprung up in the stagnant waters, providing homes for other kinds of wildlife. Consequently, British Waterways undertook wetlands

The National Sea Life Centre, located near the intersection of the Birmingham and Brindley Loop canals, is one of a series of attractions that bring visitors from throughout the U.K. to Brindleyplace. *Argent Group plc*

The preservation of landmarks and habitats will continue to influence development along the canals. There are over 1,000 listed (landmark) structures on the waterways in and around Birmingham, as well as ancient monuments and sites of particular scientific interest such as reed beds and endangered species' habitat. And the fish are back.

Brindleyplace Development Strategy

During the 1980s the city spent £6 million assembling the Brindleyplace site; in 1987 it issued a request for proposals with three main directives:

■ Increase the viability of the plan for the city center while addressing the city's requirement for a mix of uses that will promote a high level of pedestrian activity;

■ Ensure that the site, as the natural extension of the west end of the city center, is integrated into its surroundings and has strong pedestrian links to the traditional prime office zone;

■ Create a workable plan for the development, including a substantial increase in office space, that will lend itself to phased implementation.

The city also wanted to make the most of the canal system and to open it as much as possible to increased public use. Given that the canals have an average width of about 15 feet (4.6 meters) and are located some 15 feet (4.6 meters) below the city grade, they were an asset that would have been easy to obscure. Any designs would need to carefully take into account both the opportunities and constraints presented by the canals. (For example, to avoid creating the effect of canyons, development would have to be layered away from the canals.) To ensure that the developer would be guided more by concern for quality than by concern for profit, the city opted to forgo an opportunity to sell the property for its maximum market value, in favor of finding a developer who would maximize the site's overall development potential.

The developer selected, Rosehaugh plc, acquired 17 acres (seven hectares) at Brindleyplace, adjacent to the canal, on a 150-year lease for £23.3 million. The acquisition price included monies earmarked for the construction of the International Convention Centre (ICC) and Symphony Hall, which were to be located across the canal from Brindleyplace. Under this arrangement, Brindleyplace plc, a subsidiary of Rosehaugh, would be the master leaseholder, provided that it met various development obligations. A project manager was appointed from within the city government to coordinate activities across departments and cut through red tape.

Initially, the key component of the city's vision for Brindleyplace was a 250,000-square-foot (23,225-square-meter) festival marketplace; the £80 million development was to include an arts and crafts market and a leisure center, as well as a 2,000-space parking garage that would link the ICC to the proposed national aquarium. Despite the city council's enthusiasm, opinions were divided about the prospects for the marketplace: even James Rouse reportedly thought it was a bad idea. And, since the economy was in the grips of a recession, lenders were reluctant to bankroll the plan. With the festival marketplace apparently a nonstarter, Rosehaugh submitted a second proposal for an office development.

The Rosehaugh office development was based on a 1991 master plan, created by Terry Farrell and John Chatwin, that had drawn heavily on the Highbury principles and the BUDS. The plan was organized around a system of public squares, linked to one another and to the rest of the city center by pedestrian pathways. Density would be high, to maintain the urban character, but building heights would be in keeping with the four- to five-story buildings on adjacent Broad Street, Birmingham's traditional main street. The stone and brick that were characteristic of Birmingham buildings would be the favored building materials.

In 1992, Rosehaugh went bankrupt; in 1993, its assets were purchased by Argent plc for £3 million. Under the original agreement with the city, five years still remained to develop Brindleyplace. The fire-sale price meant that Argent had more money available than Rosehaugh to invest in the redevelopment of the site. Thus, Argent was able to undertake a higher-quality, higher-cost development than Rosehaugh might have been able to afford.

Nevertheless, financing the project became a challenge. Aside from the recession and the site conditions, lenders tend to be suspicious of mixed-use development, a factor that had an important implication for Brindleyplace: the lenders' requirements meant that housing had to be more segregated from retail and office uses than the developers had originally planned, which created a more "horizontal" rather than "vertical" arrangement of uses. The phased development required by the city in its request for proposals became a key part of the project's financing strategy: capital for subsequent phases was negotiated as each prior phase reached completion.

Building Brindleyplace

Under the agreement with the city, Argent was required, at its own expense, to build the first 60,000 square feet (5,575 square meters) of speculative retail and restaurant space at the Water's Edge site, across the canal from the ICC, as a gateway into the main Brindleyplace development. The developer was also required to refurbish the Oozells Street School building (a landmark constructed in the decorative style known as Ruskinian Gothic), and to lay out the main square. The addition of these requirements meant that Argent's investment rose to nearly £8 million before any income could be realized.

Fortunately, the phased construction and funding approach proved successful, and allowed the next several phases of mixed-use office development to proceed. The Water's Edge development was completed and partially leased by 1994, with full lease-up in 1995. Designed by Benoy Architects and Designers, the project consists of shops, restaurants, and bars situated around a piazza on the pedestrian thoroughfare that passes through Brindleyplace to the main square.

After the completion of Water's Edge, British Airways Pension Trustees acquired one parcel of Brindleyplace and agreed to provide initial funding for the speculative construction of Number One Brindleyplace. Happily, general confidence in the economy was rising along with the buildings of Brindleyplace, making subsequent phases more attractive to investors. Sales of the surrounding land—to Berkeley Homes, Greenalls Pubs, and the Institute of Electrical Engineers—provided the capital for the construction, in 1995, of the main square and the major infrastructure. As the larger development area began to take shape in

Number Three Brindleyplace is prominently located at the head of the square. The building's civic facade fronts the square, and the rear of the building steps down three stories toward the canal. *Argent Group plc*

1996, Argent was able to prelease 120,000 square feet (11,150 square meters) of office space to British Telecom, which made possible the construction of Number Five. Also in that year, the sale of land to the National Sea Life Centre and a prelease to Lloyd's TSB Bank underwrote the construction of Number Two.

The Argent Development Consortium was formed, in 1997, with a loan from a consortium of German banks; the partners are Argent plc, the British Telecom Pension Scheme, Citibank, and the United Bank of Kuwait (UBK; now Ahli United Bank). The Argent Development Consortium financed the construction of two additional speculative office buildings, a multistory parking garage, and a theater.

Surrounding Brindleyplace Square

The main square, which is surrounded by the initial buildings of the development, is the heart of Brindleyplace. The square was designed by Townshend Landscape Architects to be a natural extension of the series of public spaces that run through the center of the city, and to provide an organizing element for the buildings that would surround it. It features a fountain, a terraced area that can be used as a performance space, and a café designed by Piers Gough. Townshend took advantage of the three-foot (0.9-meter) slope across the site to create a series of distinct spaces within the square.

The buildings surrounding the square (Two, Three, Four, Five, and Six Brindleyplace) were the work of different architects but were all designed to address thoughtfully the public space and one another, and to fit into Farrell and Chatwin's master plan. The selection of the architectural firms was itself a key part of the design approach. The developers wanted to avoid large commercial firms that "churn out commercial space by the square

Set on a triangular site across from the Brindley Loop Canal, Symphony Court offers flats and townhouses with parking. The footbridge connects to Brindleyplace. *Argent Group plc*

foot" and to work instead with smaller firms, for whom the Brindleyplace commissions would represent a significant portion of their practice.[1] The developers also sought out firms with which they could collaborate, by working directly with the designers and making their vision under-

stood firsthand. The result is a collection of buildings that, although generated simultaneously, have an organic quality as though they have been assembled over time. The buildings are harmonious without being individually anonymous, and bear a strong family resemblance to one another without being clones.

Two Brindleyplace (Allies & Morrison Architects) provides 75,000 square feet (6,965 square meters) of office space on six floors that surround a full-height atrium. To accommodate the diagonal cut of the route from Water's Edge, an indentation was made in the building's principal facade, which overlooks the main square and features a freestanding, fully glazed stair tower and a 20-foot- (six-meter-) high colonnade with a double-height entryway. The colonnade forms the base of the building's three-part composition; the middle is formed by the office grid and the top by a recessed floor surrounded by terraces.

At Two Brindleyplace, the details of each facade differ slightly to reflect their surroundings. The front is the most formal and deliberate, while the side facing Oozells Street is slanted and asymmetrical. The simpler back is the service side, providing access to the parking garage and loading docks. The exterior walls are of load-bearing brick on a steel frame. Fenestration in silver-gray painted metalwork forms a continuous lattice, serving as both a counterpoint to the masonry and a link to the white-plastered interior. The recessed upper story and the back wall of the colonnade are also painted white to enhance the sense that the building has an inner layer.

Three Brindleyplace (Porphyrios Associates, Architects), at the meeting point with Water's Edge, dominates the main square, and its 164-foot- (50-meter-) high tower has become a Brindleyplace landmark. It offers 91,500 square feet (8,500 square meters) of office space on six floors (stepping down to three stories on the canal side). The main entrance leads through a double-height arcade into a foyer—which, in turn, leads to a seven-story glazed central atrium. A ground-level arcade clad in ashlar stone surrounds the atrium. The middle section is ringed with columns that reach to an upper loggia with a glazed roof. Broad balconies overlook the atrium, and office ceiling heights are nine feet (2.7 meters). The interior post-and-spandrel construction contrasts with the bulkiness of the exterior, which is of self-supporting brick masonry and ashlar stone. Reconstituted stone was used in all the architectural projections and rusticated surfaces. The entry portals, with half-round arches descending into load-bearing Doric columns, are almost Venetian in design.

Four Brindleyplace (Stanton Williams Architects) is by far the most modernist of the buildings fronting the square. The exterior of this seven-story, 114,000-square-foot (10,590-square-meter) building makes use of glass and Belgian brick in almost equal measure, and the colonnade at the base of the building is formed of precast concrete. Designed for multitenant occupancy, the building has a range of environmental control systems, including natural ventilation, and excellent views from its 20,000-square-foot (1,860-square-meter) open-plan offices. Three service cores run through the building, and a glazed atrium, 130 feet (40 meters) long and 99 feet (30 meters) high, provides light and air to the building's center. A 10,000-square-foot (930-square-meter) restaurant occupies the ground floor, extending outdoors onto the square in the front of the building and to the canal behind the building. The basement includes a two-story parking garage.

Five Brindleyplace (Sidell Gibson Partnership), at the western edge of the main square, is also organized around an atrium. Occupants of all seven floors have good views of the square; lit at night, the heart of the building is plainly visible from across the square. The energy-efficient building includes upflow air conditioning and window openings that were kept as small as practical. Towers mark the entrance of the castlelike construction of brick and reconstituted stone. Because the building is deeper than it is wide—114 feet by 279 feet (35 by 85 meters)—its interior has a slightly cavernous appearance, an effect that is enhanced by stepped balconies at the far end of the atrium that are draped with green hanging plants. Designed in consultation with the tenant, British Telecom, the interior is intended to create spaces in which staff and visitors will feel welcome and congregate naturally. Visible circulation, glass elevators, a prominent spiral stair near the entrance, and dramatic bridges traversing the atrium all contribute to the feeling of openness.

Number Six (Allies & Morrison Architects) faces both the main square and Oozells Square. The seven-story building contains 94,000 square feet (8,730 square meters) of office space, 4,500 square feet (420 square meters) of restaurant space, and basement parking. The entrance through the three-part facade leads from the main square through a colonnade and lobby to a raised atrium illuminated by a glazed roof. Balconies open on three sides of the atrium. The service core forms the fourth wall. The red-brick facade is offset by deeply recessed windows in gunmetal gray.

Surrounding Oozells Square

Oozells Square, by Townshend Landscape Architects, was designed to counterbalance Brindleyplace Square. Flanked by cherry trees, the square features a small inlet of water that diagonally bisects the site and leads the eye to sculptures designed by Paul de Monchaux. The surrounding art galleries and restaurants activate the otherwise calm square.

The square is surrounded by the Ikon Gallery and by buildings Nine, Eight, Ten, and Seven. To convert the historic and architecturally notable Oozells Street School into the Ikon Gallery, Levitt Bernstein, the designer, transformed the large, light-filled classrooms on the first and second floors into 44,800 square feet (4,160 square meters) of exhibition space. A shop, a café, and administrative offices are located on the ground floor. Argent donated the school building to the Ikon Gallery, which then obtained construction funding from the National Lottery and the European Regional Development Fund.

Number Seven (Porphyrios Associates) straddles both Brindleyplace Square and Oozells Square; it has 85,000 square feet (7,895 square meters) of office space set around a courtyard entrance.

Several nonoffice projects round out the Brindleyplace development. Symphony Court, with 143 apartments and townhouses lining the Brindley Loop and Canal, was the first to offer city-center living. Rents for one- and two-bedroom units range from £950 to £1,750 per month. The National Sea Life Centre, designed by Sir Norman Foster, features 38,700 square feet (3,595 square meters) of exhibition space and offers the largest collection of marine creatures in Europe. The Crescent Theatre, original to the Brindleyplace site, was rebuilt by Argent

Number Five Brindleyplace, which houses the headquarters of British Telecom, is positioned at the western side of the square. The atrium reduces the perceived bulk of the building and creates a sense of continuity with the public realm. *Argent Group plc*

Number Nine (Associated Architects) is a mixed-use building that bridges Broad Street and Oozells Square. The building's design complements the adjacent Presbyterian church, built in 1849, and provides 43,000 square feet (3,395 square meters) of office space and 26,800 square feet (2,490 square meters) of restaurant space. The restaurant space can easily be subdivided to meet tenant needs.

Numbers Eight and Ten, both by Sidell Gibson, were the last two office buildings to be developed. Number Eight is a mixed-use structure with 13 floors: the first eight floors offer 92,000 square feet (8,545 square meters) of office space; the five floors above are occupied by 35 apartments. To minimize the apparent height of the building, the residential floors are stepped back, but they still provide views of Birmingham and the surrounding countryside. Number Ten features 62,000 square feet (5,760 square meters) of high-quality office space and serves as a transition between Brindleyplace and Broad Street, marking a definitive end to the development.

The shops, bars, and restaurants of the Water's Edge, which were inspired by the 200-year-old canal system, are arranged around a piazza and a pedestrian walkway that leads to Brindleyplace Square. A footbridge over the Birmingham Canal leads to the International Convention Centre. *Argent Group plc*

on a corner site near the canal, providing the theater with much-needed backstage space. The City Inn Hotel, offering 240 rooms and a restaurant terrace that overlooks the Crescent Theatre, opened in 2001.

With a total project cost of over £250 million, the site offers two major public open spaces (Oozells Square and the main square), 1.1 million square feet (102,220 square meters) of office space, residential apartments and townhouses, two hotels, an art gallery, restaurants and cafés, a health club, and ample parking for residential and commercial uses. Within ten years of the Rosehaugh bankruptcy, a formerly isolated and derelict site had become a major hub of activity in the city center and one of the city's choicest office locations. Brindleyplace is a true mixed-use, in-town community, with offices, retail, condominium apartments and townhouses, and ample active public space.

Lessons Learned

The Birmingham experience demonstrates that even a modest body of water can be a major development asset when the surrounding development is carefully planned. The success of Brindleyplace has firmly established the importance of the canal system as an organizing element: it will continue to be the backdrop for urban regeneration as the process makes its way through the rest of the city.

Brindleyplace also has shown that master planning can be used to foster, rather than undermine, innovative building design. Each building features a unique style and character while clearly functioning as a part of the whole. High-quality design is essential to the creation of lively, round-the-clock environments that function as "people places" while lending prestige to the surrounding buildings. Building tenants also care about good design and are willing to pay for it: at £25 per square foot (£269 per square meter) for offices and £30 per square foot (£323 per square meter) for retail, average commercial rents at Brindleyplace are among the highest in the U.K.

The development has also been the catalyst for another significant transformation in downtown Birmingham: people—especially wealthy people who would never have seriously considered city living before—are choosing to live in the city center. Brindleyplace has generated other in-town residential projects along the canal, including the Mailbox, which opened in December 2000 and forms a second key destination along the canal, just 600 yards (548 meters) from Brindleyplace. In the "vertical" mixed-use tradition once rejected by lenders, the Mailbox—Europe's largest mixed-use center—is a 1.4 million-square-foot (130,060-square-meter) former general post office that now features 200 luxury apartments, 247,578 square feet (22,999 square meters) of office space, and high-end retail.

Brindleyplace has benefited from the flexibility of its master plan, which provided overall structure yet allowed for innovation and nuance—and for adaptation by developers, architects, and end users. The result is a development that can be said to please everyone, yet that retains its internal logic and integrity. It was also important that the developers chose to work with architects and designers who were willing to participate in a dynamic planning process.

Finally, Brindleyplace proves the importance of linking a site to the rest of the city. Pedestrian routes in and out of the site, although carefully analyzed and strictly engineered, feel natural, and are experienced as part of a continuum with the chain of squares and streets beyond.

The city's commitment, through the master-planning process, to creating links not only within the project but between Brindleyplace and the rest of the city (including the downgrading of the ring road) is consistently cited as the key to the development's success. Connectivity was also a theme in the design of the open spaces and the buildings that surround them, which were conceived as both independent elements and thematically linked features. Similarly, the links between the canalside sites and the waterway were designed to complement, rather than overwhelm, the canals. As Birmingham continues the redevelopment of its canals, this system of connections will continue beyond Brindleyplace.

Note

1. Ian Latham and Mark Swenarton, eds., *Brindleyplace: A Model for Urban Regeneration* (London: Right Angle Publishing, 1999).

Project Data: **Brindleyplace**

Land Use Information

Site area (acres/hectares)   17/7

Site or Building	Type of Space	Square Feet/ Square Meters	Number of Residential Units
Water's Edge	Retail and entertainment	60,000/5,575	
The Mailbox	Retail Office Residential	1,400,000/130,065 247,578/23,000	200
Number One	Office	68,600/6,375	
Number Two	Office	75,000/6,965	
Number Three	Office	91,500/8,500	
Number Four	Office Restaurant	114,000/10,590 10,000/930	
Number Five	Office	120,000/11,150	
Number Six	Office Restaurant	94,000/8,730 4,500/420	
Number Seven		85,000/7,895	
Number Eight	Office Residential	92,000/8,545	35
Number Nine	Office Restaurant	43,000/3,995 26,800/2,490	
Number Ten	Office Retail	62,000/5,760 5,000/464.5	
National Sea Life Centre	Museum	38,700/3,595	
Ikon Gallery	Art Gallery	44,800/4,160	
Symphony Court			143

Project Timeline

1989	Site leased by Rosehaugh
1991	International Convention Centre built
1993	Argent buys Rosehaugh's assets
1995	Water's Edge opens
	Brindleyplace Square completed
	Number One completed
1996	Number Five completed
	National Sea Life Centre opens
	Symphony Court completed
1997	Argent Development Consortium formed
	Number Two opens
	Ikon Gallery opens
1998	Oozells Square completed
	Number Three opens
	Crescent Theatre opens
1999	Numbers Four, Six, and Nine completed
2000	Number Eight and the City Inn Hotel open
2002	Construction begins on Number Seven and Number Ten
2004	All construction completed.

Contacts

Argent Group plc
5 Albany Courtyard
Piccadilly, London, U.K. W1J 0HF
+44 (0)207 734 3721
www.argentgroup.plc.uk; www.brindleyplace.com

Townshend Landscape Architects
London, U.K.
+44 (0)207 562 0007
www.townshendla.com

John Chatwin, Architect
Oxfordshire, U.K.
+44 (0)1993 823875

Allies & Morrison
London, U.K.
+44 (0)207 921 0100
www.alliesandmorrison.co.uk

Benoy Architects
London, U.K.
+44 (0)207 404 7666
www.benoy.co.uk

Terry Farrell & Partners
London, U.K.
+44 (0)207 723 7059
www.terryfarrell.co.uk

Porphyrios Associates
London, U.K.
+44 (0)207 580 9594
www.porphyrios.com

Sidell Gibson Partnership
London, U.K.
+44 (0)207 284 9005
www.sidellgibson.co.uk

Charlestown Navy Yard

Boston, Massachusetts

William P. Macht

lthough the tale of Charlestown Navy Yard reveals many successes, it is also the story of public initiative stymied by underfunding, overregulation, and private litigiousness.[1] The Navy Yard occupies 135 acres (55 hectares) of the eastern waterfront of the Charlestown section of Boston, just across the inner harbor from downtown Boston. The site is surrounded by barriers on all sides—the confluence of the Charles, Mystic, and Chelsea rivers; an elevated expressway; the Tobin Bridge, and a long granite wall. The site has been under the control of the Boston Redevelopment Authority (BRA) since 1978; the agency is responsible for redeveloping both the historic structures and the vacant land. The redevelopment plan incorporates a broad mix of uses, including luxury and affordable housing, office, restaurant, retail, hotel, recreational, industrial research, and interpretive uses. The Navy Yard is also the anchor of the Harborpark planning initiative (which emphasized jobs, affordable housing, and public access) and is the key site for Harborfest, Boston's annual celebration of the Fourth of July.

Rich in History

A National Historic District that includes the 30-acre (12-hectare) Boston National Historic Park, Charlestown Navy Yard has a rich history. The Massachusetts legislature originally established the Boston Naval Shipyard in 1800, to honor the 25th anniversary of the Battle of Bunker Hill. Shipbuilding was underway by 1813, but it was not until 1826 that a 2,400-foot- (732-meter-) long granite wall cut off the site from the rest of Charlestown.

The basic plan for the yard, designed in 1828 by Colonel Laommi Baldwin, consisted of large, rectangular buildings situated on five avenues. Alexander Parris, the designer of Quincy Market and one of Boston's most celebrated architects, designed the yard's classic granite buildings, including the Ropewalk, which is over one-quarter-mile (0.40 kilometers) long. The building supplied rope to the Navy continuously for 125 years, until 1955, when it ceased operations. In 1815, the first naval training school was established at the yard; it became the parent institution for the naval academy at Annapolis. Ironically, the USS *Constitution* was both the first and last occupant of the yard; it now draws more than 1.1 million visitors annually. Dry Dock 1, built in 1827, is one of the two oldest dry docks in the country.

Charlestown Navy Yard was a major Navy base during World War II and was continuously active in the years that followed. In 1968, however, the Navy determined that the yard's tight layout and relatively small buildings were inadequate to maintain the huge ships of the modern Navy. In 1973, as part of a nationwide reduction in military bases, the Pentagon announced that the yard would be closed. When the President decommissioned the yard, in 1974, about 5,000 workers lost their jobs.

A Challenging Development

Boston was ready to act, and the city had strong allies. Charlestown's congressional representative, Thomas P. (Tip) O'Neill, was House majority leader, Speaker of the House, and the most powerful man in Congress. Massachusetts senator Edward M. (Ted) Kennedy was also a major supporter. Because it is both the city's planning agency and its development arm, the BRA was and is one of the most powerful redevelopment agencies in the country.

The BRA already had a strategy for gaining control of the site from the federal government, as well as a plan to transform the yard into a mixed-use development. In 1968, the entire Navy Yard had been placed on the National Register of Historic Places. Although the site's historic status made it more likely that the BRA could acquire it for a reasonable price, federal review would be required for *all* development on the site.

In 1974, as part of the Boston National Historic Park Act, the southernmost section of the Navy Yard—a 30-acre (12-hectare) area that included the site of the USS *Constitution*—was designated as a National Historic Park, which meant that this portion of the yard would be operated by the National Park Service (NPS). In 1976, the BRA incorporated the Navy Yard into the Charlestown Urban Renewal Plan, thereby assuming responsibility for the development of the area. Simultaneously, the BRA initiated

Charlestown Navy Yard was continuously active from 1800 until it was decommissioned in 1974. In this photo, a ship is visible in Dry Dock 2, which dates from the 1890s. (Dry Dock 2 has since been opened and permanently flooded.) The Yard was the site of the first "ship houses," which allowed ships to be built under cover. In the 20th century, ships housed at the Navy Yard were converted for antisubmarine duty or equipped to carry guided missiles; the Yard was also used as a construction site for submarines. *BRA Photo*

and negotiated the transfer from the federal government of the remaining 105 acres (42 hectares), under an agreement that contained different terms for each of the three remaining sections.

The 30-acre (12-hectare) Historic Monument Transfer Area was transferred at no cost to the BRA in return for an agreement, between the BRA and the Department of the Interior, that all 25 buildings in the area, with the exception of some World War II additions, would be restored and maintained as a historic district. The buildings in this area,

At the end of the Rowhouses is a cylindrical five-story tower with a copper roof, a quintessential seacoast form that celebrates the water's edge and serves as a landmark on the boardwalk. Of the 50 units, 47 have water views. Most units are designed so that natural light penetrates both the front and back of the unit. *Steve Rosenthal Photo*

Flagship Wharf's 201 luxury condominiums adjoin Pier 4, which functions as the town landing—a public docking facility for tour boats, commuter boats, and water taxis. The Massachusetts Bay Transportation Authority operates a commuter shuttle every half hour to Long Wharf, in downtown Boston, that takes only five minutes. *Peter Vanderwarker Photo*

which are offered to private developers on an "as-is" basis for redevelopment on long-term ground leases, range in size from the small, hexagonal 1852 Muster House, which has only 6,000 square feet (555 square meters), to Building 149, a brick and concrete structure built in 1919 that has over 650,000 square feet (60,385 square meters).

The 17-acre (seven-hectare) Shipyard Park recreational area was transferred at no cost to the BRA in return for a commitment that the area would be used for public recreation in a way that would support the national park area to its west. Shipyard Park offers two types of space: a 6.5-acre (2.6-hectare) landscaped park faces Dry Dock 2 (Dry Dock 2, which dates from the 1890s, has been opened and permanently flooded); and Pier 4, which adjoins Dry Dock 2, serves as a public docking facility for tour boats, commuter boats, and water taxis.

The Massachusetts Bay Transportation Authority operates a commuter shuttle to Long Wharf, in downtown Boston, that takes only five minutes and costs $1.25. The city water taxi is also available on a demand basis for about $10 per person. These water-transit options have provided important infrastructural support for residential development in the Navy Yard.

Early development of Shipyard Park, at a cost of over $6.1 million, was an important element of the overall development strategy. The project won several design awards, created critical mass for the project, helped catalyze a change in the public's perception of the site, and offered important early evidence of visible success.

The atrium of Building 149 is a focal point for Massachusetts General Hospital (MGH), the anchor tenant of the largest building in the Navy Yard. In 1986, MGH agreed to lease 650,000 square feet (60,385 square meters) for biomedical and biotechnology research and development, a field experiencing major growth in the Boston area. MGH also leased a 1,386-space parking structure developed within the old facilities. *DiMella Schaffer Associates Photo*

The 58-acre (23-hectare) New Development Area was transferred to the BRA by the General Services Administration (GSA) under a negotiated sale at a price of $1.74 million. This area was intended for mixed-use development on less restrictive terms for both new and rehabilitated structures.

Even with extensive planning, it took four years for the BRA to negotiate the land transfer agreements; it did not actually take possession of the site until 1978. The reason that the approval process took so long was that many federal agencies—including the GSA, the Department of the Interior, the NPS, and the Department of Housing and Urban Development—monitored the transfer.

The major problem was the difficulty of funding the initial purchase from the GSA. Although it was relatively easy, with assistance from Senator O'Neill, to obtain federal funds for park development, the BRA found it very difficult, in a time of fiscal austerity, to obtain the $1.74 million to acquire the New Development Area. To raise capital, the BRA was forced to turn to the private sector—and, at that time (the mid-1970s), the Boston real estate market was poor, interest rates were rising, and urban renewal funds were being cut. As then-mayor Kevin White said, "Nobody could conceive of development over there; they weren't building in downtown, so why should they build in Charlestown? The city was exhausted and there was no lending. Jim Rouse couldn't get the banks to lend him $3 million for Fanueil Hall."

As a result, the BRA had a difficult time trying to attract developers. When no local developer was willing to take an interest in the site, the search was widened. Eventually the BRA found Immobiliare New England, which was a joint venture of two large Italian development and construction firms that had developed the Watergate, in Washington, D.C., and Marina del Rey, in California. The cash-starved BRA was forced to negotiate what has proven to be a very costly deal. Under the phased land disposition agreement, Immobiliare loaned the BRA $1.74 million to buy the 58-acre (23-hectare) New Development Area from the federal government, in exchange for exclusive development rights within the area. As Immobiliare undertook the development of each parcel, the BRA's repayment obligation would be reduced according to what was then the appraised value represented by that phase.

The decision to use a master developer proved to be difficult as well as expensive. Immobiliare used a conservative development strategy of building one project at a time and using the proceeds of each project to fund the next. This strategy, combined with slow demolition, a weak market, poor access, and unwelcoming security (visitors had to pass through a checkpoint established by Immobiliare), led Immobiliare's development efforts to have limited success. By the mid-1980s, Immobiliare had completed only one major project: converting the two warehouses in the 300,000-square-foot (27,870-square-meter) Building 42 into 367 rental units called Constitution Quarters.

As bank loans evaporated for developers during the real estate recession of the early and mid-1980s, Immobiliare invested its own capital in a 150-slip marina in order to raise interest in the 64 townhouses, called Constellation Wharf, that it had developed on Pier 7. (The wood-frame townhouses, built over at-grade parking at the water's edge, later became a rallying point in the fight by activists to halt waterfront development.) Perhaps because of a shortage of berths in the inner city, the marina complex sold well, and began to pique local interest. The Raymond Group, an aggressive local developer, bought out Immobiliare and proceeded to develop Flagship Wharf, 201 luxury condominiums on a spectacular site in front of Shipyard Park, directly facing the waterfront and the basins surrounding Piers 4 and 5. Absorption was not as strong as anticipated, however, and many buyers withdrew after the 1987 stock market crash. When the construction lender collapsed, the building went into receivership.

After a decade of difficulties (and despite some successes), the BRA approved the assignment of Immobiliare's exclusive development rights to LDA Acquisition, a limited-liability company (LLC) headed by New York developer Martin Oliner and a limited partnership whose interests are held by wealthy investors (reportedly including Laurance Rockefeller, Warren Buffett, and the sultan of Brunei). While Oliner was apparently able to sell out the Flagship Wharf units, his further development plans were anathema to the BRA and to other Bostonians, and the BRA sought to have Oliner's LLC "de-designated" as exclusive master developer. The LLC subsequently sought protection through a Delaware bankruptcy court. The developer's litigious approach on this and other issues has not only delayed resolution of the issue of development rights but has also brought to a halt all new development within the New Development Area.

A Landmark on the Boardwalk

To meet the city's linkage requirements for affordable housing, Immobiliare surrendered to nonprofit developers the development rights for a portion of the land within the New Development Area. There, the Bricklayer's Union developed an innovative affordable housing project—the 50-unit Charlestown Navy Yard Rowhouses—that proved to be the most successful in the Navy Yard. Both that project and the $5 million Building 104 rehabilitation, which created 46 units of affordable housing for seniors, were developed by an improbable team. William L. Rawn III is an urbane, intellectual Boston architect (and former Washington, D.C.,

Shipyard Park, developed at a cost of over $6.1 million, was an important element of the Boston Redevelopment Authority's development strategy. The park acted as a catalyst, helping to change the public perception of the site. Building 42, Constitution Quarters, a 367-unit rental apartment complex, is visible beyond the park. *Anton Grassi Photo*

lawyer) celebrated in Tracy Kidder's best seller *House.*[2] Thomas McIntyre, the leader of the Bricklayers Union, had years of hardheaded construction experience, which he used to tightly control costs. Together they conceived and developed low-cost projects that set new standards for the design and development of affordable housing. While the BRA "sold" the three-quarter-acre (0.30-hectare) site to the non-

Building 42 was part of a warehouse complex that Immobiliare New England converted, in 1979, into Constitution Quarters. The exposed structure of an old boiler plant provides a forecourt for the surrounding residential complex.
BRA Photo

profit for $1, the larger cost benefit came from the low-interest loan the union was able to negotiate with the bank where it keeps its pension funds.

Rawn's plan was based on the two urban patterns embodied in the historic plan for the Navy Yard: the two-sided main street, called First Avenue, which runs parallel to the waterfront, and the finger piers that run perpendicular to it. He designed a massive, five-story brick structure with a two-story arcade at its base, arched and ganged windows at its center, and a large front gable. Appended to this large structure—in a long, pierlike form—are townhouses stacked like interlocking letter "Cs" in three stories. Most units are designed so that natural light penetrates both the front and back of the unit. At the building's end is a cylindrical, five-story tower with a copper roof (paid for with a $25,000 grant from the city), a quintessential seacoast form that celebrates the water's edge and serves as a landmark on the boardwalk.

Of the 50 units, 47 have water views. Despite the concrete floors, brick walls, and union labor, construction costs were held to $67 per square foot ($721 per square meter). The units sold for under $100,000 in 1988 and won numerous design awards. To keep the units afford-able, resale prices are capped by deed restrictions, and the BRA has right of first refusal. However, the desirability of the units has led to abuses: in an infamous 1999 case, for example, the BRA's chief of staff bought one for $158,000 and was later forced to resign.

Searching for Anchor Tenants

The BRA made a significant effort to bring the New England Aquarium, a major public attraction, to the Navy Yard. The aquarium's management was interested in relocating because it would then be possible to sell the facility's valuable downtown waterfront site for a price that would allow the construction of what they termed "the world's largest aquarium." The first plan was to use the historic Dry Dock 2 as the main tank and some of Shipyard Park for ancillary facilities. The Charlestown Neighborhood Council expressed dismay, however, at the loss of Shipyard Park—and about having apparently been excluded from the planning process. In the face of concerted opposition, the aquarium was relocated to Yard's End, on Parcel 5, at the east end of the Navy Yard. Adjoining the aquarium would be a 390-room hotel, a use that had long been sought by the BRA.

The opposition and the resulting changes in the plan delayed the process by 14 months. By the time the deal was near consummation, the real estate market had plummeted, depressing the value of the aquarium's downtown site, and the recession had dampened hopes for major private fundraising. The New England Aquarium withdrew its interest, and the loss of the aquarium doomed the hotel.

There have been notable successes in the Historic Monument Area, where the BRA has acted as the master developer. Although it took the BRA three years to complete essential infrastructure improvements and another five to begin to interest historic redevelopers, in 1986 a well-connected local developer secured a highly desirable anchor tenant for Building 149, the largest building in the Navy Yard. Massachusetts General Hospital (MGH) agreed to lease 650,000 square feet (60,385 square meters) for biomedical and biotechnology research and development, a field undergoing major growth in the Boston area. MGH also leased a 1,386-space parking structure developed within Building 199. Most of the 5,000 jobs created at the Navy Yard can be attributed to the MGH facilities and to spin-off research companies.

The architects who worked on Building 104, transforming it into 46 units of housing for seniors, and who also designed the newly constructed Charlestown Navy Yard Rowhouses to its east, were inspired by the original scale and detail of Building 104. *Steve Rosenthal Photo*

The successful rehabilitation of Building 114 is an exemplary saga of a celebrated historic redeveloper overcoming intransigent opposition through experience, skill, patience, and sheer determination—over a period of 15 years. Robert H. Kuehn Jr. is president of the Cambridge-based Keen Development Corporation, a board member of the National Trust for Historic Preservation, and the redeveloper of over 3,000 housing units, a community college, research labs, and artists' lofts.

In 1986, Kuehn and the BRA agreed that Kuehn would rehabilitate Building 114, the former joinery shop in Yard's End, which had been damaged by fire and had been vacant since the yard closed, in 1972. Kuehn obtained an agreement from MGH to lease the entire 120,000-square-foot (11,150-square-meter) structure as a biomedical laboratory dedicated to Alzheimer's research. He also facilitated the issuance of $40 million in tax-exempt bonds by the Massachusetts Development Finance Agency to pay all development costs.

In 1986, Kuehn applied for a waterway development permit from the State Department of Environmental Protection (DEP) under what are known as Chapter 91 regulations. Chapter 91 codifies the ancient "public trust doctrine" that protects public access to the shoreline. While Chapter 91 had previously been administered according to a flexible standard that weighed public benefits against public detriments, new DEP regulations, passed in 1990, included a rigid requirement that the entire ground floor of all buildings within 100 feet (30.5 meters) of the water's edge be used for "facilities of public accommodation." The Alzheimer's lab could obviously not meet that requirement. Although the regulations ostensibly permitted variances, none had ever been granted. And the argument that Building 114 was a historic building within a historic district on an isolated site that would be used for a public purpose fell on deaf ears.

Through a long and arduous process, a municipal harbor plan was created that ultimately broke the deadlock, superseding the application of Chapter 91 and allowing the DEP to issue the permit. When an intransigent group of 20 citizens filed an appeal that would have extended the adjudication process by another year, Kuehn settled by agreeing to provide another $100,000 of waterfront improvements, bringing his soft costs for attorneys and consultants to well over $1 million. Despite his recognized—and often-awarded—skill and experience as the developer of historic properties, Kuehn vowed not to attempt any further projects that were subject to Chapter 91.

The BRA's planning decision to maintain and reinforce the street grid, and thereby limit the size of the development parcels in the Historic Monument Area, may largely account for the fact that development in that area has been more extensive, diverse, and successful than on the waterfront.

Progressive Development

By 2000, over 2.3 million square feet (213,675 square meters) of new and rehabilitated space had been completed in the Navy Yard. Some of the most challenging buildings remain to be developed, however. Although the granite Ropewalk, for example, is only about 114,000 square feet (10,590 square meters) in size, its narrow width, its length (one-quarter-mile—0.40 kilometers), and its location at the rear of the site have prevented developers from creating a marketable use for the building. In the case of the 72,000-square-foot (6,690-square-meter) Chain Forge Building, the cost of the hazardous materials cleanup and the NPS's insistence on devoting a large portion of the 50-foot (15.3-meter) interior space to interpretive use have delayed rehabilitation. This situation may change, however: the BRA has obtained $6.5 million for environmental remediation, and the NPS appears to be more amenable to a modified plan.

The BRA's early decision to insist on a "once-and-for-all" approval of historic design guidelines for the entire Historic Monument Area obviated the need for a building-by-building review of each project by NPS officials, but it also led to initial delays in the approval process. As noted by Robert Kenney, then the director of the BRA, "There are problems when you want to change the guidelines, but the alternative was to have a federal bureaucrat second-guessing every move you make."

The design guidelines have produced buildings that are compatible with their surroundings; the mass and finishes of the five-story YMCA building, for example, reflect the scale and texture of neighboring granite structures. In the hands of sensitive architects (such as Rawn Associates), the guidelines have been used to foster creative rehabilitation. At Building 104, for example, which was redeveloped as housing for seniors, portions of the building were removed to create courtyards that narrow the building's width, bring light into the building, and conceal parking. But the guidelines have produced unintended conse-

The 50 affordable units of the Charlestown Navy Yard Rowhouses were designed and developed by an innovative team led by William Rawn, an architect, and Thomas McIntyre, of the Bricklayers Union. The massive, five-story brick structure has a two-story arcade at its base, arched and ganged windows at its center, and a large front gable at its top. Appended to this large structure—in a long, pierlike form—are townhouses stacked like interlocking letter "Cs" in three stories. *Steve Rosenthal Photo*

quences and delayed new construction on infill sites such as Parcel 39A, where the request for proposals prescribes height, mass, density, setback, roof shape, cornice and ridge lines, masonry finishes, parking size and location, through-block interior and exterior pedestrian access, and permissible location of uses. As a result, the submitted proposals were nearly identical. And, because parking was forced underground in an area with a high water table, the cost of building a watertight underground parking structure escalated to nearly $30,000 per space (in 2001 dollars), making most proposals infeasible.

Lessons Learned

Powerful political allies can assist with initial acquisition, but bureaucracies can impede implementation. The fact that the Navy Yard was in Tip O'Neill's district and in Ted Kennedy's home city and state greatly facilitated land transfers from the military to the city, and the subsequent flow of funds for some public projects. However, even the involvement of political heavyweights cannot prevent the long delays that often result from oversight by multiple federal bureaucracies.

When master developers lose money, they often lose interest. The very size and scope of master developers' organizations enable them to seek more profitable projects in other locations. Local developers are forced to be more cautious before committing, and more determined thereafter. They simply cannot afford to misjudge the market or to abandon projects, and they can be more nimble in finding profitable market niches.

Granting exclusive development rights compounds risks. To mitigate the risks involved in assigning rights, land disposition agreements should usually include clauses providing that, in the event that developments of an approved scale and character are not completed within prescribed time frames, the development rights revert to the original owner. At the very least, such agreements should provide for the termination of exclusive development rights upon the expiration of reasonable time periods. Any of these provisions would have saved the BRA from the long and continuing battle to regain possession of its waterfront land from the successors to its original master developer.

Urban waterfronts may need special development corporations or subsidiaries. A single-purpose subsidiary development corporation (public or quasi-public) can coordinate the management of large urban waterfront projects. Because of its own size and responsibilities, the BRA, which is both the planning and development agency for Boston, may have failed to provide the time and the staffing power that would have been necessary to accelerate the pace of development. Given adequate authority, a single-purpose development corporation can offer both the flexibility needed to respond to market changes and the stability needed to satisfy capital markets.

Complicated projects need flexible development plans that can be changed administratively, rather than a "master plan" that must pass through a protracted public process—and is therefore likely to be modified infrequently. The 1978 master plan, which emphasized luxury housing, was changed significantly by the 1984 Harborpark planning initiative, which emphasized jobs, affordable housing, and public access. The master plan was not changed again until 1990, after a lengthy public process. Eleven years

later, that plan had still not been revised (even though major components, such as the aquarium and the hotel, were no longer feasible).

Delays arising from public involvement alone can defeat developments. Mayor Kevin White's decision to open the process to the Charlestown Neighborhood Council led to major changes in the plan for the aquarium and hotel—and the resulting delays ultimately killed the project, because the real estate market depressed the value of the downtown assets that the aquarium had planned to sell in order to finance relocation and expansion.

Market changes can wreak havoc with development plans. The real estate recession of the early 1980s made housing nearly unmarketable, which led to the departure of the original master developer. When an aggressive local developer sought to capitalize on the recovery of the mid-1980s, he was caught short by the local housing recession that occurred after the 1987 stock market collapse. By 2001, the condominiums that could not be sold in 1987 were resold, at premium prices, to baby boomers flush with cash from the stock market boom of the 1990s.

Development timing changes development options. At the time most of the residential development occurred at the Navy Yard, the most common residential form was a traditional rental apartment, which was difficult to fit into the large floor plates of factories and warehouses. By the early years of the 21st century, a live/work residential loft condominium had become one of the most popular options in residential design; it would have been particularly well suited to the historic factory and warehouse buildings in the Navy Yard and would have produced many more feasible economic projects. Offering such a product within the context of a secure, water-oriented community five minutes from downtown Boston would not only have drawn more young urban professionals and empty nesters, but would also have achieved faster absorption than traditional products.

Slow decision making stands in the way of development opportunities. The cyclical nature of real estate markets means that a public development agency must act quickly when a window of opportunity opens. In the development of the Navy Yard, slow decision making led to significant opportunity costs: the BRA itself was slow to make decisions (often a problem with agencies that are as large as the BRA); the foreign master developer was slow to react to market changes; and the intricate historic-design guidelines that the BRA was forced to devise slowed progress further.

Large-scale development projects need major anchor tenants. MGH's commitment to lease 650,000 square feet (60,385 square meters) for biomedical and biotechnology research and development was crucial to the redevelopment of enormous buildings with large floor plates. MGH's expansion and biomedical spin-offs have been responsible for the redevelopment of several other smaller facilities.

Overregulation can increase development costs and even halt projects. Inflexible administration can also confer on a few citizen activists the power not only to single-handedly stop projects but also to demand expenditures that, according to some independent observers, are tantamount to extortion. In the case of the Navy Yard, the inflexible interpretation of regulations by a state agency had devastating effects, not only generating a 15-year delay and cost overruns for the rehabilitation of Building 114 but also persuading both the project developer and other developers not to participate in any waterfront project subject to the same regulations.

Increased public parking can ensure more shared parking. Because of a parking cap set by the BRA, the average amount of parking provided on site is less than one space per 1,000 square feet (93 square meters) of developed area. Because the site is neither fully urban nor fully suburban, the parking cap has slowed development. Although the BRA has prudently retained ownership of the public streets, it has not maximized the use of on-street parking to increase the quantity, efficiency, and convenience of shared parking.

Water transit can stimulate development pace, change the image of an area, increase land values, and reduce dependence on automobiles. By arranging for regular and frequent water shuttles and taxis to the Navy Yard early in the development period, the BRA was able to transform the psychological distance from downtown Boston into a pleasant, five-minute water ride and increase the market for high-end residential condominiums.

Alexander Parris, one of Boston's most celebrated architects and the designer of Quincy Market, designed several classic granite buildings for the Yard, including Building 34, which was constructed in 1837 (shown here after its conversion to office space). Parris also designed the Ropewalk, which is over one-quarter-mile (0.40 kilometers) long.
Anton Grassi Photo

Contaminated public sites need public remediation. When accepting land from the federal government—especially the military, which uses hazardous materials—it is best to insist on environmental remediation before taking possession. In the view of the development community, when the public sector has contaminated a site, it is unreasonable to turn it over to the private sector for remediation.

Short-term profits can overwhelm long-term strategy. Selecting a private sector master developer can shift the formulation of a development strategy from the long-term objectives of the public development agency to the short-term profits of the private developer. It is unlikely, for example, that the BRA would, on its own, have allowed the development of Constellation Wharf, the relatively low-density, wood-frame, 60-townhouse condominium project on Pier 7. In fact, it may have been the fact that such a public waterfront site was relegated to exclusively private use (and that a pier deck was used for parking) that emboldened citizen activists and environmental regulators to draft onerous new Chapter 91 waterway regulations and to take an inflexible position on their interpretation.

Leasing land to developers rather than selling it strengthens control over development. Leasing also enables public developers to share equitably in the increase in land values. In return for a loan of $1.74 million, the master developer was granted exclusive development rights to the BRA's undeveloped land; as the master developer undertook the development of each parcel, the BRA's repayment

Project Data: **Charlestown Navy Yard**

Land Use Information (Acres/Hectares)

Total site area	135/55
Boston National Historic Park	30/12
Shipyard Park	17/7
Historic Monument Transfer Area	30/12
New Development Area	58/23

Economic Information (in Millions)

Site acquisition cost	$1.74
Initial site improvement cost	$11

Project Timeline

1968 The Navy determines that the Charlestown Navy Yard's tight layout and relatively small buildings are inadequate to maintain the modern Navy's huge ships.

1968 The entire Navy Yard is placed on the National Register of Historic Places.

1973 The Pentagon announces that the yard will be closed as part of a nationwide reduction in military bases.

1974 The president decommissions the Charlestown Navy Yard; about 5,000 workers lose their jobs.

1976 The Boston Redevelopment Agency (BRA) incorporates the Navy Yard into the Charlestown Urban Renewal Plan.

1978 The BRA executes a land disposition agreement with Immobiliare New England (INE).

1978 The BRA acquires title to the New Development Area's 105 acres (42 hectares) of land for $1.74 million.

1978 The BRA starts development of Shipyard Park; cost: $6.1 million.

1982 INE converts Building 42 into a rental apartment complex called Constitution Quarters; cost: $28 million.

1982 INE converts Building 40 into a parking structure; cost: $2 million.

1982 INE refurbishes Pier 6, transforming it into a marina with slips for 170 boats; cost: $3.5 million.

1984 INE starts construction of 48 condominiums known as Shipways I and II; cost: $9.2 million.

1985 INE converts Building 103 into the Anchorage, a housing development for seniors; cost: $6.9 million.

1986 The Raymond Group starts construction on Building 197—Flagship Wharf—which will house 201 luxury condominiums and 26,000 square feet (2,415 square meters) of office and retail space; cost: $25 million.

1986 The Parris Building, No. 34, is rehabilitated to create 50,000 square feet (4,645 square meters) of office and retail space.

1986 The Keen Development Corporation (1) reaches an agreement with the BRA to rehabilitate Building 114 and (2) obtains an agreement from Massachusetts General Hospital (MGH) to lease the entire structure as a biomedical research laboratory dedicated to Alzheimer's research.

1986 The Keen Development Corporation applies for a waterway development permit from the State Department of Environmental Protection (DEP) under Chapter 91 regulations.

1987 On Pier 7, INE completes Constellation Wharf, 64 townhouse condominiums located above at-grade parking for 113 cars.

1987 INE completes a second marina for 180 boats on Pier 8; cost: $4 million.

1988 Flagship Wharf goes into receivership.

1988 The BRA approves the transfer of the exclusive development rights in the New Development Area from INE to LDA Acquisition, LLC, which is controlled by New York developer Martin Oliner and a limited partnership held by wealthy investors.

1988 The Bricklayers Union completes the 50-unit Charlestown Navy Yard Rowhouses, an affordable-housing project.

1988 The New England Aquarium expresses interest in relocating to the Navy Yard.

obligation would be reduced by the value of that parcel. While the land disposition agreement provided that the price paid by the master developer for the land would be adjusted to market value at the time of the draw down, there was apparently no reciprocal security for the BRA that would have required timely performance on the master developer's side. Nor was it clear whether market value would be based on allowable building area or on land area. However, the BRA was to be paid 4 percent of the sales price of condominiums sold by the master developer.

Waterfront development can succeed despite many missteps. Despite setbacks and remaining problems, the redevelopment of the Charlestown Navy Yard can be regarded as a qualified success. In the space of 25 years, more than 5,000 permanent jobs were created at wage rates that far exceeded those lost in 1974. Redevelopment also created more than 2,000 construction jobs. Public sector investment of over $30 million successfully leveraged private investment of well over $600 million, sharply increasing the tax revenues derived from a federally owned site that had been totally tax-exempt. More than 1,200

1989	Building 149 is rehabilitated and transformed into 650,000 square feet (60,385 square meters) of biomedical and biotechnology research space for MGH, and Building 199 is rehabilitated and transformed into a parking structure for MGH; combined cost: $61 million.
1990	The BRA undertakes a new master plan.
1990	The Charlestown Neighborhood Council leads concerted opposition to the new master plan, requiring the relocation of the proposed aquarium to Yard's End.
1990	Under new DEP regulations, the entire ground floor of all buildings within 100 feet (30.5 meters) of the water's edge must be used for "facilities of public accommodation."
1991	The New England Aquarium withdraws its interest in the Navy Yard. The loss of the aquarium attraction dooms a proposed adjoining hotel.
1991–2001	Development in the 58-acre (23-hectare) New Development Area is halted when the BRA attempts to "de-designate" the Oliner group as master developer and to terminate its exclusive development rights.
2001	After 15 years, the Keen Development Corporation finally gets a waterway development permit and completes the rehabilitation of Building 114 as a biomedical research laboratory.

Major Project Participants

Boston Redevelopment Authority
Boston, Massachusetts
Web site: www.ci.boston.ma.us/bra/

Keen Development Corporation
Cambridge, Massachusetts
Web site: www.keencorp.com

William Rawn Associates, Architects
Boston, Massachusetts
Web site: www.rawnarch.com

Gadsby Hannah, LLP
Boston, Massachusetts
Web site: www.ghlaw.com

Goulston & Storrs
Boston, Massachusetts
Web site: www.goulstorrs.com

Martin Oliner, P.C.
New York, New York

Young Conaway Stargatt & Taylor, LLP
Wilmington, Delaware
Web site: www.ycst.com/

Massachusetts General Hospital
Boston, Massachusetts
Web site: www.mgh.harvard.edu/

Charlestown Navy Yard
Charlestown, Massachusetts
Web site: www.nps.gov/bost/Navy_Yard.htm

housing units were developed, of which nearly 30 percent are affordable, and space remains for at least 400 more. More than 500 marina slips were developed, and there is room for many more. Over 13 acres (five hectares) of open space were dedicated and improved, and the 8,000 linear feet (2,438 meters) of Harborwalk provide public waterfront access. More than 1.1 million visitors a year visit the USS *Constitution* and its associated facilities. The Navy Yard is a new hub for biomedical research, a burgeoning field. Although still somewhat isolated from the larger area (it was designed to be one of the first military "gated communities"), the Navy Yard is now linked by water transit to downtown Boston and to Charlestown, which has become increasingly gentrified.

Notes
1. Portions of this case study were based on David L. A. Gordon, "Implementing Urban Waterfront Development in an Historic Context: A Case Study of the Boston Naval Shipyard," *Ocean and Coastal Management* 42 (1999): 909–931.
2. Tracy Kidder, *House* (New York: Avon Books, 1985).

South Bank

Brisbane, Queensland Australia

Guy Gibson

South Bank is a 104-acre (42-hectare) development area that stretches three-quarters of a mile (1.2 kilometers) along the Brisbane River; it lies within South Brisbane, directly across the river from the Brisbane central business district.[1] For years, South Bank—a prime piece of land in the center of the city—was no more than a port and a home to old hotels and industrial buildings. It was given new life, however, in 1984, when it was chosen as the site for World Expo 1988—a massive operation that involved creating an environment that would last for just six months. After the Expo, redevelopment plans were scrapped in favor of the community's plans for the site; what has evolved is truly a world-class amenity, distinctively designed and deeply appreciated by the community.

With a city population of about 900,000 and a metropolitan population of 1.5 million, Brisbane is the third-largest city in Australia. A river port, the 470-square-mile (1,220-square-kilometer) city straddles the Brisbane River and is 12 miles (19 kilometers) by land from the river's mouth, in Moreton Bay, on the Pacific coast.

South Bank includes parklands, the Brisbane Convention and Exhibition Centre, an international hotel, the state library, a museum, an art gallery and performing arts complex, institutions of higher education, residential apartments, commercial development, and a range of restaurants and retail outlets.

Prime Real Estate

In the earliest times, the South Brisbane area was covered with lush vegetation, including a rain forest and native pines, and was a meeting place for Australia's indigenous people. The land was traversed by a number of Aboriginal pathways, some of which were later used by early settlers to forge roads through the area. The first European use of the South Bank area occurred soon after the establishment of the Moreton Bay penal settlement, in 1825. When Brisbane became open for free settlement, in 1842, South Bank became the commercial and shipping center of the city. After 1850, however, when the customs house was built on the north side of the river, South Bank's commercial district began to founder, although the area's attractiveness as a residential address continued to grow, particularly during the boom of the 1880s. Beginning with the depression of the 1890s, however, South Brisbane began a long and gradual economic decline that was exacerbated by major floods in 1893, which forced much of the commercial activity to move to the north side of the river. As the years went on, shipping relocated downstream, and new cross-river links diverted traffic around the area, further weakening local businesses.

World Expo 1988

At the time that South Bank was selected as the site for World Expo 1988, it consisted largely of poorly developed riverside parkland, run-down commercial and industrial premises, low-cost and rental housing, and railway land, including rail yards and the interstate passenger-rail station. A large proportion of the land was owned by the Commonwealth and Queensland governments and the city of Brisbane, and a maritime museum was being developed at the downstream end of the site. Covered fairly uniformly in low buildings, South Bank offered a range of building forms and types that reflected the history of the area from the earliest days of European settlement to the present day.

The Queensland Government established the Brisbane Exposition and South Bank Redevelopment Authority (known as the Expo Authority) to acquire and develop the site for World Expo 1988, market and manage the event, prepare a plan for the site's redevelopment afterward, and dispose of the site. The Expo Authority compulsorily acquired 66 private properties. The passenger terminal and the rail yards were relocated to the central business district (CBD), and the Expo Authority took control of this land, as well as of other city and state government land holdings within the site, including approximately 12 acres (five hectares) of riverbank parkland that the city had purchased over a period of four decades.

The waterfront site was a major factor in the success of World Expo 1988. It was centrally located, highly accessible, and boasted an impressive river outlook from almost every aspect. The Expo, in turn, was crucial to the

The 104-acre (42-hectare) South Bank development area is directly across the Brisbane River from the Brisbane central business district.

emergence of Brisbane as a major Australian city, attracting 18 million visitors in six months (including a large number of out-of-state and overseas tourists), creating considerable economic and other positive impacts, and generating a level of goodwill that is difficult to calculate.

After World Expo 1988, the government planned to sell off the land to commercial interests, and the Expo Authority was given the statutory obligation of achieving "a net financial result that will not impose a burden of cost on the Government of Queensland." A preferred developer was chosen from among 13 candidates who had submitted plans in response to a request for proposals. The selected project, submitted by the River City 2000 Consortium, was to feature two hotels with provision for a casino, a 50-story world trade center, an exhibition and convention center, a space and science center, offices, residential uses, and tourist-oriented retailing. The proposal also involved creating an island in the Brisbane River by constructing a canal through the Expo site.

The people of Brisbane had other ideas, however. In a remarkable display of extraparliamentary democracy, they successfully lobbied for the site to remain a "people's place." One of the guiding principles of World Expo 1988 had been that Brisbane should be left with a lasting physical memorial, in the form of a "landmark" post-Expo redevelopment. The Queensland state premier withdrew preferred-developer status from the consortium and announced that a fresh start would be made. Under this new initiative, planning excellence would be the driving force, not merely the financial imperative of ensuring that Expo had been staged at no cost to taxpayers.

An interim committee, under the auspices of the Expo Authority and with representation from the Queensland Government and the city of Brisbane, was established to determine appropriate planning policies and legislation requirements. The Sydney Cove redevelopment and the Darling Harbour development in Sydney, New South Wales, were both reviewed for possible lessons that could be applied to South Bank. Various overseas schemes were also reviewed, including La Villette, in Paris; the Cologne Cathedral Area Redevelopment Scheme; Tivoli Gardens, in Copenhagen; Battery Park City, in New York; Faneuil Hall Marketplace, in Boston; the Portland Development Commission's park projects; and the redevelopment of downtown Long Beach, in California. A major lesson of these reviews was that inner-city renewal and waterfront park development require substantial public sector intervention, in the form of public funding and development incentives.

The South Bank Corporation

In 1989, under legislation passed by the Queensland Government, the Expo Authority was extinguished and the South Bank Corporation was charged with planning and facilitating the development and operation of a successful, world-class leisure, business, and residential precinct for the enjoyment of South Bank visitors and the economic benefit of Brisbane's community and investors.

The primary activities of the corporation, which includes members from the state and city government, the professions, and the business community, include
■ Maintaining and administering the South Bank Corporation Area Approved Development Plan;
■ Coordinating the development of land within the corporation area;
■ Disposing (by lease) of land vested in or under the control of the corporation;
■ Promoting, organizing, and conducting tourist, educational, recreational, entertainment, cultural, and commercial activities within the corporation area;
■ Marketing and promoting South Bank as an appealing and entertaining precinct for leisure, tourism, and convention activities for Queensland residents and out-of-state and international visitors;
■ Promoting South Bank as an attractive and viable residential and commercial address for investors, financiers, and business operators.

Several architectural firms—Media Five Australia (later DBI Design Corporation), John Simpson and Associates, and Denton Corker Marshall—have played key roles in the planning and development of the site.

The first task of the South Bank Corporation was to produce a ten- to 20-year plan to develop the area. The Approved Development Plan was published in April 1990 and had the following features:
■ Historic buildings would be retained in their entirety, with the former Stanley Street (which had been removed for the Expo) reestablished as a plaza in the vicinity of two historic buildings.
■ Development would include approximately 40 acres (16 hectares) of public open space, including 3.5 acres (1.4 hectares) resulting from river reclamation.
■ Facilities would include 4,758,000 square feet (442,030 square meters) of gross floor area, including 1,965,000 square feet (182,555 square meters) of commercial space; 484,000 square feet (44,965 square meters) of convention space; 734,000 square feet (68,190 square meters) of hotel space; 907,000 square feet (84,265 square meters) of residential space (645 units); 267,000 square feet (24,805

A lagoon and beach were part of the parklands that opened in 1992.

square meters) of retail, food, and beverage facilities; and 5,900 parking spaces.

■ Most of the built development would be located along the rear of the site (including air-rights development over the railway line).

■ The area would offer recreational features such as a rain forest, a lagoon, and a family beach accommodating up to 750 swimmers.

■ Grey Street would be reconstructed as a two-lane bus corridor, with provision for later widening to four lanes for general traffic. A boulevard for pedestrian use would be constructed directly above the bus corridor.

To emphasize that the people-oriented spaces and facilities were more important than the buildings themselves, the phrase "the park within the building within the park" was used to capture the urban design theme of the proposal.

The corporation spent $105 million clearing the site and building a new South Bank.[2] Two historic buildings, a boardwalk, and a Nepalese pagoda—a gift from Nepal to Brisbane, after Expo—were all that remained.

The 42-acre (17-hectare) parklands, which opened in June 1992, consist of a beach and a lagoon, where visitors can explore the rocky creeks and shady hollows or swim in enough water to fill more than five Olympic swimming pools; a rainforest; garden walks; more than 20 restaurants and cafés; free picnic and barbecue areas; and several paid tourist attractions. More than 40 million people have visited the parklands since they opened.

The corporation also started selling long-term leases on the land surrounding the parklands, and various sites were developed. The most significant was the Brisbane Convention and Exhibition Centre, which officially opened on Queensland Day, June 6, 1995. The convention center covers 18.5 acres (7.5 hectares) and features four exhibition halls; the 4,000-seat Great Hall; the Grand Ballroom, with

The Brisbane Convention and Exhibition Centre opened in 1995.

a capacity of 2,000; and 16 meeting rooms. The center is also equipped with the latest audiovisual, lighting, communications, and other technical equipment. Connected to the convention center by a 660-foot- (201-meter-) long plaza, above the railway line, is the $60 million, 305-room Rydges South Bank Hotel, which opened in May 1996.

Other projects include Park Avenue, South Bank's first residential condominium building, completed in February 1995; the Thiess Centre, a $30 million global headquarters that houses some 300 employees of one of Australia's leading building contractors, which opened in June 1999; the $35 million premises of Griffith University's Queensland Conservatorium of Music and Opera Queensland, which is located between the Queensland Performing Arts Complex and the Piazza and was completed in May 1996; and Cinema Plus Ltd, Brisbane's first IMAX theater, which opened in January 1999. A spectacular $20 million architectural feat, the building is also home to Hoyts South Bank Cinemas, a four-cinema complex.

In Need of a Face-Lift

By 1997, five years after it had opened, South Bank had begun to look a little dated and tired; in addition, several major problems had emerged, and it was time to consider improvements:

■ Access was difficult: the aboveground parking lots were reached by means of bridges over a canal, which posed difficulties for seniors and people with baby carriages.

■ A continuous access loop was needed to link the southern end of South Bank with the CBD and the Royal Botanic Gardens.

■ South Bank had become known as a weekend destination. Sales soared on the weekends and slumped during the week.

■ Tourist attractions, including a wildlife sanctuary, an environmental center, and a canal-based ferry service, were not financially viable and had closed down.

■ The development community was dissatisfied with the Approved Development Plan, first because of the plan's restrictive requirements for building envelopes, and second because the plan favored sectors (including tourist-oriented retailing and commercial recreation facilities) in which developers had little interest.

A new plan, the $81 million South Bank Master Plan, was launched in 1997; its principal planning strategies were as follows:

■ Remove the busway on Grey Street.

■ Reroute pedestrian and motor vehicle activity so that it occurs at grade.

■ Create legible entry points.

■ Encourage access to the site and permeability within the site.

■ Realign Grey Street and open cross-streets to reestablish the traditional street pattern of South Brisbane.

■ Provide additional open parkland for passive recreation.

■ Provide active street edges to encourage pedestrian interaction with the uses fronting the street.

■ Open links to the river and the city.

■ Consolidate and augment uses within the park.

■ Encourage links to adjacent uses.

■ Create improved development parcels as traditional city blocks.

■ Intensify activity at the river's edge.

The launching of the master plan was followed by a four-week public consultation period. Overall, the community generally accepted the plan. The component of the plan that addressed bridges for pedestrians and bicycles was launched, in October 1998, for a two-month consultation period, which included comment on proposed landing spots. The next stage of the planning process involved rigorous consultation with precinct neighbors to ensure that effective linkages were achieved.

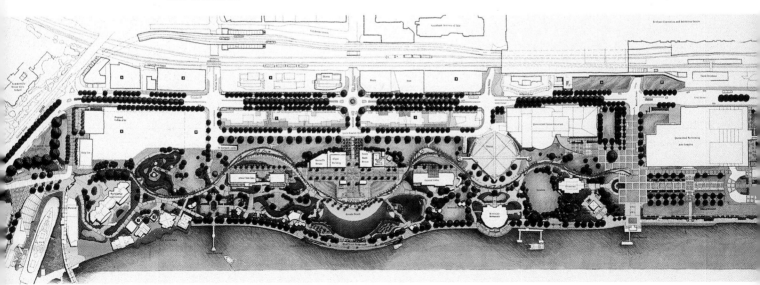

Site plan.

In general terms, the value of land at South Bank has increased dramatically since the completion of the 1997 master plan. Before 1997, vacant development land was valued at $6 million; its 2003 value was $58 million.

Sites were and are being released on an individual basis, for maximum market exposure. The South Bank Corporation determines prospective uses and provides developers with extensive briefs for their submissions—including, in some cases, preliminary concepts. Sales are based on desired uses, design concepts, capability of the developer, and price.

Development Tools

The development and use of land in the corporation area are controlled by the South Bank Approved Development Plan. The plan contains general provisions that address

■ The development aims and intentions of the corporation;

■ Overall development intensity;

■ Urban design themes and guidelines;

■ Implementation provisions (including the designation of planning areas and precincts, and development principles and urban design requirements for each precinct);

■ Special issues, including parking, bikeways, vehicular circulation and access, service and emergency vehicle access, and pedestrian thoroughfares.

The corporation has an urban design advisory panel whose role is to assess development proposals and provide advice to the corporation's board.

Urban Design

The corporation's goal for the South Bank precinct is to create a distinctive urban leisure area that incorporates opportunities for development within a parklands setting. Developments are expected to adhere to a high standard of design and to be compatible with each other and their environment.

The master plan is based on three spines that run through the site: a street spine (Grey Street), a park spine (the Arbour), and a river spine (corresponding with the river's edge). Each spine offers a variety of development options while improving access to locations within the site. The master plan incorporates planning and urban

The serpentine ENERGEX Brisbane Arbour forms the park spine. A 0.62-mile- (one-kilometer-) long trellis of pleached bougainvillea connects the 400 galvanized steel arches.

design principles from successful redevelopment projects and cities around the world; these include

■ A comprehensive urban design approach;

■ High-quality design;

■ An emphasis on detail;

The river spine maximizes public use of the river, contributing to an overall 20 percent increase in attendance.

CBD's Royal Botanic Gardens and adjoining educational facility, the Queensland University of Technology. Known as the Goodwill Bridge, after the CNN-sponsored games of the same name (which convened in Brisbane in 2001), the bridge provides an architectural centerpiece for the river. Construction started in May 2000, and the bridge opened in October 2001.

Grey Street

Grey Street has been recreated as a grand, tree-lined boulevard edged by shops, hotels, theaters, cinemas, cafés, apartments, and offices. A vine-covered pergola stretches along

- Making the most of public spaces;
- Permeability;
- An emphasis on public art;
- An emphasis on the civic landscape.

The next eight sections describe a number of South Bank's noteworthy design elements.

The ENERGEX Brisbane Arbour

The ENERGEX Brisbane Arbour, a colorful canopy of flowers that winds the full length of South Bank, was built as a new landmark for Brisbane. Constructed of 403 galvanized steel columns, each with a bougainvillea at its base, the arbor provides an easy-to-access walkway from one end of South Bank to the other, with no steps. Work started in November 1998 and was completed in November 1999.

Pedestrian and Cycle Bridge

A 1,300-foot- (396-meter-) long pedestrian and cycle bridge, believed to be the world's longest, provides a vital link between the southern end of South Bank and the

The 1,300-foot- (396-meter-) long Goodwill Bridge provides a pedestrian and bicycle link across the Brisbane River.

the two blocks closest to the parklands. Phase I (south of Glenelg Street), in which Grey Street was realigned and lined with trees, was completed in late December 1998. Phase II, from Glenelg to Melbourne Street, followed the demolition of the boulevard between Rydges and the Queensland Conservatorium. Grey Street was completely open in early November 1999.

South Bank House

The new, 18,000-square-foot (1,670-square-meter) South Bank House is situated in the heart of the parklands, between two buildings that are on the UNESCO World Heritage List, and has been designed to complement the historic buildings that flank it. South Bank Corporation staff moved to the new building in late October 1999, and other tenants have also taken up residence there.

IMAX

The $20 million IMAX theater, on Grey Street, opened in January 1999, and Hoyts South Bank Cinemas opened in March 1999.

Thiess Centre

National building contractor Thiess Contractors Pty., Ltd., built its ten-story, $30 million, 108,000-square-foot (10,035-square-meter) national headquarters right next to IMAX. In June 1999, more than 300 staff moved in.

Queensland College of Art

Griffith University's Queensland College of Art (QCA) was relocated to a site that also includes South Bank House and the adjoining parking garage. The QCA refurbished an existing building and constructed additional facilities on the rest of the site. Work on the $33 million project began in June 2000, and the college moved to its new facility in late 2001.

Arbour on Grey and the Galleria

Arbour on Grey is a $120 million residential, retail, and commercial development being undertaken by Mirvac. Phases I and II of the residential component, consisting of 172 condominium apartments, have been sold. The retail component of the project involves a joint venture between Mirvac and the South Bank Corporation for 43,000 square feet (3,995 square meters) of retail, dining, and entertainment facilities. A second residential development, the Galleria, on a 999-year lease, constructed by Honeycombe Group, sold its 68 units within a few months of release to market.

A 100-unit multifamily building on Little Stanley Street contains four levels of residential above street-level shops and restaurants.

Lessons Learned

One of the key lessons learned from the South Bank redevelopment is that planning and institutional arrangements for major redevelopment projects need to evolve in response to changing needs. The climate for development in Brisbane, particularly commercial development, has altered significantly during the 14 years since planning began for the project. The master plan for South Bank has had to adjust to the changed conditions while maintaining a long-term commitment to creating and sustaining high-quality public spaces. The parklands created as part of the project are a valuable asset for the residents of Brisbane, and South Bank is arguably one of the world's most successful redevelopments of an Expo site.

A key aspect of South Bank's success was the willingness of the South Bank Corporation to acknowledge that the original master plan was lacking in a number of respects and to address the problems that had arisen. In doing so, the corporation also responded to the develop-

The redevelopment program, completed in 2000, has increased land values fourfold in the precinct and has resulted in a 27 percent increase in retail sales.

ment community's sense that the original plan was an obsolete product of an earlier development cycle, and that a slavish attempt to realize the original design intentions would not satisfy either the commercial objectives of the corporation and the state government, or the objective of creating a world-class public amenity.

Some of the recreation elements included in the original scheme were not only commercially unviable but also unsatisfactory in terms of access and urban design. It is important, in planning such projects, to ensure that proposed activities are justified in terms of both need and demand. The current plan still provides for a wide variety of leisure activities, from the lagoon and beach area to the state art gallery, the museum, and the library complex, but the facilities are now better matched to the aspirations of the local community and to the demands of out-of-state and overseas tourists.

The current master plan has the advantage of being more robust, and allowing for changes in the nature and extent of demand for development. Extending the original street pattern of South Brisbane into the site has improved access to locations within the site, improved access to the parklands, and created more valuable development parcels.

Because, under the new master plan, each development parcel has its own lease and is fully serviced in terms of infrastructure and access, staging of development is now easier, as individual parcels can now be developed more or less independently of each other. The new master plan also has more clearly defined precincts, which facilitates the marketing and promotion of various areas, including the parklands, commercial and retail premises, food and beverage outlets, educational and cultural facilities, and events venues.

One of the main ingredients of the corporation's current successful development program is the use of partnerships to achieve commercial and planning goals. Partnerships have been established with the state and city governments, local businesses and developers, educational institutions, and community and cultural organizations. All have been successfully enlisted in the task of implementing the new vision for South Bank.

The South Bank precinct has provided Brisbane and Queensland with a number of signature features, which assist in marketing and promoting the city and the state to visitors. These elements have respected the local culture and lifestyle and the unique architecture of the city. The project is now better linked to the city center on the north bank of the river, and the facilities at South Bank complement the tourist accommodations and attractions of the CBD. The place making that has occurred at South Bank has yielded a dividend for the project, and also for the city and state, and has demonstrated the community benefit of high-quality, mixed-used development in an inner-city riverside environment.

All images in this case study are courtesy of South Bank Corporation.

Notes

1. The author gratefully acknowledges the assistance of the staff and consultants of the South Bank Corporation in the preparation of this case study—in particular, Marcia Gray, special projects manager; Graham Robinson, planning manager; Bill Grant, chief executive officer; John Simpson, consulting master architect—as well as Bill Corker and Adrian FitzGerald, of Denton Corker Marshall.
2. Unless otherwise noted, all dollar amounts in this case study are in Australian dollars.

Project Data: **South Bank**

Land Use Information

Site area (acres/hectares)	104/42
Parks and open space (acres/hectares)	42/17
Parking spaces	3,000

Land Use Plan

Use	Square Feet/Square Meters
Brisbane Convention and Exposition Centre	805,860/74,870
South Bank House	18,000/1,670
Thiess Centre	108,000/10,035
Retail (Arbour on Grey)	43,000/3,995

Residential Information

Condominium apartments, Arbour on Grey	172
The Galleria	68

Project Costs (Millions)

Site clearing (South Bank Corporation)	$105
Rydges South Bank Hotel	$60
Thiess Centre	$30
Queensland Conservatorium of Music and Opera	$35
Queensland College of Art, renovations and addition	$33
IMAX	$20
Arbour on Grey	$120

Project Timeline

1984	South Bank chosen as World Expo 1988 site
1988	World Expo
1995	Brisbane Convention and Exhibition Centre opens
1996	Rydges South Bank Hotel opens
1999	IMAX and Hoyts South Bank Cinemas open
1999	Thiess Centre completed
2001	Queensland College of Art renovation and addition complete

Major Project Participants

Denton Corker Marshall
49 Exhibition Street
Melbourne, Victoria 3000
Australia
+61 3 9654 4644
Web site: www.dcm-group.com

DBI Design Corporation
Level 5, 46 Cavill Avenue
Surfers Paradise
Queensland 4217
Australia
+61 07 5539 9788

John Simpson & Associates
236 Crown Street
East Sydney, New South Wales 2000
Australia
+61 02 9331 6188

Mirvac
Level 5, 40 Miller Street
North Sydney, New South Wales 2060
Australia
+61 02 9080 8000
Web site: www.mirvac.com.au

South Bank Corporation
Level 3, South Bank House
South Bank, Queensland 4101
Australia
+61 07 3867 2000
Web site: www.south-bank.net.au

Charleston Waterfront Park

Charleston, South Carolina

Anne Frej

Charleston Waterfront Park is a 12-acre (five-hectare) green space that serves as a transition between the Cooper River and the historic downtown of Charleston, South Carolina. Located at the city's eastern shoreline, the park is an inviting public space that is easily accessible to the city's residents and visitors.

The park opened in May 1990, after a more than ten-year planning and construction process that was interrupted by Hurricane Hugo. Careful planning and attention to detail are the hallmarks of the project, which features a 1,200-foot- (366-meter-) long riverside promenade, walking paths, grassy lawns, and intimate seating areas shaded by groves of live oaks.

The park is designed both to serve as an unprogrammed, peaceful refuge and to offer opportunities for recreational activities such as strolling, jogging, and fishing. A fishing pier and a 400-foot- (122-meter-) long wharf provide easy access to the water, and the wharf's three shade structures offer shelter to those who wish to fish or relax. The park's fountains offer opportunities for other informal activities. The pineapple fountain, designed by Sasaki Associates, Inc., serves as the park's centerpiece and is a popular meeting spot. The shallow pool and spraying water jets of the second fountain, located near the northern entrance, draw children and adults alike to cool off on hot days.

From Port to Pineapple Fountain

Waterfront Park is located in a section of Charleston that was once a dynamic center for maritime commerce. The city was one of the country's leading ports for the transport of cotton, rice, and other commodities, and as early as the 1700s, warehouses, offices, and residences had developed along the waterfront. After an 1886 earthquake struck the Charleston peninsula, causing considerable damage, many structures were rebuilt. The waterfront remained active until the early 20th century, when the introduction of larger ships shifted most port traffic to the north. Over time, the historic docks in the area decayed and disappeared. Although some buildings continued to be occupied by small businesses, much of the former port was vacant and underused.

A portion of what is now the Waterfront Park site was once used by the Clydeline Steamship Company, which provided passenger and freight service along the Atlantic coast. The Clydeline terminal was destroyed by fire in 1955 and was not rebuilt. With little economic activity nearby, the

The water edge of the park was formalized with decorative railings, light fixtures, and rows of trees. *David Soliday*

Those who want to fish—or just to relax—have ample opportunity: Charleston Waterfront Park offers a fishing pier, a 400-foot- (122-meter-) long wharf, and three shade structures. *Landslides*

site languished, and was used only as a parking area for many years. In the late 1970s, a real estate developer purchased the site, intending to redevelop it as a high-rise commercial and residential district. The prospect that this major development could change the city's historic skyline and remove the last undeveloped waterfront property from public access mobilized the community. Intensive negotiation with the developer, backed up by the threat of condemnation, prompted the sale of the site to the city, in 1979. Two generous private donations and a matching grant from the U.S. Department of the Interior funded the acquisition.

In 1983, preliminary work—which consisted primarily of stabilizing and strengthening the soil—began on the park. The second phase of construction began in 1988 and was well underway in September 1989, when Hurricane Hugo hit the city. Although ornamental elements of the new park sustained considerable damage, its underlying structure withstood the hurricane, and the remaining work continued. Charleston Waterfront Park opened on May 11, 1990.

An Urban Retreat

When the city of Charleston first began exploring possible development strategies for the Waterfront Park site, the potential for a city park was not immediately apparent. Given the site's characteristics—a silted-in shoreline, rotting pilings from long-gone wharves standing offshore, and abandoned buildings and parking lots—a strong concept would be needed to complete the transformation.

From the beginning, the project was envisioned as more than just a new city park. Waterfront Park would be a stimulus and a key component in efforts to upgrade the eastern edge of the city and provide public access to the city's waterfront areas. It was also decided early in the design process that the park would function as an urban retreat for Charleston residents and visitors. Unlike many other waterfront redevelopment projects undertaken in the United States during the 1980s, it was not intended to

The pineapple fountain is the centerpiece of the park. *Sasaki Associates*

To acquire background for the creation of the master plan, the designers looked carefully at the area's history and origins—at how the site had functioned in its early days and how it was related to the fabric of the historic downtown. The area had been an important commercial center that drew people from other parts of the city on an east-west axis that led into the park. To maintain the site's relationship to the rest of the city, the designers tied the park's

become a festival marketplace or an entertainment-oriented destination. Instead, the goal was to create a place of natural beauty that would serve as a counterpoint to Charleston's dense downtown area. As Charleston mayor Joseph Riley Jr. noted at the park's opening ceremony, "This is to be a quiet park . . . a place of repose along the water's edge for all citizens to enjoy."

This approach favored intimate seating areas over amphitheaters, and walking paths and piers over marinas and boat tie-ups. No public events, such as concerts or plays, are held in Waterfront Park. Instead, visitors have the assurance that they are always welcome to use the park for walking, jogging, fishing, or just relaxing.

An aerial view of Charleston Waterfront Park. The park was designed to provide a place of natural beauty and serenity that would serve as a counterpoint to the dense urban character of the nearby downtown. The marshlands lining the waterfront were enhanced and filled in with native grasses. *Landslides*

Natural and Historical Elements

The design of Waterfront Park is the result of a strong collaborative effort between the city of Charleston and an internationally respected team of designers: Sasaki Associates, Inc.; Edward Pinckney/Associates; and Jaquelin Robertson. Recognizing that the proposed park must fit into the context of the entire city, the design team addressed not only the park design but also opportunities and constraints throughout the larger peninsula area. The resulting master plan pays close attention to context, addressing areawide issues such as traffic, parking, the impact of tourism, and linkages between areas; it also takes account of urban design features: streetscapes, existing open spaces, proposed projects, and undeveloped blocks.

pedestrian walkways to the existing street system and used special paving techniques to emphasize the connection. While the park is seamless at its city edge, with no formal dividers to separate it from the city, these walkways help direct visitors to the park at key access points.

Preserving and enhancing environmental conditions in the vicinity of the park was another element in the planning process. The park's location on the tidal, saltwater portion of the Cooper River meant that coastal forces such as flooding, salt spray, wind, and hurricanes would have to be taken into account. The poor and unstable soil conditions that are typical of many city harbors also had to be mitigated.

The park's relationship to the water was also debated. The designers decided to build up the park to a level above the water and to use decorative railings and rows of trees and lampposts to create a defined edge along the water. At the same time, the marshlands lining the waterfront were enhanced to incorporate natural elements into the park's edge and to preserve natural wildlife habitats. To accomplish this goal, land had to be filled in to the correct elevation to allow for periodic flooding; native grasses were then planted by hand on the filled-in land.

All elements of the park, from landscape materials to furniture, reflect attention to detail. The "Charleston benches" found throughout the site are based on traditional park benches but have been redesigned and enlarged to provide more comfortable seating. Even the raised walls that serve as borders for the green lawns were built at a suitable height for informal seating.

The materials selected for the walkways throughout the park vary from hard surfaces, such as the blue stone typical of older Charleston sidewalks, to a softer gravel finish. This gravel is unique to Waterfront Park and was produced specially from a mix of stones selected for color, texture, and permeability.

Until it was determined that, particularly in its early years, the park itself should function as the primary design theme, the designers considered placing artwork throughout the park. But with an eye to the later evolution of the park, the designers installed a series of pedestals to provide future "art opportunities." When the park was first opened, a five-year moratorium on the installation of art was imposed; new works can be added only every ten years.

The concept for the redevelopment of the blocks facing the park has evolved over time, as the city worked to find the appropriate type and scale of development. Construction on one of the last pieces of land facing the park was initiated in 2001. This project, One Vendue Range, is a luxury residential condominium complex being developed by Vendue/Prioleau Associates, a partnership between local resident Walter Seinsheimer Jr. and East/West Partners, of Beaver Creek, Colorado. The architects are Schmitt Sampson Walker, of Charleston.

The planning and design process for Waterfront Park started in 1980 and took four years. Construction, which was interrupted by Hurricane Hugo, was completed in 1990. *Sasaki Associates*

The project includes 50 units, ranging in size from 1,100 to 3,500 square feet (100 to 325 square meters), and is designed to blend in with neighboring historic structures: the exterior of the complex features brick and cast stone, with a stucco base. To avoid blocking the east-west view corridors or the walkways that connect the city center with Waterfront Park, the project is designed as six separate structures. At the center of the complex is an 8,000-square-foot (745-square-meter) art gallery that the developer agreed to donate to the city. According to Seinsheimer, the project benefits enormously from its proximity to Waterfront Park, which the buyers view as a spacious and green frontyard. Any potential negative impacts of the location are mitigated by the fact that the city closes the park at dark and pays close attention to safety and maintenance there.

Another undeveloped block, at the northern edge of the site, is currently occupied by warehouses and port-related uses. Future plans call for a mixed-use development with residential, retail, and office uses.

A Successful Collaboration

Creating a waterfront park to serve Charleston residents and visitors was the long-term vision of Joe Riley, who had been the city's mayor since 1976. But despite the fact that the site was overgrown and underused, plans for redevel-

Spraying water jets and a shallow fountain at the park's northern entrance provide visitors with relief on hot days. *Sasaki Associates*

opment had to proceed slowly and carefully because of the historic character of the city and the environmental issues associated with a waterfront setting. During the four-year planning and design process that began in 1980, the city held numerous public meetings and work sessions with owners of adjacent properties and with others who were concerned about the future of this area of Charleston. The construction process also required a measured approach. Because the soil conditions were so poor, it was necessary

to preload the soils (to wick out moisture and minimize settling) before installing the paving and landscaping.

Funds for the design and construction of the park, totaling nearly $13.0 million, were provided by a combination of private donations, federal assistance, county funds, and city funds; the city's funding came from several sources, including tax increment bonds. An endowed perpetual maintenance fund supports maintenance, and capital improvements are funded from the interest on that fund. Routine maintenance is funded through the city's general fund.

Many of the ambitious goals set for Waterfront Park have been met. Not only did the city succeed in creating a popular waterfront destination for city residents and visitors, but, during the past ten years, it achieved the larger objective of stimulating revitalization in the surrounding blocks. The city can take credit for many of the factors that have spurred private sector investment in the area, including the creation of Waterfront Park; the provision of new, structured parking facilities in the area; investment in public improvements; and the development of design guidelines and an architectural review process to guide new infill development. At the same time, a strengthening economy and improving market conditions also helped the revitalization process.

Efforts to provide public access along the city's perimeter waterfront have led to the construction of a waterfront promenade that begins several miles north of Waterfront Park, at the South Carolina Aquarium, and continues past the Charleston Maritime Center, through Waterfront Park, to the Battery and Ashley River Walk. Waterfront Park's portion of the promenade runs the length of the park and provides unrestricted views of the water.

Lessons Learned

Mayor Joseph Riley's commitment to the project was key to the success of Charleston Waterfront Park. His vision for the park and its surrounding neighborhood helped establish the development concept and keep the project on track over a relatively long design and construction period.

Project Data: **Charleston Waterfront Park**

Land Use Information

Site area (acres/hectares)	12/5
Length of promenade (feet/meters)	1,200/366
Length of wharf (feet/meters)	400/122
Number of residential units facing park	50
Area of residential units (square feet/square meters)	1,100–3,500/100–325
Area of art gallery (square feet/square meters)	8,000/745

Project Costs

Land acquisition	$3,000,000
Architecture and engineering, survey, construction administration	400,000
Site preparation	1,200,000
Construction	11,400,000
Total project cost	$16,000,000

Funding Sources

City funds (tax increment financing bonds)	$6,500,000
City funds (other)	1,000,000
Federal and state grants	5,000,000
Private contributions	3,500,000
Total	$16,000,000

Project Timeline

1970s	Site purchased by developer for a potential commercial and residential project
1979	Site sold to the city of Charleston
1983	Preliminary construction begins
1988	Phase II of construction begins
1990	Waterfront Park opens

Major Project Participants

City of Charleston Department of Parks
823 Meeting Street
Charleston, South Carolina 29403
843-724-7324

Sasaki Associates Inc.
64 Pleasant Street
Watertown, Massachusetts 02472
617-926-3300
www.sasaki.com

Edward Pinckney/Associates, Ltd.
14 Westbury Park Way
Bluffton, South Carolina 29910
843-757-9800
www.pinckneyassociates.com

Cooper, Robertson & Partners
311 West 43rd Street
New York, New York 10036
212-247-1717
www.cooperrobertson.com

Waterfront Park proves that the successful revitalization of an urban waterfront area does not require an entertainment or commercial focus. In this case, public investment in a major park and attention to the immediate surroundings helped reposition all of downtown Charleston.

Waterfront projects require sensitivity to environmental issues in both the design and construction phase. It is important to recognize that unforeseen events, including natural disasters, can add considerable time and expense to a major project.

Attention to detail and the use of high-quality materials pay off over time. The iron railings, light fixtures, benches, and other furniture used in Waterfront Park have held up well and have required only routine maintenance.

International Financial Services Centre

Dublin, Ireland

Virginia Sorrells

My beloved subjects, a new era is about to dawn. I, Bloom, tell you verily it is even now at hand. Yea, on the word of a Bloom, ye shall ere long enter into the golden city which is to be, the new Bloomusalem in the Nova Hibernia of the future.

—James Joyce, *Ulysses*

Early Celtic settlements lined the River Liffey before the Vikings founded Dublin in the ninth century. The name was derived from the Irish name for the point where the River Poddle joined the Liffey in a "black pool," or "dubh linn." The Vikings were followed by the Anglo-Normans, who built atop the Viking town; the medieval city grew around this nucleus. The Georgian ascendancy, during the 18th century, was a boom time for Dublin, when it grew to be the second-largest city in the British Empire after London. Aggressive city planning in the 18th and 19th centuries created the form of modern Dublin, with its Georgian residential squares, wide streets, neoclassical townhouses, and quays lining the Liffey. The Custom House, to the east, and Dublin Port, beyond, were also built during this period.

Until the 19th century, the city was contained by the Royal Canal to the north and the Grand Canal to the south; even in the 20th century, "true Dubliners" were said to be those born within the confines of the two canals. In the 19th century, expanding rail lines encouraged development along the southeast coast, as far as the port of Dun Laoghire, and the city became increasingly suburbanized.

As Dublin's population grew in the early part of the 20th century, and many of its more affluent residents moved to the suburbs, the traditional neighborhoods within the confines of the canals went into decline. New arrivals from rural areas were packed into aging residential buildings, and poverty, crime, and malnutrition increased. In particular, the communities north of the Liffey, bordering the Custom House Docks area, became increasingly crowded and poor.

In 1914, two pioneering urbanists, Patrick Geddes and Robert Unwin (one of the founders of the Garden City movement), helped the city organize a competition to solicit planning ideas designed to combat urban decay. Patrick Abercrombie's winning design incorporated many Garden City principles and was the first to envision a major civic gateway at the Custom House Docks. Abercrombie's scheme remained the basic planning framework for the city well into

Two of the four main buildings at the International Financial Services Centre: the North Block (foreground) and the South Block. The buildings are constructed from Irish limestone, accented by green-tinted glass. *Davison and Associates LTD*

the 20th century, but many of its physical components were set aside as the government focused instead on the urgent need for adequate social housing. Although some of the city's slums were rebuilt, the high costs of land led to the construction of new social housing in the suburbs.

Suburban expansion continued into the 1960s. The Myles Wright Plan, created in 1966, leapfrogged the inner-ring suburbs and called for new towns west of the city. The further development of an outer-ring motorway, shopping centers, business parks, and regional amenities steered private investment away from the inner city. In the 1970s, in an attempt to stem the exodus, the city council, known as the Dublin Corporation, began investing in inner-city social

housing. Between the end of the war and 1996, the population grew from approximately 600,000 to over 1 million.

Anna Livia, James Joyce's evocation of the spirit of the Liffey, gradually became a river more conducive to poetry than to navigation. At Dublin Port, changes in passenger handling and a shift from labor-intensive manual handling of cargo to mechanical processes led to a dramatic decline in employment. In a reflection of worldwide sectoral shifts, large-scale industrial users also abandoned the Docklands area. By 1986, with inward capital investment at a standstill, Ireland's economy was on the verge of collapse. Despite a highly educated workforce, the national unemployment rate was 17 percent. According to one planning official, a large part of Ireland's economic development policy at this time consisted of helping college graduates to process their green-card applications as quickly as possible so that they could find jobs in the United States.

Revitalizing a Sputtering Economy

By the mid-1980s the Irish national government, through the Investment and Development Agency (IDA), had launched a new strategy to reverse the country's brain drain and turn the sputtering economy around. The strategy involved focusing investment on two key industries: pharmaceuticals and international finance. At the same time, the Urban Renewal Act of 1986 shifted the national planning focus to the preservation and regeneration of historic cities.

The decline of industrial and port uses presented Dublin with the perfect location in which to begin the restructuring of the Irish economy: the Dublin Docklands, 1,300 acres (526 hectares) of former industrial land lining the north and south banks of the River Liffey. Adjacent to the eastern portions of Dublin's central business district, the massive redevelopment site connects downtown with Dublin Harbour and the Irish Sea. The Docklands can be subdivided into two subareas: the Custom House Docks, north of the Liffey, and the Grand Canal Docks, south of the river.

The Custom House Docks Development Authority (CHDDA—now the Dublin Docklands Development Authority, DDDA), Ireland's first public/private development partnership, was established in 1986 as a response to the Urban Renewal Act. The 1,300 acres (526 hectares) under the control of the DDDA constitute approximately one-tenth of the total area of the city between the canals. Backed by the force of the new IDA strategy, local planners decided to locate a special financial services district at the Custom House Docks.

Allied Irish Banks Capital Market is headquartered on West Block. Designed by Burke-Kennedy Doyle Architects, this five-story building, with its own car park, was completed in 1990.
Davison and Associates LTD

Established in 1987, the 27-acre (11-hectare) International Financial Services Centre (IFSC) followed a "free port" model, offering significant tax incentives to businesses engaged in a range of activities related to the capital markets. To be eligible to locate within the IFSC, businesses must be engaged in one of the following:

- Banking, asset financing, and leasing;
- Corporate treasury management;
- Fund management, investment management, custody, and administration;
- Futures and options trading;
- Securities trading;
- Insurance, assurance, reinsurance, captives, and brokering.

The definition can be expanded to include any activity that can be broadly defined as a financial service. All activities must be carried out on behalf of non-Irish residents and in non-Irish currencies.

The Irish national legislature created an unprecedented package of tax incentives for developers and businesses locating in the IFSC. For all new buildings, building owners do not pay property tax for ten years; for all expanded or improved buildings, building owners do not pay property tax for ten years after the increase in build-

The South Block of the International Financial Services Centre (IFSC), viewed from across the River Liffey. There are two channels of water inside the IFSC: the Inner Dock, and Georges Dock, which is connected to the river by a narrow inlet. *Barry Mason Photography*

ing valuation. Building owners in all targeted areas are able to write off 100 percent of capital expenditures for commercial development. Under a double rent allowance, tenants are able to deduct from their income taxes 200 percent of their rent for the first ten years of occupancy. To promote the construction of rental units, residential developers are able to write off their construction costs. Finally, corporate tax obligations were sharply reduced. At a time when the Irish national corporate tax rate was 52 percent, international financial services and associated service businesses locating in the Custom House Docks area were eligible for a 10 percent corporate tax rate.

The Dublin City Development Plan of 1991 designated several declining areas of the central city as "rejuvenation areas," granting the city condemnation powers and providing special incentives for new development. Two of these areas—the Custom House Docks and the Temple Bar—were placed under the control of "special project organizations." Modeled after development authorities in the United Kingdom, these organizations have the power to develop plans within the framework of the larger city plan and to solicit and negotiate specific development proposals within their project areas.

By the late 1990s, the emphasis in Dublin planning policy had shifted to social and economic welfare, partly in response to the "development at any cost" approach that had characterized attempts to attract tourism and financial services investment in the mid-1980s.

The depression of the late 1980s through the early 1990s took its toll on the economy, with unemployment peaking at 13 percent. A fast economic expansion in the mid-1990s, driven by high-tech exports, fueled a property boom.

Ireland has a strong history of homeownership: approximately 80 percent of Irish people own their own homes, and very little rental housing is available. Housing construction could not keep pace with demand; as a result, homelessness increased and prices remain high, even today. Given the high cost of housing in Dublin, eligibility for affordable housing is broad. To alleviate the need, 20 percent of housing land or units must now be set aside for social or affordable housing throughout Dublin. To achieve this goal, the planning department promotes infill development that is in character with the surrounding architecture.

Developments within the rejuvenation areas are eligible for "fast-track" approval, provided that their plans conform with the plans that the special project organizations have crafted. Designed to give comfort to investors by clearly defining the rules upfront (and avoiding delays down the road), the fast-track system also helps developers navigate Dublin's traditionally lengthy and cumbersome "third-party appeals system," under which any member of the public can protest planning decisions. The Dublin planning authority maintains responsibility for the review of plans outside the fast-track areas—and even within the fast-track areas, owners have the option of applying to the planning authority for special review of nonconforming plans. Within the Docklands, infrastructure is still provided by the Dublin Corporation, although development levies are assessed for major infrastructure.

Development of the IFSC

With the tax package in place, the CHDDA prepared a master plan for the site and, in 1987, issued a request for proposals, seeking a development partner. Custom House Docks Development Company Limited—a consortium of British Land Company plc, Hardwicke Limited, and McInerney Properties plc—was selected from among 16 submissions. A master project agreement was signed in 1988, formalizing the public/private partnership. Under the agreement, the CHDDA provided the land, tax incentives, and planning powers, while the developer designed, built, and financed the project.

The site is cut off from the river by a quayside roadway that provides the main east-west access from the city to the docklands north of the Liffey. Thus, the IFSC's dominant features are two other water bodies: George's Dock, which is connected to the Liffey by a narrow channel, and the Inner

Dock, to the west. Many of the features of the two historic docks are of architectural interest, including the paving and the cut-stone walls. Throughout the site, stone pillars and blocks—remnants of other buildings that once ringed the docks—have been integrated into the landscape.

Care was taken to integrate historic elements into the redesign of the site and to preserve two historic buildings. The Harbourmaster's House has been reborn as a pub and restaurant. Stack A, a former wine warehouse that was an engineering marvel in its day, is noteworthy for its cast-iron roof and interior columns.

Ground was broken in 1988 for the first new building, the West Block, designed by Burke-Kennedy Doyle Architects. By 1990, the West Block was occupied by Allied Irish Banks. The North, South, and East blocks were con-

The North, South, and West blocks, as seen from Georges Dock. Stone pillars and blocks—remnants of buildings that once lined the docks—have been integrated into the landscape. *Davison and Associates LTD*

structed later. Work on the site roared ahead as the Irish economy took off: demand for additional office space had increased substantially by 1994, and by the end of 1997, the original 27-acre (11-hectare) site had been expanded to 39 acres (16 hectares), including over 1.2 million square feet

A ring fence surrounds the International Financial Services Centre (IFSC), setting it apart from the inner city. The view shown is from across the River Liffey; West Block is on the left, North Block on the right.

(111,485 square meters) of office space; 333 apartments; a Jury's Hotel; the Dublin Exchange Facility; retail (including the Harbourmaster Pub and other restaurants); and a multistory parking garage. Today, the IFSC development includes 2 million square feet (185,805 square meters) of offices; 850,000 square feet (78,965 square meters) of residential development; 50,000 square feet (4,645 square meters) of retail; and 70,000 square feet (6,505 square meters) of space dedicated to cultural uses. Plans for Stack A would transform it into a 160,000-square-foot (14,865-square-meter) community cultural center. Currently employing approximately 14,000 people and some 370 international financial companies, the IFSC houses the offices of more than half of the world's top 20 insurance companies and half of the world's largest banks: it now ranks as one of the world's leading centers for international banking, fund management, and insurance.

The IFSC has also had significant spillover effects. Demand for office space is so strong that the citywide vacancy rate is now around 2 percent. Far from exporting

its college graduates, Dublin has had to import workers, particularly in the services sector. Dublin businesses, which once provided back-office services to the United States and Europe, are now shipping back-office jobs to Eastern Europe to meet still-increasing demand.

Any new development in the Docklands—and, indeed, throughout Europe—will be undertaken without the substantial tax benefits that Dublin was able to offer early on. As a member of the European Union (EU), Ireland will need to conform to the EU's fiscal policies, which take a dim view of incentives designed to alter the competitive landscape. In future, deep subsidies will likely be reserved for the neediest member nations, such as the incoming countries of Eastern Europe. However, because of the EU's requirement for level tax rates, corporations throughout Europe will be subject to a 12 percent corporate tax rate, only slightly above the 10 percent currently levied within the IFSC.

Whether or not the Docklands is the "Bloomusalem," capital of the New Ireland foretold in James Joyce's vision, it has opened a whole new development frontier within the city. Further expansion plans are underway within the Docklands, to the east of the IFSC. A draft plan released early in 2001 called for an additional IR£2 billion ($2.14 billion) in development, between the IFSC site and the harbor, that would include 4 million square feet (371,610 square meters) of office space; 3,000 apartments and townhouses; hotels; and cultural and community spaces. A new light-rail system, dubbed Luas, would connect points within the greater Docklands area to the central city. However, the plan also called for building heights and densities that in some cases exceed those allowed in the current area plan. The would-be developers maintained that, given the lack of subsidies, the increased densities are necessary.

If these differences cannot be overcome, the area between the IFSC site and the harbor might be destined to become a very large urban park.

Lessons Learned

The Dublin Docklands experience demonstrates that when a redevelopment project of this scale is undertaken, it pays to identify—and market to—a well-defined niche. When appropriately used, tax incentives can help to spur development. In this case, the tax incentives were merely a powerful lever: had it not been for the government's careful assessment of how to position itself in the international financial services market, no amount of incentive would have been adequate.

By matching the available land with an abundant human resource—a highly educated, English-speaking workforce—planners were able to take advantage of the economic boom times of the 1990s, and perhaps to extend the area's economic prominence well into the future. Fast-track development powers also proved useful, reassuring developers that if they followed a few easily understood rules, they could implement their designs in a timely fashion. Significant value has been added to the area: land within the Docklands is now the most expensive in Dublin, and price has not yet become an obstacle to development.

At the outset of the Docklands redevelopment, public subsidies were more influential than the waterfront location, but the location itself has since become very important. New paths and waterfront attractions have increased awareness of the Liffey, which was previously all but ignored. Moorings along one mile (1.6 kilometers) of the river can now accommodate smaller cruise liners, and the DDDA is exploring the creation of a dedicated cruise port to accommodate craft with drafts of greater than 16 feet (five meters). To increase enjoyment of the river, the DDDA is also considering "static vessels," such as floating restaurants, and the establishment of a system of water taxis to take passengers between the riverfront developments and out into the harbor.

As the site continues to grow, however, and the city center shifts east to meet it, automobile traffic will become an increasing problem. The two roads lining the Liffey—the main routes in and out of the site—are always congested with cars and trucks. Discussions are underway for a tunnel that would take traffic from the port to the M-50 ring roadway.

The future success of Dublin's Docklands will naturally depend on the continued strength of the global economy. But should economic trends remain positive, Dublin appears equipped, with land and infrastructure, to capture its fair share of foreign investment.

Project Data: **International Financial Services Centre**

Land Use Information

Site area (acres/hectares)	39/16

Development by Type of Use

Use	Square Feet/Square Meters
Office	2,000,000/185,805
Residential	850,000/78,965
Retail	50,000/4,645
Cultural facilities	70,000/6,505 (230,000/21,365 planned)

Major Project Participants

Dublin Docklands Development Authority
Custom House Quay
Dublin 1
Ireland
+35 1 818 3300

Dublin City Planning Office
Civic Offices
Wood Quay
Block 4, Floor 3
Dublin 8
Ireland
+353 1 672 2222
Web site: www.dublincity.ie

Project Timeline

1986	Urban Renewal Act passed; Custom House Docks Development Authority established
1987	International Financial Services Centre (IFSC) established
1988	West Block, the first building of the IFSC, completed
1997	The IFSC expands to 39 acres (16 hectares)
2001	Plans for further expansion released

Project Web site

www.ifsc.ie

Custom House Docks Development Company Limited
14 Wellington Road
Dublin 4
Ireland
+353 1 668 3791

Jones Lang LaSalle
10/11 Molesworth Street
Dublin 2
Ireland
+353 1 679 4622
Web site: www.joneslanglasalle.ie

RiverPlace

Portland, Oregon

William P. Macht

Because of the location and the complexity of such projects, the redevelopment of urban waterfronts is a long-term undertaking. RiverPlace, in Portland, Oregon, shows how a development agency can learn to adapt to changes in planning practices, development concepts and strategies, markets, developers, and real estate cycles.

A mixed-use urban waterfront development on 73 acres (30 hectares) adjacent to downtown Portland, RiverPlace is located on a site formerly occupied by a lumber mill and by a steam plant that supplied heat and power to the downtown. Almost complete after more than 20 years of development, the project will offer three hotels with 450 rooms; over 800 housing units; 240,000 square feet (22,300 square meters) of office space; 50,000 square feet (4,645 square meters) of street-level retail space, half of which is on a waterfront esplanade; a 3,000-square-foot (280-square-meter) floating restaurant; a 47,000-square-foot (4,370-square-meter) athletic and rowing club; a 203-slip marina; a five-acre (two-hectare) grassy amphitheater; and a four-acre (1.6-hectare) waterfront park with a total of approximately 1,500 parking spaces.

Maverick City Planning

Portland's modern urban waterfront development began with a decisive act: the removal, in 1976, of a four-lane expressway to make way for Waterfront Park. "Nothing in the history of the city did more to establish Portland's reputation as a maverick in city planning than the jack-hammering of Harbor Drive to establish this 22-block stretch of greenway on the west bank of the Willamette River," writes *Oregonian* urban design critic Randy Gragg. Taking down the expressway was the culmination of planning efforts begun by activist mayor Neil Goldschmidt in the 1972 Downtown Plan, which had been developed in concert with the Willamette River Greenway Plan championed by maverick Governor Tom McCall, for whom Waterfront Park was later renamed.

While most of the Portland waterfront remained an open-space park, the creation of Waterfront Park was the first step in transforming the industrial south waterfront area into a mixed-use urban development. In 1978, the city council extended the downtown urban renewal district to include 73 acres (30 hectares) of undeveloped waterfront land between the Marquam and Hawthorne bridges. The most visible piece

Among its initial investments, the Portland Development Commission improved access to and from downtown on Front Avenue; dredged a natural basin to create a marina; created a five-acre (two-hectare) terraced meadow and swimming beach; and extended the riverfront esplanade one-half mile (0.8 kilometers), from the Hawthorne Bridge to a newly constructed Montgomery Street. Initial development completed in 1985 and 1990 included condominiums, rental units, the luxurious RiverPlace Hotel, the RiverPlace Athletic Club, retail, restaurants, structured parking, and the marina. *William P. Macht*

of waterfront property in the city, it was also one of the last still-vacant downtown sites of significant size. Extending the urban renewal district was a pivotal move because it allowed the use of the same economic resource—tax increment financing—that the city had used to successfully revitalize other downtown areas. In 1979, the city council adopted the South Waterfront Development Program, which had been prepared by the Portland Development Commission (PDC), and asked the PDC to acquire the 73 acres (30 hectares). The development arm of the city, the PDC is run by a semi-independent board of five commissioners who are appointed by the mayor and are predominantly from the private development sector.

As early as 1973, private interests had begun to view the area as a logical extension of a revitalized downtown and had proposed a number of projects for the area, primarily commercial office projects. Because of a number of factors, however—including poor access, very poor soil conditions,

the extensive utility lines that laced the site, environmental contamination, and traffic noise from the two-level Marquam Bridge—these proposals all foundered.

As noted earlier, the site had been the location of a lumber mill and a steam plant. Mountains of sawdust—over 40 feet (12 meters) deep—had been used as fill, and chemicals and fuel oils had saturated the accumulated layers of sawdust. Every structure that has been built on the site, including wood-framed structures, has required piling. Because the firmest rock foundation is a hard-packed gravel that undulates below the site, it has been difficult to predict the necessary depth of the piling, and construction has been costly.

It was clear to the PDC that development could not proceed without substantial improvements to the infrastructure. After acquiring the land for $3.9 million, the PDC spent $5.6 million for marina and park improvements and $4.1 million on street improvements and utilities.

The esplanade is lined with retail shops and a restaurant. Condominiums above the retail shops enjoy unfettered views of the marina. Because it is separated from downtown, the retail component lacks the critical mass that is necessary to support a diversified tenant mix. *William P. Macht*

These investments, which were funded primarily through tax-exempt tax increment bonds, included improving access to and from downtown on Front Avenue; dredging a natural basin to form and construct a marina enclosed by a floating breakwater and a fishing pier; creating a five-acre (two-hectare) terraced meadow and swimming beach; and extending the riverfront esplanade one half-mile (0.8 kilometers), from the Hawthorne Bridge to a newly constructed Montgomery Street.

In 1987, Pacific Power and Light (PP&L) closed its steam plant and donated the plant and the surrounding area (approximately half the total area of the site) to the PDC. The PDC was obligated to pay for demolition and environmental remediation and assumed liability for the underground storage tanks. PP&L agreed to relocate its major power substation to the southwest corner of the site.

Finding the Right Mix

The initial development objectives for RiverPlace were to reinforce the downtown revitalization plan; to catalyze private investment through waterfront development; and to provide year-round public access, and a variety of active uses, to attract residents and visitors. The initial plan, which was devised by consultants retained by the PDC, had three principal components: (1) the creation of a park and grassy amphitheater in a natural bowl on the northernmost portion of the property, south of the Hawthorne Bridge and opposite the new Marriott Hotel; (2) the development of a mix of uses, including hotels, restaurants, retail and office space, a marina, and some of the first downtown waterfront housing; (3) the develop-

ment of low- and mid-rise office space at the southern end of the site, adjacent to the Marquam Bridge. The first part of the north RiverPlace area to be developed was the grassy amphitheater breaching the seawall. The PDC made an early decision not to challenge or renegotiate an open-space deed restriction.

Given the time period—the late 1970s and early 1980s—the PDC can be said to have pushed the envelope in two respects: it sought to develop downtown housing for middle-income households where there had been very little, and to create waterfront retail where there had been none.

In January 1983, the PDC began a competitive process in which developers were required to meet minimum use and density requirements. The request for proposals called for 500 units of housing over the first two phases, 45,000 square feet (4,180 square meters) of office and retail space, and a 150-slip marina. The six proposals yielded two finalists. Cornerstone Development Company, of Seattle, owned by Weyerhaeuser Real Estate Company and Cornerstone's president, Paul Schell (later mayor of Seattle), submitted a proposal for 510 residential units, primarily one-bedroom condominium units; a 75-room hotel; two restaurants; 20,000 square feet (1,860 square meters) of retail space; a 30,000-square-foot (2,785-square-meter) athletic club; a 207-slip marina; and 768 structured parking spaces. The second proposal was from Bill Naito, a widely respected Portland developer who proposed to build 608 residential units—predominantly two-bedroom rentals—more restaurants, an athletic club, a marina, less retail space, no hotel, no office space, and a Ferris wheel in a public plaza.

The criteria for selection included project economics, the strength of the development team, the quality of the architectural design, and the competitiveness of the business offer. Despite strong support from the local business and architectural community for the idea of using a local developer, and the fact that the reviewers found Naito's design concept to be superior, the PDC selected Cornerstone, citing Weyerhaeuser's offer to sign a $20 million negotiable letter of credit as security against the $40 million performance of Phase I. Although it was not apparent at the time, Naito had a better understanding of the local market. Cornerstone was later forced to rent condominiums that it could not sell, and to combine one-bedroom units in order to create the two-bedroom units that the market demanded. Both the office and retail components also faced market resistance.

Under Cornerstone's disposition and development agreement (DDA) with the PDC, the sales price of the land was $20 per square foot ($215 per square meter) for

The RiverPlace Hotel, a 74-room boutique hotel, was built in the first phase. The RiverPlace Hotel will face direct competition from a 100-room boutique hotel that will be located on the waterfront, adjacent to South Waterfront Park. *William P. Macht*

the projected gross leasable area of the retail and office space, and $2,000 per unit for each of the residential units. Because the per-unit cost reflected some land-cost writedowns from the PDC, the agreement included an innovative surcharge of 10 percent for all sales prices in excess of $120,000, which would enable the PDC to recapture some of its subsidy.

Initial Implementation

In 1985 and 1990, respectively, the first two phases of Cornerstone's development were completed, at a cost of approximately $80 million. The RiverPlace I and II projects encompassed 8.7 acres (3.5 hectares) and featured 180 condominiums; 108 rental units; the 74-room luxury Alexis Hotel (now called RiverPlace Hotel); a 47,000-square-foot (4,370-square-meter) athletic club (originally built for the YMCA, it is now operated by a Seattle company as the RiverPlace Athletic Club); 995 parking spaces; a 203-slip marina (120 of whose slips are dry dock); and 38,500 square feet (3,575 square meters) of retail and restaurants, including the Newport Bay floating restaurant, the 250-seat, 7,000-square-foot (650-square-meter) Stanford's, and the Harborside Restaurant, which has the Full Sail Brewery Pilsner Room attached.

The first phases of RiverPlace did not perform as expected. Cornerstone attempted to spread the risk by selling a 50 percent interest to the Columbia Willamette real estate arm of Portland General Electric Company, forming a joint venture named Cornerstone Columbia Development Company. The venture faced a variety of difficult problems, however, including the following:

■ High construction costs associated with vast common areas;

■ Cost overruns for the extensive piling that was necessary to create the concrete platforms of the parking structures, which support the wood-frame construction above;

Almost complete after 20 years, RiverPlace is a mixed-use waterfront development that will include three hotels, housing, office space, street-level retail, a floating restaurant, an athletic club, a 203-slip marina, a five-acre (two-hectare) grassy amphitheater, a four-acre (1.6-hectare) waterfront park, and approximately 1,500 parking spaces. *Bergman Photographic Services*

■ The combination of high interest rates, a weak state economy, and a soft market for condominiums;

■ Resistance to for-sale units in a pioneer location;

■ A mix of units that was weighted too heavily in favor of one-bedroom units which, though popular in Seattle, were rejected by the Portland market.

Furthermore, it proved so difficult to "sell an empty neighborhood" as a residential location that it took over five years to sell 158 units. Naito's plan, which anticipated such difficulties, was designed to establish the neighborhood as a successful residential location before attempting to convert rental units to condominiums or to build for-sale units. Eventually, Cornerstone was forced to take Naito's route, and at great expense—including high initial unit costs, high vacancy rates, high turnover expenses, conversion costs, and extended selling costs. Although Cornerstone received a ten-year property tax abatement by promising that rents on a significant portion of the units would remain affordable to households earning 80 percent of the median income, the move lowered the company's potential income and may have stigmatized

The 400-room downtown Marriott Hotel (right) is located adjacent to the development area, near the RiverPlace Hotel, a 74-room boutique hotel (left). *William P. Macht*

the complex. Recently, the values of the Phase I condominiums were depressed by a special assessment of approximately $2 million for dry rot and other repairs.

The retail component, meanwhile, a virtual island on the fringe of downtown, is isolated from all other retail, has limited patronage, and has always performed poorly. Single-loaded and facing the water, it violates the basic retail tenet that calls for two-sided retail streets. Moreover, it lacks the critical mass necessary to permit a diverse tenant mix. The limited number of parking spaces—one per 1,000 square feet (93 square meters)—are located in private garages with pay parking, far from the retail space. The retail season peaks during the good-weather months of June through September and almost entirely misses the crucial Christmas shopping season. Lack of business has led to considerable tenant turnover; and the absence of anchors, which draw repeat business, reinforces the weakness of the retail location.

The athletic club was another major disappointment. Constructed at a cost of $7.5 million, the building was intended to be a turnkey facility for the local YMCA. In January 1987, only a year after signing a 20-year lease with Cornerstone, the YMCA defaulted on its $56,000-a-month lease because its membership had fallen far below expectations. At the same time, the YMCA was being attacked politically by the operators of suburban athletic clubs, who contended that by running an elaborate, high-profile athletic club, the YMCA was violating its tax-exempt status and creating unfair competition.

The YMCA's default forced Cornerstone to search for a new tenant, to spend $1 million to renovate the club and pool, and to assume risk it had never foreseen. Although Cornerstone did succeed in persuading a Seattle company to operate the since-renamed RiverPlace Athletic Club (RAC), it was forced to do so on a management contract rather than on a lease, which meant that Cornerstone was saddled with further unanticipated risk. Although the club eventually broke even, it took a long time to overcome the negative publicity that had attended the earlier default. Since 1994, the RAC has been operated successfully by Northwest Club Management as a private, full-service facility featuring a restaurant, health services, and a fitness program; the club draws its members from a wide geographic area that includes downtown workers and suburban residents. The RAC has also benefited from the proximity of the river: it runs the River-Place Rowing Center, in the marina, where rowing shells are launched. RAC membership is near full capacity, and use is limited more by access and parking constraints than by the size of the building.

Cornerstone had a one-year option to negotiate with the PDC for the purchase and development of additional land on the site of the steam plant, and thought that it could recoup some of it losses by building a 12-story, lux-

The second phase included rental townhouses with private tandem garages, private street entrances, and no corridors, elevators, or other enclosed common areas. The first floors of the units, along the public streets, were designed as separate home offices. *William P. Macht*

ury high-rise residential tower there, but the owners of the buildings to the west of the proposed tower contended that it would block views of the water. Fearing protracted litigation—and subsequently becoming skeptical about the luxury high-rise condominium market—Cornerstone abandoned its plans. The developer's fears about the market were not unfounded: it took the market about eight years to absorb the 44 luxury high-rise condominium units in the KOIN tower. The development manager for

Cornerstone, which had enjoyed great success with similar products in Seattle, said, "We discovered that high-end tower living was deathly in Portland, which was definitely not the case in Seattle. It demonstrated that you couldn't carry assumptions 200 miles [322 kilometers] and expect them to be transferable."

One element that markedly affected the development of RiverPlace was the fact that the project changed ownership during development. Shortly after Cornerstone was selected as the initial developer, Portland General Electric purchased a 50 percent interest in the company. As a publicly held corporation, the new owner had a decidedly different philosophy of asset management—one that was focused more on cash flow and short-term earnings than on the longer-term capital returns sought by Weyerhaeuser. By 1989, the joint venture of Portland General Electric and Cornerstone had sold an 85 percent interest to Sansei America, Inc., for a reported $34.4 million. The purchase included an 85 percent interest in the office and retail space, the hotel and athletic club, 380 parking spaces, and 32 condominiums. In 1991, after a protracted court battle, Sansei took over the remaining 15 percent of Phase I in exchange for a 50 percent share in a Washington State industrial park. Portland General Electric had sold its share of Cornerstone Columbia in 1990, after reportedly writing off a very substantial loss. Weyerhaeuser proceeded to liquidate its assets in the venture and sold the second phase of the project to Trammell Crow Residential (TCR), a subsidiary of the Dallas-based company, in a joint venture with Prudential Realty Pension Fund. This phase, which sold for $14.8 million, consisted of 108 rental apartments, 13,332 square feet (1,240 square meters) of ground-floor retail and restaurant space, a 302-space parking garage, the air rights above the parking structure, and the 2.73 acres (1.1 hectares) of land adjacent to the structure.

TCR assumed Cornerstone's obligation to develop 200 units of housing. Because the market had been exceptionally slow to absorb Cornerstone's products, but the 108-unit apartment project had only a 2 percent vacancy rate when TCR acquired it, in the summer of 1993, TCR chose to develop rentals rather than condominiums. A market study by Robert Charles Lesser suggested that a "lifestyle" project in a unique location could generate premium rents and could be converted to condominiums later.

TCR used GGLO Architects, of Seattle, to design the RiverPlace Square project, which consisted primarily of rental townhouses with private tandem garages and private on-street entrances; the project had no corridors, elevators, or other enclosed common areas, which reduced both development costs and operating expenses. The first floors of the units that were situated along public streets were designed as separate home offices. Even after design changes requested by the PDC (which were intended to open the project more to the street grid) caused a reduction in the number of units, the efficient design of the three-story buildings (182 units on 2.7 acres—1.1 hectares) yielded a density of 67 units per acre (166 per hectare).

The design features traditional pitched and gabled roofs, wood and stucco siding, and heavily landscaped trellises, which have the combined effect of reducing the apparent scale of the project. With a unit mix of predominantly one- and two-bedroom units and areas up to 1,300 square feet (120 square meters), TCR has been able to keep vacancy rates below 2 percent, even with monthly rents of as much as $1,650 (in 2001). Permanent financing was obtained through a joint venture with Prudential Realty Pension Fund, which holds 85 percent of the equity as a limited partner; TCR, as general partner, holds the remaining 15 percent and retains a management contract. In the event that the units are converted to condominiums, the PDC will be paid 10 percent of the sales proceeds in excess of $120,000, in partial recompense for the public subsidies for the project, which included infrastructure development, ten-year tax abatements, and land-cost writedowns to $2,000 per unit.

All the rental and condominium units benefit from the proximity of the RAC and its extensive facilities, which include a large pool. Because the RAC was adjacent to the residential units, TCR did not bear either development or

Weyerhaeuser sold the second phase, including 108 rental apartments, 13,332 square feet (1,240 square meters) of ground-floor retail space, a 302-space parking garage, the air rights above the parking structure, and the adjacent 2.73 acres (1.1 hectares) of land, to Trammell Crow Residential. The decision to construct only private parking garages, which charge among the highest rates in the downtown, has hindered both retail use and public access. *William P. Macht*

operational costs for recreational facilities. Joggers, reinforcing the synergies of the mixed-use location, make heavy use of the extensive pathway along the waterfront greenway.

Between 1993 and 1995, the PDC turned an unsolicited inquiry about the Portland labor market into an eight-story, 106,000-square-foot (9,850-square-meter) corporate headquarters for Pacific Gas Transmission (PGT—now known as PG&E Gas Transmission NW), the largest U.S. transporter of Canadian natural gas. Looking to relocate its headquarters from San Francisco to the Northwest, the company challenged the PDC to lower the construction costs enough to make them competitive with a site in suburban Vancouver, across the border in Washington State. The PDC induced the Oregon Office of Energy to use tax-exempt bonds to lower development costs and helped arrange an efficient turnkey development agreement with a local developer, Robert K. Gerding, to bring the $21 million project in on time and within budget. At a price of

The café of the Harborside Restaurant extends onto the esplanade in front of the marina. *William P. Macht*

$20 per square foot ($215 per square meter), the PDC also provided a waterfront site on which it had recently completed years of environmental remediation.

Pioneering Development

As the redevelopment progressed, the PDC became more opportunity driven—choosing, for example, to locate the PGT corporate headquarters on a waterfront site, which might have been more valuable for a hotel and housing, rather than to lose the development.

By the late 1990s, in its revised development strategy, the PDC recognized that "markets are constantly changing, some peaking while others are emerging. With long-term urban development projects like RiverPlace, it is essential to assess past expectations and balance them with current and near future trends." In July 1997, the PDC convened a workshop with development experts from Portland, San Diego, San Francisco, and Seattle to formulate a new development strategy for its four remaining parcels. By that time, major downtown projects were in

development and competing for office and retail tenants; six downtown hotel projects were bringing nearly 2,000 rooms on line; and the downtown residential market had strengthened: rental vacancy rates were low, and condominium sales were brisk.

In this environment, the PDC decided to continue the checkerboard development strategy it had followed previously by offering a waterfront site (Parcel 5) for an extended-stay hotel, even though it was its least desirable site, and offering an inland site (Parcel 8, opposite the PGT building) for another job-rich regional headquarters. For the last inland project (Parcel 3, which was next to the power substation), the PDC sought affordable rental housing above a full-line grocery store. For its last waterfront site (Parcel 6, later redesignated Parcel 1), which was over two Portland city blocks in size, the PDC sought a capstone project that would include a full-service hotel and upscale condominiums.

In January 2000, after a two-year solicitation process, the PDC closed on the sale of Parcel 5 under a redevelopment agreement with InnVentures, Inc., a northwest franchisee for Marriott Residence Inns, for the construction of a 258-room Marriott Residence Inn. The $2 million transaction for the 1.55-acre (0.6-hectare) site represents the largest cash land sale, at almost $30 per square foot ($323 per square meter), that the PDC had closed since the beginning of the RiverPlace project. Because the site is immediately adjacent to the double decks and ramps of the Marquam Bridge, it cannot be used for permanent housing: at 75 decibels, noise levels from the bridge substantially exceed the 65-decibel limit set by the U.S. Department of Housing and Urban Development. Because site constraints and piling costs limited parking to only 139 spaces (a ratio of only 0.5 spaces per unit), the hotel had to increase its operational expenses by offering valet parking, at least until the PDC is be able to lease land from the state for parking under the interstate bridge. The $35 million hotel opened in June 2001.

In the fall of 1998, the PDC requested proposals for the remaining three parcels in RiverPlace. Parcel 3, in the southwest corner of the site, is planned for a mix of more than 200 market-rate and affordable units. In addition, the PDC is requiring development of a full-line, ground-floor grocery of between 25,000 and 35,000 square feet (between 2,325 and 3,250 square meters). This site will be released for development in fall 2003.

Parcel 8, just west of the PGT building, is offered as a site for a Class A corporate or regional headquarters with a minimum area of 100,000 square feet (9,290 square meters) and a maximum parking ratio of 2:1. The PDC's minimum land price is $25 per square foot ($269 per square meter).

Through a combination of luck, timing, and planning, the PDC's capstone project for RiverPlace is Parcel 1. The luck stems from the fact that geotechnical problems and delays in environmental remediation prevented the waterfront site from being available during periods when the market was weaker. More than two and one-half Portland city blocks in size, Parcel 1 is the largest remaining site, the last waterfront site, and the site with the best views; it is also adjacent to the new South Waterfront Park, com-

pleted in October 1999 at a cost of $4.3 million. Parcel 1 is planned for a full-service, 110-room hotel and high-rise condominium housing. The $76 million proposal is the result of an August 2001 development agreement between the PDC and RiverPlace Partners, which is represented by Homer Williams, a leading developer of downtown housing in Portland's successful Pearl and River districts. Plans call for two buildings, one with 11 floors and the other with eight floors, on the west side of the property. The condominiums are expected to be sold at over $300 per square foot ($3,229 per square meter). Construction is slated to begin in the late summer of 2003.

RiverPlace Partners is working with developer Gordon Sondland, of the Seattle-based Aspen Group, on the hotel. Sondland, who developed downtown Portland's new Westin Hotel, is negotiating with Inter-Continental Hotels, a worldwide chain of nearly 200 hotels, to operate the hotel. The hotel and condominium complex will include a public plaza connected to South Waterfront Park. The PDC expects to add visitor parking under the Marquam Bridge.

Lessons Learned

Short-term market pressures can overwhelm long-term objectives. Cornerstone's long-term development objectives, for example, were compromised by the short-term demands of its joint-venture partner. While most people agree that the public goals for the redevelopment of scarce waterfront land assets should not change annually to respond to short-term business cycles, maintaining focus is not always easy. The PDC, for example, had to resist the temptation to sell a prime hotel site for office or residential use when those segments of the market were hot and hotels were not.

Long-term objectives need periodic reality checks. By 1996, 15 years after construction began, the PDC recognized that its plans for the buildout of the remaining parcels needed to reflect a vastly changed real estate market.

To ensure that the decisions it would make over the next five to seven years would have the support of its private volunteer board and the city's elected officials, the PDC convened a group of public and private development experts to reexamine the strengths of the remaining parcels, to evaluate the types of uses that would be successful from a market perspective, and to consider strategies that would strengthen the mixed-use character of the emerging neighborhood.

Local developers may often plan and develop more marketable projects than out-of-town developers. Bill Naito's understanding of the local market led him to propose plans that omitted most retail and focused on two-bedroom rentals rather than one-bedroom condominiums, and Naito's perceptions turned out to be right. Cornerstone was forced to rent condominiums that it could not sell, and to combine one-bedroom units in order to create the two-bedroom units that the market demanded.

Early planning decisions can overpower development logic. The decision to develop the at-grade extension to downtown as a large, grassy, amphitheater park, rather than as mixed use, made RiverPlace an island—separated by distance, grade, and highway ramps from the downtown core. If the amphitheater had been juxtaposed with the retail, restaurant, housing, office, hotel, and marina uses at the terminus of the four downtown streets at the higher elevation, closer to downtown, pedestrian connections and retail uses would have been much stronger. If the downtown grid had been functionally extended along those four higher streets—rather than symbolically extended in the plan, but not in the elevation, at the lower grades, farther south—density could have been increased, and the prospects for the retail component could have been improved. Furthermore, the apparent continuation of the street grid through RiverPlace Square, the TCR townhouse project, is foiled by mazelike private streets. The result is a triumph of form over substance: few public streets are aligned with the Portland street grid, and there is minimal on-street public parking.

Changes in planning practice that occur during long-term development projects affect urban waterfront density. The long time frame for the development of RiverPlace—nearly a quarter-century—meant that the more suburban planning conventions and conceptions popular in the 1970s were carried over into a period when both planning principles and the market had become more urban. The lower-density superblocks that were subsidized in the earlier years of the project, for example, would be precluded now. Similarly, plans that limited the project's connection to the downtown, and the decision not to challenge or renegotiate a deed restriction, led to a much more suburban, auto-dependent, low-rise development than would have resulted if River-Place had been conceived as an extension of down-

InnVentures, a northwest franchisee for Marriott Residence Inns, completed construction of a 258-room Marriott Residence Inn in June 2001. The hotel adjoins the eight-story, 106,000-square-foot (9,850-square-meter) corporate headquarters for PG&E Gas Transmission NW, the largest U.S. transporter of Canadian natural gas. Foreground: 57 surface spaces and the 164-space parking structure for the office building.

town rather than as an extension of Waterfront Park. Moreover, the proposed development of a 12-story, 150-unit condominium building on the waterfront generated opposition from residents of the three-story, suburban-style residential units upon which RiverPlace was initially based.

Adequate and convenient public parking is essential to support waterfront retail, restaurants, athletic clubs, hotels, and other uses. Although the substantial parking problem at RiverPlace may be a sign of its success, the fact that the city limits retail parking to a 1:1 ratio (one space per 1,000 square feet—93 square meters—of gross leasable area) has proven to be a severe impediment to both the development and operation of retail space. In addition, the decision to build only private parking garages, which charge among the highest rates in the downtown, has hindered both retail use and public access. Similarly, the fact that cost constraints limited the Marriott Residence Inn to a parking ratio of only 0.5:1 places a difficult burden on the operator. While shared parking may be feasible for office and restaurant uses, it is difficult for restaurant and residential uses, which compete for parking in similar peak periods. And, in the case of condominium uses that require some assigned parking or rental townhouses that have attached private garages (of the type developed by TCR), shared parking is particularly unlikely to work. In hindsight, PDC officials would have built larger public parking structures and negotiated more extensive shared parking arrangements. However, agreements with the office developers stipulate that the PDC does retain the right to arrange shared parking for other users during nonpeak evening and weekend periods.

Public transit in the area is currently marginal; although it is not ever likely to be adequate to serve retail needs, improving public transit might at least assist with employee recruitment. As the North Macadam area, to the south of RiverPlace, is developed, the PDC plans to

South of the marina, the Portland Development Commission completed South Waterfront Park in October 1999 at a cost of $4.3 million. To the south of the park is the site for the construction of 150 condominiums and a 100-room hotel. *William P. Macht*

extend the new streetcar system that is intended to run adjacent to RiverPlace.

A waterfront-inland development sequence can maximize values. A checkerboard pattern of development—hopscotching from waterfront site to inland site and back to waterfront site—is relatively effective in stimulating demand for inland sites that are adjacent to the waterfront and increasing the value of the waterfront sites that are developed later in the process. The disadvantage of this approach, however, is that when a financially strong developer or corporate anchor tenant, like PGT, indicates a strong preference for a waterfront site, it is very difficult for a public agency to resist the temptation to negotiate a development agreement on such a site—even when the public development agency would prefer an inland site. Deferring environmental remediation on waterfront sites until the market value of the land has increased (and thereby covering the cost of cleanup) may fortuitously assist the public agency in saving the best sites for the last and reinforce the desired checkerboard sequence. However, the public agency must take care to complete the entitlement process for all waterfront sites because changes in environmental rules may increase setback and other requirements in such a way as to make the sites undevelopable under any reasonable conditions. In fact, some of the developed waterfront sites, including the floating restaurant at the RiverPlace marina, would likely be precluded under current rules.

Using master developers can slow the pace of development and hinder market capture. In the case of RiverPlace, the master developers were subsidiaries of large corporate parents that were moving into and out of the real estate development business and were unfamiliar with local markets. Their decision to create for-sale rather than rental housing products was not responsive to local markets. Ironically, the financial strength that was so appealing to the PDC may have eliminated the market discipline to which canny local developers would have been subject.

Smaller parcels can be used to diversify developers. Limiting the size of development parcels allows the development agency to increase the number of local developers, improve its ability to address market niches, spread the risk among more committed developers, and lessen the damage caused by inevitable project shortfalls. Smaller local developers survive only if they know markets well and act nimbly to capture them. Spreading the risk among a number of local developers actually lowers the risk for the public agency, which would otherwise be drawn to the apparent financial stability of master devel-

opers. The diversity of developers will also increase the diversity of the architecture, creating a more naturally urban and urbane experience.

Long-term development may entail substantial risk for public development agencies, as well as for the private developers who depend upon them. Midway through the development period, the PDC's authority to issue tax-exempt tax increment bonds was compromised by a successful statewide initiative put forth by tax limitation groups. The PDC was then forced to pay off bonds with revenues from the general fund, which severely limited its ability to structure deals and to make further public investments. Fortunately, by 1996, phenomenal growth in property valuations in the central city had helped the PDC to overcome a negative cash flow, and a new tax measure had virtually restored the PDC's ability to collect the full tax increment to support the issuance of new bonds. Because the PDC is a particularly strong agency, led by commissioners who have considerable private development experience and political independence, it has been able to avoid many of the kinds of difficulties that plague other, less experienced development agencies.

Developers, owners, and tenants from earlier phases will gain a vested interest in the project that often conflicts with the plans of public development agencies. At RiverPlace, for example,

■ The owners and tenants of existing three-story condominiums and apartments objected to development of a 12-story luxury condominium tower, sought by the PDC, that would have blocked their views of the water.

■ The owners of the RiverPlace Hotel objected to the fact that the PDC later recruited and offered incentives to a direct competitor—one that was even closer to the water.

■ When the PDC proposed the construction of new restaurants and hotels, on the theory that the new uses would support public transit, owners of existing restaurants and shops (already crippled by inadequate and expensive parking) objected, contending that the new uses would also have inadequate parking, and that their anticipated effects on public transit use were unproven.

■ When the PDC proposed the removal of the Montgomery Street traffic circle, existing residents objected, claiming that the circle is essential for traffic flow and visitor parking.

■ Existing businesses insisted that the PDC provide public restrooms to ease visitors' use of their facilities; the same businesses also protested the PDC's failure to include them in development strategy workshops.

Favorable participating mortgages can replace land-cost writedowns. If the development agreements had been undertaken today, the PDC might have sold the land at full market value, rather than at the more restricted "fair reuse value," and used the proceeds to make a loan to the developer, in a participating mortgage, under favorable terms. Such an arrangement may have been more palatable to the public than land-cost writedowns, which the public perceives as subsidies, and may have offered the PDC a greater share of the proceeds from successful projects.

Significant synergies can be achieved in mixed-use development, especially when one owner owns several uses. For example, RiverPlace LLC, the current owner of the Cornerstone projects, owns the RiverPlace Athletic Club, whose facilities are available, at no charge, to guests in the RiverPlace Hotel, as well to users of the RiverPlace Marina, which conducts rowing classes for athletic club members and rents slips to residents. RiverPlace LLC also owns parking facilities, which it makes available, at reduced rates, to patrons of the restaurants and retail shops that it owns, and to the tenants in its office build-ings. Such synergies are much harder to achieve when different uses have different owners.

Without subsidies, geotechnical and environmental problems can make development projects economically infeasible. The unstable fill of the waterfront land—which consisted of 40-foot- (12-meter-) deep layers of sawdust saturated with fuel oils and other chemicals—required all structures, including parking slabs, to be on deep piling. To reduce the costs of eliminating environmental damage, public agencies need to work with private developers to create and subsidize innovative techniques, such as augur cast piling.[1] Without the support of a public agency, private developers would have a much more difficult time securing approvals for the use of such innovative methods. The increased setbacks that environmentalists are seeking in connection with salmon recovery efforts have also reduced the potential for waterfront development in Portland. As a result of both environmental complexities and economic constraints, RiverPlace may remain an island of urban waterfront development, albeit one that has gained a reputation for livability and is a symbol of waterfront renaissance.

Note

1. In this technique, concrete is forced, under pressure, into holes that have been dug in contaminated soils, in such a way as to instantly seal the holes, thus preventing any leakage of environmental contaminants.

Project Data: **RiverPlace**

Land Use Information

Site area (acres/hectares)	73/30
Site acquisition cost	$3.9 million
Site improvement cost	$16 million

Project Information
RiverPlace I

Developer	Cornerstone Columbia Development Company
Year completed	1985
Site area (acres/hectares)	6/2.5
Total investment	$64 million

Use	Square Feet/Square Meters	Number and Type of Units	Number of Parking Spaces
Hotel	68,266/6,340	74 rooms; 10 condominiums in adjacent building (used for hotel guests)	98
Housing	178,494/16,580	180 condominiums	267
Office	38,515/ 3,580		Mill Street Circle garage: 38 exclusively for office tenants; 60 for office use on weekdays
Retail	20,147/1,870		Montgomery Street garage: 42 public spaces, none dedicated to retail
Floating restaurant	3,121/290		No dedicated parking
Athletic club	47,000/4,370		75
Marina	N.A.[a]	83 wet slips; 120 dry dock	N.A.
Total	355,543/33,030		580

a. Not applicable.

RiverPlace II

Developer	Cornerstone Columbia Development Company
Year completed	1990
Site area (acres/hectares)	3.3/1.3
Total private investment	$16 million

Use	Square Feet/Square Meters	Number and Type of Units	Number of Parking Spaces
Housing	119,610/11,110	108 rental units: 56 one-bedroom; 24 two-bedroom, one-bath; 28 two-bedroom, two-bath	115 in garage, of which 26 are tandem (shared) spaces
Retail	6,332/590		
Restaurant	7,000/650		302 in public garage
Office	2,700/251	Rental	
Total	135,642/12,600		417

RiverPlace Square Townhouses

Developer	Trammell Crow Residential, Pacific Northwest
Year completed	1995
Site area (acres/hectares)	2.7/1.1
Type of use	Residential
Number and type of units	182 rental units: 22 studios; 5 one-bedroom flats; 74 one-bedroom townhouses; 79 two-bedroom townhouses; 2 three-bedroom townhouses
Area (RiverPlace II housing and RiverPlace Square Townhouses; square feet/ square meters)	244,590/22,725
Number of parking spaces	211
Total private investment (approximate)	$15 million

PG&E Gas Transmission NW

Developer	Gerding Investment Company
Year completed	1995
Site area (acres/hectares)	1.2/0.48
Type of use	Office headquarters
Area (square feet/square meters)	106,158/9,860
Number of parking spaces	164 structured; 57 surface
Total private investment (approximate)	$15 million

South Waterfront Park

Developer	Portland Development Commission
Year completed	1999
Site area (acres/hectares)	4/1.6
Type of use	Open space with retail kiosk and public restroom
Area (square feet/square meters; kiosk only)	210/20
Parking	No dedicated parking; approximately 80 on-street public parking spaces in the RiverPlace area
Hard construction costs	$4.3 million
Total public investment	$4.3 million

Residence Inn by Marriott

Developer	InnVentures, Inc.
Year completed	2001
Site area (acres/hectares)	1.55/0.6
Type of use	Extended-stay hotel
Number and type of units	258: studios, one-bedroom, and two-bedroom
Area (square feet/square meters)	277,054/25,740
Parking	139 structured spaces on site; 75 planned off site
Total private investment	$35 million

Project Data: **RiverPlace** (Continued)

Pending and Future Development

Site	Acres/Hectares	Planned Use	Area (Square Feet/ Square Meters)	Number and Type of Units	Number of Parking Spaces	Cost (Millions)
Pending Development						
		Boutique hotel	80,000/7,430	100–120 rooms	67	$16
Parcel 1	2.6/1.05	Retail	2,000/185	1 restaurant	0	
		Housing	300,000/27,870	150 condominiums	249	$57
Future Development						
Lot 8	1.2/0.48	Commercial office headquarters	100,000/9,290		Maximum according to code is 2/1,000 square feet	
		Grocery	25,000/2,320		Maximum according to code is 1/1,000 square feet	
Parcel 3	2.1/0.85					
		Residential	200,000/18,580	200 rental units	Maximum according to code is 1/bedroom	

Note: All figures except those for the site area are estimates.

Project Timeline

1978	Portland City Council extends the Downtown Urban Renewal District to include 73 acres (30 hectares) of undeveloped waterfront land	1985	Cornerstone completes Phase I
		1987	Pacific Power and Light donates the steam plant and the surrounding area
1979	City council adopts the South Waterfront Development Program, which was created by the Portland Development Commission (PDC)	1990	Cornerstone-Columbia completes Phase II
		1995	Trammell Crow Residential, in a joint venture with Prudential Realty Pension Fund, completes RiverPlace Square
1982	The PDC begins land acquisition	1995	Gerding Investment Company completes Pacific Gas Transmission Headquarters
1983	The amphitheater and marina basin are completed		
January 1983	The PDC issues requests for qualifications to seek qualified developers	1997	The PDC revises the RiverPlace development strategy
		1999	The PDC completes South Waterfront Park
April 1983	The PDC selects the Seattle-based Cornerstone Development Company	2001	InnVentures completes the Marriott Residence Inn

Source: Portland Development Commission.

Major Project Participants

Portland Development Commission
Portland, Oregon
Web site: www.portlanddev.org

Brian McCarl Company
Portland, Oregon

BBS International, RiverPlace Associates, LLC
Portland, Oregon
Web site: www.bbsinternational.com

RiverPlace Athletic Club
Portland, Oregon

RiverPlace Hotel
Portland, Oregon

Trammell Crow Residential Services
Portland, Oregon
www.tcresidential.com/communities/index.php?state=Oregon

Gerding/Edlen Development Company
Portland, Oregon
www.ge-dev.com/

InnVentures, Inc.
Bellevue, Washington

RiverPlace Partners, LLC
Portland, Oregon 97209

Waterplace Park and Providence Place

Providence, Rhode Island

William P. Macht

The renaissance of downtown Providence proves that with vision, creativity, flexibility, and shrewd determination, a city can bury railroads, move rivers, relocate freeways, and recapture waterfronts. In less than 20 years, Providence, Rhode Island, has transformed itself from a bypassed backwater into what *Money* magazine described as the most livable city in the Northeast and the *New York Times* architecture critic called "a Venice in New England." (The city was also featured in the popular television series *Providence*.) Two projects in particular, Waterplace Park and Providence Place, symbolize Providence's commitment to its rebirth—and to its waterfronts.

A Bypassed Backwater

The gem of Providence's waterfront—the Cove Basin, which had been surrounded, in the mid-19th century, by the wide Cove Promenade—gradually became polluted by overflowing sewers and by the wastes from woolen mills, textile-dyeing plants, and meat-packing plants. Over time, the cove was filled to build rail yards; the three rivers—the Providence, the Woonasquatucket, and the Moshassuck—that converged in the downtown were covered with parking decks; through-streets were terminated; elevated tracks severed the historic capitol building from downtown; and downtown retailers left for the suburbs.

Providence's decline was best symbolized by the closure, in 1975, of its beloved Biltmore Hotel—an event that galvanized the city's corporate leaders. Led by Bill Miller (then chairman of Textron, later chairman of the Federal Reserve Board and then Secretary of the Treasury), a private group of civic leaders purchased, rehabilitated, and reopened the elaborate landmark hotel. Formalizing its commitment to downtown revitalization, the group formed the Providence Foundation to target catalytic investment opportunities.

The Providence Foundation was initially chaired by Bruce Sundlun, who had had a storied career—World War II bomber pilot shot down over Germany, Harvard-educated lawyer and head of a 23-person Washington, D.C., and Providence law firm, former assistant attorney general in the Truman administration, chairman and chief executive officer of Outlet Communications, and later a two-term governor of Rhode Island. One of the foundation's first projects was to address the problem of the elevated railroad tracks, known as the "Chinese Wall," that had long separated downtown from the elaborate statehouse designed by preeminent architects McKim, Mead & White. The architectural and planning firm of Skidmore, Owings & Merrill (SOM) was retained to produce the Capital Center Plan, which would bury the railroad tracks under an exten-

The Riverwalk runs the entire length of the revitalized riverfronts, past the Citizens' Bank headquarters and under graceful new bridges. Metal braziers suspended above the river are used for *Waterfire*, a site-specific artwork conceived for the Riverwalk. *William P. Macht*

sion of the statehouse lawn, construct a new railroad station above the submerged tracks, and transform the parking lots ringing the south end of the lawn into development parcels. From the frequent flights Sundlun piloted between Washington and Providence, Sundlun knew that his passenger, Senator Claiborne Pell, had a fear of flying but was a confirmed railroad buff. Sundlun's connection to Pell and knowledge of Pell's railroad predilections made it possible for him to get Pell to facilitate a $5 million federal grant to help bury the tracks and relocate the station.

Although the Capital Center Plan tackled the railroad problem and included a major downtown interchange at Route I-95, a short boulevard, and the 35-acre (14-hectare) Capital Center Development District, it did not address the traffic congestion on the decks covering the rivers, nor the funding for the design and implementation of a four-acre (1.6-hectare) waterfront park.

Three young architects who were members of the design review commission were displeased with the flaws they found in the SOM plan, but they were not successful at persuading the commission to change it. While drowning their sorrows at what they termed a "memorial burial dinner," the three colleagues from RISD—the Rhode Island School of Design—developed a radical solution, broad in scope, that would move the rivers, relocate the I-195 freeway, recapture the jewelry district, and line the rivers with walkways all the way to Providence Harbor, on Narragansett Bay. According to Friedrich St. Florian, who was among the three at the dinner, it was only Bill Warner who, of the three

Along Francis Street, which leads from downtown to the capitol, 160,000 square feet (14,865 square meters) of street-level retail and restaurants spill out onto a wide side-walk. *Peter Goldberg*

young architects, had the vision, shrewdness, and tenacity to turn that plan (sketched on a napkin that now hangs on St. Florian's wall) into a river renaissance realized.

A Radical Solution

Bill Warner is an urban enthusiast who presides over an atelier of young architects in a small historic cotton mill in rural Exeter, Rhode Island. Warner knows the power of simple ideas and the importance of communicating them simply. He reasoned that the key to changing minds and securing funds was to describe the architects' plan as a solution to a transportation problem. In the spring of 1982, he met with the directors of the state transportation and environmental management departments. Pointing out that the Capital Center Plan had failed to address traffic congestion or waterfront access, Warner persuaded the directors that a study of the larger picture of waterfront access could yield approaches to improving congestion not only in the Capital Center but also along the remaining Providence waterfront. Both Warner and the directors knew that the National Endowment for the Arts (NEA) had funding available for urban design studies that involved the public in the process, but they needed a sponsor quickly.

Seeking support to obtain federal funds to help revitalize downtown, Warner approached the Providence Foundation. As Sundlun describes it, because he had recently seen the San Antonio River Walk (which was located near one of his television stations) and understood what it had done for that city, Warner's description of a riverfront walkway for Providence piqued Sundlun's interest, and the foundation immediately agreed to sponsor the study. On May 18, 1983, the NEA and state, city, and business entities announced $125,000 in funding for the Providence Waterfront Study.

Warner worked quickly, and in less than five months he had not only assembled a 20-member working team of major stakeholders (including city, state, and federal agencies—environment, transportation, city planning, state planning, and historic preservation—as well as key private sector organizations, among them the Providence Foundation), but also produced a plan they all accepted as their own. A six-month deadline set by the Providence & Worcester (P&W) Railroad, the principal landowner along the rivers, motivated the group to work quickly and cooperatively. Unless an alternative was proposed within the specified period, the railroad intended to go ahead with its prior development plans, which were completely inconsistent with the proposal to move the river.

Relocating the River

In accordance with the plan, the river was moved out from under the post office, and the confluence of the rivers was relocated nearly 100 yards (91 meters) to the east. Those changes made it possible to extend Memorial Boulevard, on solid ground, between the post office and the rivers' new confluence. Finally, the decking to the south of the post office was removed, uncovering the Providence River, and Memorial Boulevard was extended south to Crawford Street, along the downtown side of the Providence River. This scheme included the following additional features:

■ An independent river walkway system: Providence River Park—a Y-shaped, landscaped river corridor—was created at the center of the city to connect existing parks, accommodate boat traffic, and establish an independent walkway system from the Capital Center and the statehouse to Kennedy Plaza and Crawford Street. A new federal program established in 1984 provided 100 percent funding for independent walkway systems.

■ Circulation: All existing decking was removed, making possible the construction of 12 elegant bridges to reconnect the existing east-west streets and pedestrian routes. In addition to improving aesthetics, the bridges clarified the circulation patterns and relieved congestion.

■ Navigation: To accommodate boat traffic, the rivers were dredged, and a uniform clearance under the bridges was established. Three docking places were provided for boats to discharge and take on passengers. Between these boat landings, cleats for boat lines, conveniently spaced along the Riverwalk, provided access for visiting boats.

■ Memorial Park: Anchoring the southern portion of the project, the two-acre (0.8-hectare) Memorial Park provided the historic courthouse setting for the World War I Monument that was relocated from a treacherously congested traffic circle (which Warner referred to as Suicide Circle). The northern edge of the park is defined by the historic brick Market House; this and other RISD buildings line 650 linear feet (198 meters) of the Riverwalk and are accessible from it.

■ Waterplace Park: A four-acre (1.6-hectare) park was created at the western terminus of the walkway system; it features a 30-foot- (9-meter-) high fountain, an amphitheater, several smaller plazas with seating, two pedestrian bridges, and a pavilion that houses a restaurant and a visitors' center.

Warner had a keen sense of history, and had been careful from the start to include historic preservationists in his planning. The circular basin that became Waterplace

Visitors to the Waterplace Park basin may walk to Old Union Station via an arched underpass. *William P. Macht*

The four-acre (1.6-hectare) Waterplace Park, which punctuates the western terminus of the walkway system, features a 30-foot-(nine-meter-) high fountain, an amphitheater, and a pavilion building that accommodates a restaurant and visitors' center. Providence Place spans the Woonasquatucket River and the main Amtrak line, which leads to a new domed railroad station (shown here on the right, below the capitol). *Commonwealth Development Group*

Park was based on the historic elliptical Cove Basin, created from a natural cove that, in the mid-19th century, was surrounded by the Cove Promenade, a wide structure with cast-iron railings and seats. Constructed between 1846 and 1856, the promenade was the result of a public/private partnership between the P&W Railroad and the city, and became the site for all kinds of gatherings, from circus performances to holiday celebrations. During the next three decades, however, the cove became so polluted that the railroads succeeded in their efforts to fill the "filthy cove"—and then built rail yards and the Chinese Wall of elevated tracks. The perception that the polluted rivers were no more than nuisances occupying valuable space in the heart of the city persisted well into the 20th century, as was evidenced by the fact that the city covered them with parking lots.

Realizing a Riverfront Renaissance

Once it became clear that the river needed to be moved to make the whole project work, it also became clear that the landowner, Capital Properties (P&W's successor), was adamantly opposed to the relocation. The opposition puzzled Sundlun, who eventually learned through an assistant, a close friend of Capital's chairman, that the former executive director of the Providence Foundation had an undisclosed development agreement to pay Capital $2 million for land on which to build a new headquarters for Citizens' Bank—land that was located on the site to which the river was to be moved. To break the deadlock, Sundlun got a $2 million commitment from the publisher of the *Providence Journal* to buy the land. Sundlun then persuaded Capital's chairman that if the company went ahead with the original development deal, Capital would have to wait almost two years to get paid, but that he was prepared to pay immediately. Sundlun's proposal changed Capital's decision, but the firm declined the immediate payment, preferring to get considerably more by holding onto the land and waiting for condemnation. Capital also profited from the relocation of the bank to a nearby site that was now located on the point of the new confluence of the three rivers—and that was now also a much more valuable waterfront site.

In 1984, the city, the state, and the Federal Highway Administration (FHA) committed to funding the project. In 1985, Warner and a group of engineers designed the River Relocation Project. Phased construction began in 1987, on the first of five contracts, the last of which was completed in 1996. The total cost of the project, including the Memorial Boulevard extension, all the bridges, the Riverwalk, the parks and plazas, the relocation of the rivers, and the construction of Waterplace Park, was $66 million, most of which was funded by the FHA. The project had been "sold" as a transportation project, and the waterfront improvements were a by-product but had been written into the contract documents.

Although the arrangements may have been unusual—having an architect maintain design control over what was primarily an engineering project—the result is striking, featuring graceful bridges; varied parks and plazas at different elevations; and classic street lighting, furniture, and finishes. Warner even took care to match the construction materials to their surroundings—using granite, for example, near the Old Stone Bank and the Custom House, brick near the courthouse, and concrete near the Textron headquarters. The entire project was knit together by a series of tile plaques and graphic panels, incorporated along the Riverwalk, that create a self-guided tour that explains and celebrates the city's waterfront heritage. Warner's staff based the panels on historic photos, maps, and engravings supplied by the Rhode Island Historical Society. Even cost-saving measures were based on historical precedent: bridge piers and granite blocks were reused where possible, and bronze railings were employed to eliminate the need for repainting. The amphitheater and the restaurant use—and disguise—the

40-foot- (12-meter-) high wall that had been left by the earlier construction of the underground tracks and a new road. Warner points out that simply removing the earlier disruptions to the underlying grid pattern improved traffic flow.

Architects celebrated the river by building a deeply recessed glass wintergarden over it, which divides the mass of the mall in two; this approach opened the mall to the city and created a beacon of activity that is especially visible at night, when the retail and entertainment center is busiest. *Peter Goldberg*

Providence Place

Although the rivers ultimately affected the city's form, the largest development project on the new waterfront was brought to Providence not by the rivers but by the highways. Providence is at the intersection of two major interstate highways—I-95, which runs north-south, and I-195, which runs east-west. With the new downtown ramps just a short distance from each other, downtown Providence—at the center of a trading area of 1.1 million, with 40 percent less department store space than the national average—was a natural location for a regional mall. The downtown offered only minimal retail space and no department stores, yet was only a short distance from most of Providence's neighborhoods. In addition to easy access, the area also offered unmatched visibility: a 13.2-acre (5.3-hectare) site that adjoined I-95, was immediately adjacent to the Capitol building, and was held by only two owners—one of which was the state.

The food court at Providence Place overlooks downtown and the Waterplace Park basin. Beneath the wintergarden and above the five tracks of the Amtrak main line, concrete steps and pedestrian ramps line the river. *William P. Macht*

Leading mall developers Melvin Simon and Nathan Landow won development rights to the site but ultimately sold the opportunity, for $7 million, to another experienced developer, the Syracuse-based Pyramid Companies. On the last day of his term, Governor Bruce Sundlun and colorful veteran Mayor Vincent (Buddy) Cianci negotiated and signed a development agreement with Bob Congel, chief executive officer of Pyramid, and one of Congel's chief lieutenants, Dan Lugosch. Under that agreement, the state and city agreed to build a 4,500-car parking garage. The garage would be funded primarily by federal transportation funds, which were available because a large number of the

spaces would be reserved for high-occupancy vehicles (HOVs) carrying downtown daytime workers, a strategy that was intended to reduce congestion.

The state would relocate the outmoded building that housed the University of Rhode Island (URI) Continuing Education School and donate to the project the seven acres (three hectares) on which the building had been sited. Sundlun had learned, meanwhile, that it would cost more to rehabilitate the continuing education building than to acquire the vacant Shepard's department store, which had double the floor area, so he made that win-win deal, injecting life into a declining downtown. Unexpectedly, Sundlun lost the Democratic primary for his third term by a narrow margin to a woman who was then defeated by Republican candidate Lincoln Almond, who had run on a platform against the development agreement and for a special public vote on it.

Congel, realizing that with the new governor in office the plan was in jeopardy, wanted to sue the state to compel enforcement of the contract and to obtain about $30 million in default penalties. Lugosch knew that starting a public/private partnership by suing your partner was inauspicious; he also sensed the risk involved in going before a Rhode Island jury to seek the transfer of funds from state resources to private pockets. Taking two other junior partners with him, Lugosch bought out Congel's interest and started Commonwealth Development Group to develop the project. Not only did this entail an immediate personal risk—Lugosch gave up a steady income to create his own firm and develop the project—but Lugosch had also, it turned out, assumed the risk of litigation from a former partner of Congel's, Alexius C. Conroy. Conroy claimed that he had right of first refusal on the retail development and contended that Congel's sale to Lugosch had triggered that right. Although Conroy's claim was eventually settled, the litigation would later delay critical financing for almost a year.

During months of long renegotiation with the new state administration, which was being pressured by business interests not to kill the project, Lugosch and economist Gary Sasse devised a clever technique to obtain a level of subsidy, without which the project could not be built, that would be equivalent to that included in the original agreement but still address the state's concerns. Lugosch's idea was that the Commonwealth Development Group and the state, as partners, would split the sales tax revenues generated by Providence Place for the first 20 years, but the developer's portion would be capitalized to pay the debt service on bonds floated to build the parking garages, which would have been built by the state in the earlier agreement.

The proposal was elegantly simple. The additional sales tax revenue could be generated only if the mall was built. No existing state funds were diverted—and in fact, the state would retain the other portion of the sales tax revenues as a bonus. Attorney Jay Gowell describes the plan as a kind of "sales tax TIF" (tax increment financing), except that it was tied to an entity, not to a district. To remove any question about its constitutionality, the plan was formally voted on in the legislature and was approved by a two-thirds vote of both houses.

Furthermore, all the construction risk—which was considerable, since the garage would be built over a river and the Amtrak main lines—was shifted to the private developer, Providence Place Group Limited Partnership (PPG, the Commonwealth Development Group's development entity for the project), which was obligated to complete it on time and within budget. The developer's portion of the annual sales tax receipts had an absolute annual cap of $3.6 million ($72 million over 20 years), or two-thirds of actual annual sales tax receipts collected from the mall, whichever came first.

PPG also paid $11 million to Amtrak for the remaining 6.2-acre (2.5-hectare) parcel and then donated it to the state. Now in possession of the full 13.2 acres (5.3 hectares), the state leased it back to the developer for $1,000 per year for 99 years, with four 99-year renewal periods. The Rhode Island Economic Development Corporation (RIEDC) could then float tax-exempt bonds for the public portions of the project. PPG leased the land on which the garage was to be built and agreed not only to assume all construction risk, but also to assume all operating risk and to fund any operating deficits of the

parking garage. PPG further agreed to make 500 spaces available as HOV spaces at deep discounts. (The HOV rate begins at 25 percent of the average daily rate and declines with each additional member of the carpool, so that a six-person carpool would pay less than 10 percent of the daily rate.) Two years after the project opened, favorable interest rates and the strength of its previous track record allowed the RIEDC to refinance $41.5 million in bonds.

The development agreement with the state was a voluminous document imposing a number of conditions on PPG; for example, the document established the identity and size of the anchor tenants, identified permissible lenders, set completion dates, established requirements for environmental remediation, set hiring standards for minorities and women, required a free minibus shuttle system to downtown, and, onerously, required personal guarantees from the developers. It also gave PPG the right to build a 300,000-square-foot (27,870-square-meter) office building, provided that it supplied additional parking. The agreement made the state responsible for public infrastructure improvements, including sidewalks, an extension of the Riverwalk, and a pedestrian bridge to the 363-room Westin Hotel and the 365,000-square-foot (33,910-square-meter) Rhode Island Convention Center, which had been built in 1993 and was owned by the state.

To understand the next steps in the Providence waterfront story it is necessary to understand a little about its longest-serving mayor, Buddy Cianci. A former state prosecutor, Cianci won the mayoral post in 1974 by running a successful campaign against an entrenched Democratic machine. Forced from office ten years later after pleading guilty to assaulting his estranged wife's boyfriend, Cianci then became a television commentator and radio talk-show host, and was reelected as mayor in 1990. Despite his indictment, in 2001, as a result of the Plunder Dome FBI sting operation, he remained mayor of Providence until his conviction in the summer of 2002,

Steps, bollards, and flagpoles define the Riverwalk as it widens near the Rhode Island School of Design. *William P. Macht*

the city half the equity for the downtown seven-screen, 1,200-seat Downcity Cinema; a city option to acquire the parking garage jointly with the state in 99 years; and a provision to participate in a 30-year, $8.8 million community reinvestment scheme. Under the reinvestment plan, when annual sales exceeded $400 per square foot ($4,305 per square meter), PPG was obligated to pay the city $200,000 annually, an amount that would increase gradually to $500,000 in the 20th year.

A River Runs through It

The Providence Place site is literally bisected by the Woonasquatucket River, a fact that affected virtually every strategic aspect of the project: its economics (because of the additional engineering costs), its architecture, its relationship to the downtown core, and its regulatory environment. As the design architect, Lugosch hired Friedrich St. Florian, a well-respected Providence architect and RISD professor, and one of the progenitors of the river relocation.[1] St. Florian, who had absorbed the European notion of contextual fit in his native Salzburg, sought ways to offset the enormous scale of the project and to avoid overwhelming its neighbor, the historic capitol building designed by McKim, Mead & White. The mall had been designed to span the river, and the developer wanted a dome on that portion of the building. St. Florian countered that a dome is a static form and that retail has always taken a dynamic, linear form. As an example, St. Florian pointed to the Arcade, a three-level, glass-covered retail building just blocks away; constructed in 1828, the Arcade is the oldest enclosed shopping center in America. St. Florian opted to celebrate the river below by building a deeply recessed glass "wintergarden" over it and dividing the mass in two—an approach that opened the mall to the city and created a beacon of activity that is especially visible at night, when the retail and entertainment center is busiest. The seating area of the food court, on the third level, fills the glazed wintergarden that overlooks the city. On the floor above are a 16-screen, 115,000-square-foot (10,685-square-meter) cinema; a 14,000-square-foot (1,300-square-meter) IMAX theater;

when he chose not to seek reelection. Cianci was a skilled and high-energy civic booster, credited by many with having created an air of excitement about the city's potential for rejuvenation. When Governor Bruce Sundlun piloted his plane to Syracuse to negotiate with Bob Congel, it was Cianci who joined him on the trip.

Cianci had attracted many talented lieutenants, including Patricia McLaughlin, who was originally his chief counsel and subsequently became his chief of staff. It was McLaughlin who negotiated a tax agreement with PPG.

With the state development agreement in hand, Lugosch negotiated a 30-year, $141 million tax stabilization plan with the city. As an inducement to PPG to make its investment, McLaughlin negotiated a provision under which payments in lieu of property taxes are paid, according to a graduated schedule, directly to PPG's lender. The specific commitments McLaughlin obtained from PPG added the following to the requirements of the state agreement: street-level retail along Francis Street; the establishment of job training and preference programs; the creation of a downtown management district; agreement to give

and a 43,000-square-foot (3,995-square-meter) Dave & Buster's entertainment restaurant. Beneath the wintergarden and mall bridge, and above the five tracks of the Amtrak main line, concrete steps and pedestrian ramps line the river and continue the Riverwalk.

The three anchor department stores—Lord & Taylor, Filene's (both May Company stores), and the only Nordstrom in the Boston region—are designed to be solid visual anchors. The mall stores, in contrast, are light, open, and faced with glass. Unfortunately, only two stores take advantage of natural light. The glass of the other stores, although lighted at night, opens to a standard mall service corridor.

Along Francis Street, which leads from downtown to the capitol building, 160,000 square feet (14,865 square meters) of street-level retail shops and restaurants spill out onto a wide sidewalk. These have proven to be much more successful than Lugosch ever expected and have achieved the permeability that St. Florian sought. Unfortunately, because the site slopes more than 30 feet (nine meters), and three continuous levels of retail were thought to be needed above parking, which also needed to bridge the river, only one of the stores on Francis Street flows through into the mall. Because Arrowstreet, the architect of record, stacked two parking levels opposite a retail level, increasing the height of the retail level to 22 feet (6.7 meters), the narrow mall, with its tall columns supporting a peaked glass roof, evokes the nave of a cathedral—an effect that is reinforced by a subdued, neutral color palette. In an unusual move, Lugosch allowed St. Florian's wife, Livia, a noted painter, to design the carpets, which have a simple pattern that is designed to fit seamlessly with, and reinforce, the structure of the mall.

The $450 million mall—with 1,350,000 square feet (125,420 square meters), 150 shops, three department stores, several mini-anchors (like Brooks Brothers, Old Navy, and

Barnes & Noble), a 16-screen cinema, an IMAX theater, and 4,500 structured parking spaces—was the largest single construction project in Rhode Island. Although the project took 13 years to develop, the time frame actually had little to do with the waterfront location. The principal source of delay, on the public side, was the necessity of securing a workable public/private financing deal and getting it enacted into legislation. Lugosch, McLaughlin, and Cianci formed a powerful coalition of labor unions and downtown business interests to counter protests from the owners of suburban malls,

Waterfire, designed by Brown graduate Barnaby Evans, combines primal elements and senses: water, fire, light, sound, and smell. Each summer evening, as the light fades at dusk, gondoliers light stacks of fragrant scrap cedar and pine in metal braziers that are suspended above the river. The smell and sound of crackling fires permeate the Riverwalk, drawing an average of 50,000 people who stroll in near-silence or sit in nearby cafés and restaurants. *Peter Goldberg*

who were concerned about unfair, state-subsidized competition. In addition, because of the waterfront location, the project fell within the jurisdiction of several major regulatory groups, further complicating the process:

■ The Rhode Island Coastal Resources Management Council (CRMC), the state's coastal zone management agency, had jurisdiction over the tidal portion of the Woonasquatucket River. The CRMC's principal concerns were to ensure that the project was compatible with historic structures in the area, to preserve visual and public access to the waterway, and to ensure that marine activities were not obstructed.

■ Because the Woonasquatucket is nominally navigable at this point, the Coast Guard had jurisdiction over any river spans.

■ The Army Corps of Engineers had jurisdiction because the river constitutes both "navigable waters of the U.S." and "waters of the U.S." The corps's principal concern, aside from ensuring that navigation was not obstructed, was to oversee the placing of any fill or structure in the waterway.

■ The Rhode Island Department of Environmental Management (DEM) had "freshwater wetlands" jurisdiction over the waterway and over a 250-foot (76-meter) buffer on either side, as well as jurisdiction over stormwater discharges into the river. Because of the riverfront location, three separate DEM permits were required.

■ The Narragansett Bay Commission (NBC), which operates the regional wastewater treatment plant, requires that stormwater be discharged into the river rather than into the sewer system. The combined requirements of the Army Corps, the DEM, and the NBC shaped the project's very unusual stormwater system.

The permitting process associated with waterfront-related regulatory requirements lasted about two years, from 1994 to 1996; some permits arrived even later. Permitting delays continued even after the state had designated Providence Place a Project of Critical Economic Concern, which entitled it to expedited permitting reviews.

In an unprecedented move, the developer allowed Livia St. Florian, a noted painter and the wife of the architect, to design the carpets for the mall. The carpets' simple pattern fits seamlessly with, and reinforces, the columns and the structure of the mall. *William P. Macht*

According to a Brown University assessment, Providence Place created 1,650 construction jobs and, within one year after opening, over 2,000 permanent jobs. Minority hiring of 12 percent exceeded projections. Taxable sales, although delayed by the late opening of Lord & Taylor, were in the range projected and were more than adequate to cover debt service on the RIEDC bonds. (Since movie tickets and most food, drugs, clothing, and footwear are excluded from the 7 percent sales tax, less than half of all mall sales are taxable.) The $300 million annual out-of-state sales leakage appears to have been reduced; and, given that one-third of the stores were new to the trading area and that the mall offered the only Nordstrom in the vicinity of Boston, some inflows appear to have occurred.

Development's "Tipping Point"

Coincidentally concurrent with the deal making on Providence Place, Brown University graduate and sculptor-photographer Barnaby Evans designed *Waterfire,* a site-specific artwork that combines primal elements and senses: water, fire, light, sound, and smell. On summer evenings, as the light fades at dusk, gondoliers light stacks of fragrant scrap cedar and pine in metal braziers that are suspended above the river. As the gondoliers move from brazier to brazier, tending the fires, the smell and sound of crackling fires permeate the Riverwalk. Free to the public, each of the 23 lightings during the summer evenings generates about $1 million from the sale of food, beverages, hotel rooms, and gas. Tax revenues total about $2.4 million each season. Since the installation of *Waterfire,* more than a dozen new restaurants have opened, hotel occupancies have risen sharply, and over 300 stories have appeared in national newspapers, magazines, and media broadcasts. The simple act of an artist has been embraced by local leaders and has become a symbol of both Providence's waterfront and its renaissance.

By the late 1990s, multiple projects—including the Biltmore Hotel, the Westin Hotel, and the Providence Place Marriott Courtyard Hotel; the Capital Center project; the new Amtrak Railroad Station; the convention center; the river relocation; Waterplace Park; the Riverwalk; Memorial Park; the Citizens' Bank headquarters, the Union Station rehabilitation; the Gateway Building; and *Waterfire*—had pushed development momentum to the tipping point. On Parcel 9, which is surrounded by Providence Place, Waterplace Park, and the Marriott Courtyard Hotel, Forest City Enterprises has an approved $75 million development plan for a 200,000-square-foot (18,580-

square-meter) office building; 70,000 square feet (6,505 square meters) of streetfront retail space; and a 265-car garage. On the other side of the Waterplace basin, on Parcel 2, to the east, Eastman Pierce has a plan for a $150 million, 225-room Hilton Hotel; 100,000 square feet (9,290 square meters) of office space; 50,000 square feet (4,645 square meters) of streetfront retail; and 150 luxury condominiums with a 500-space parking garage. On Parcels 3E and 4E, the Beacon Companies have a $55 million plan for 190 rental apartments and a 360-car parking garage. On Parcels 3W and 4W, there are plans for two office buildings, with 350,000 and 140,000 square feet (32,515 and 13,005 square meters), respectively, and associated parking.

The city has granted these newer development projects less generous tax stabilization plans, in which tax payments increase by 10 percent each year until the properties are fully taxable, in the tenth year.

The accumulated scale of the new developments is beyond the dreams of those who set the revitalization process in motion less than 25 years ago. Less than $200 million in public investment has leveraged an additional $900 million in private investment, created 6,000 jobs, built 1.5 million square feet (139,355 square meters) of retail space, started development of 1,500 hotel rooms and 500 housing units, and built 5,000 structured parking spaces. Wasteland—situated next to what was virtually a drainage ditch and worth less than $10 per square foot ($107 per square meter)—had escalated in value, by the time the Amtrak land was sold, to $40 per square foot ($430 per square meter); it would be worth many times that seven years later.

The once-moribund Downcity area, a historic district filled with elaborate granite, brick, and cast-iron buildings, is being transformed into lofts, offices, shops, and restaurants. Downcity surrounds a number of arts and educational institutions, including the Providence Performing Arts Center, RISD, Johnson & Wales University (which

The river relocation plan moved the confluence of three rivers to create a Y-shaped landscaped river corridor at the center of Providence. Providence Place connects the area known as Downcity to the state capitol. The World War I monument was relocated from an inaccessible and dangerous traffic circle to the new Memorial Park in front of the courthouse. *Commonwealth Development Group*

opments, Mayor Cianci proposed several additional plans: one would extend the promenade along the Woonasquatucket River canal to the west of Providence Place, and the other would open 200 acres (81 hectares) at the mouth of Providence Harbor to a new development called Narragansett Landing. Although these plans may be overambitious and may outrun the market's capacity for absorption, they vividly illustrate the power that has been unleashed by the simple dreams of soft-spoken architects and artists who made real the idea of recapturing the waterfront for the people of Providence.

Lessons Learned

Cities regenerate from within. Even in the depths of decline, a community that focuses on its concealed assets can regenerate its economy and its environment. In Providence, entrepreneurs and city officials seized upon the decline as an opportunity to reposition the entire city, from its public spaces to its privately held real estate. When waterfront land is bypassed and neglected, it becomes cheap enough for developers and public agencies to buy and redevelop. When office vacancies drive values low enough, they become inexpensive enough for developers to convert into residential lofts. Although federal funds were ultimately tapped, the force for regeneration came from within—from local visionaries who were able to imagine uncovering the neglected rivers and tapping the income stream that flowed along the freeways that bisected the city.

Strong leaders are essential. They move institutions forward. Shrewd business leaders with a civic conscience—like Bruce Sundlun, (chairman of Outlet Communications, then governor), Bill Miller (then chairman of Textron, later chairman of the Federal Reserve Board and then secretary of the Treasury), and Mike Metcalf (publisher of the *Providence Journal*), among many others—saw Providence's problems and used their knowledge,

specializes in culinary arts and hotel management), and the downtown facilities of URI and Roger Williams University. Brown University is a five-minute walk up College Hill. It is estimated that 20,000 college students live in or near downtown, fueling growth in restaurants, the arts, entertainment, and housing.

Funding for the relocation of I-195 will open the Providence River and Providence Harbor to further waterfront development, as well as add a 35-acre (14-hectare) development district in the old right-of-way, and bring the brick lofts of the old jewelry district back into the downtown development inventory. Beyond those devel-

contacts, and resources to solve them. Strong politicians accept political risk to obtain long-term results.

Long-term projects require long-term players. As one of the longest-serving mayors in the country, Mayor Cianci provided continuity for the revitalization of the waterfront and the downtown.

Cooperation creates catalysts. Power centers in a community need to cooperate to achieve results. Private civic leaders supported downtown revitalization by forming the Providence Foundation to target catalytic investment opportunities. The state, the city, and the foundation then reinforced their cooperation by forming the Capital Center Commission, whose members were appointed equally by all three. In contrast to the circumstances in many other cities, where public, private, and nonprofit entities are often in conflict, the state, the city, and the foundation continue to work cooperatively after more than 20 years Although these three entities do not initiate most projects, they do support them

Artists and architects can create value. If their ideas are recognized and supported by business and civic leaders, architects and artists can ignite the spark of waterfront revitalization and redevelopment, creating enormous economic value in the process. In fact, in an effort to attract more artists, the city of Providence even exempts working artists from local and state sales and income taxes.

Creatively overcome obstacles and opposition. When Dan Lugosch saw the Providence Place project almost evaporate in the face of opposition from a new governor—and saw that his irate boss was bent on litigation against the state— Lugosch bought out his boss, at considerable personal risk. Lugosch then creatively devised the idea of splitting the sales tax revenues (which could be realized only if his project was built), thereby eliminating the risk to the state and clinching the deal. Unwilling to lose a $450 million private investment, the state crafted a creative, low-risk subsidy. Even after the Providence Place agreement was renegotiated, a 1995 Brown University survey found that 66 percent of residents opposed the project and only 25 percent were in favor of it. In 2000, after the mall was opened, the numbers had reversed: 61 percent gave the project excellent or good ratings and only 17 percent rated it fair or poor. Strong politicians accept political risk, and political support often follows. Governor Sundlun notes, "Not one of my projects had public support at the time but enjoyed it later." When Governor Sundlun lost the election, he made a commitment to move the URI facility to a vacant department store, presenting the new governor with a fait accompli.

The forbidding, 40-foot- (12-meter-) high concrete cliff walls that separated Waterplace Park from the river have been transformed into a terraced café and amphitheater. The amphitheater is often the site of concerts, plays, and weddings. *William P. Macht*

Never underestimate the power of a simple idea. Bill Warner succeeded in overturning the plans of nationally renowned architects by articulating two simple ideas: first, that people like to work, live, and play along waterfronts; second, that all the city needed to do was to reopen many small, safe streets so that people could reach the waterfront without having to deal with traffic congestion.

Then, Warner used simple language and images—such as "the world's widest bridge and shortest boulevard" and "Suicide Circle"—to persuade others.

Adapt the development program to the site. The developers of Providence Place succeeded in building a familiar, three-level mall on a steeply sloping site over a river and a railroad. But the presence of the department stores demanded what is now a conventional formula: a dumbbell-shaped mall with anchors at each end and smaller stores on continuous levels in between. Applying this design to a steeply sloping urban site over a river and main rail line meant that none of the levels could be at grade, and that the only access to the river was by means of steep concrete steps. The project might have been much more dynamic, and perhaps less expensive, if the shops and restaurants had lined both sides of the waterfront and the two halves had been connected by a slender sky bridge. Such an approach might have allowed the parking structures to take greater advantage of the grade differences and eliminated the parking bridge over the river. The unexpectedly high foot traffic along Francis Street, coupled with the national trend toward street retail, suggests that innovative developers can persuade even recalcitrant department stores to change formulas. In San Francisco Centre, for example, the developer persuaded Nordstrom to place its store on the highest levels of the center, to draw shoppers up. Had a similar arrangement been tried in Providence, the mall shops, which generate the highest sales and the most profit for the developer, could have been at the street corners, and shoppers could have been led through the smaller stores to reach the department store anchors.

Diversify development risks and uses. Cities decay one block at a time and are rebuilt one block at a time. The Capital Center Commission's decision to avoid a single master developer, create multiple parcels of manageable size, spread the development risk among different local and regional developers, and pursue market-driven strategies spread the risk, diversified the uses, and accelerated the momentum. Markets create diverse opportunities that are often unrelated. The Citizens' Bank, which was eventually located on Parcel 3, was a preexisting commitment that had to be moved because of the river relocation. Center Place, an eight-story, 225-unit luxury apartment project on Parcel 5, and the Gateway Building, a four-story, 110,000-square-foot (10,220-square-meter) office building on Parcel 8, had little relationship with one another.

Be flexible. Projects can rarely survive unless both public and private partners are flexible and adapt to changing circumstances. Political, economic, financial, and market conditions always change during long-term projects. When Governor Sundlun lost reelection, both parties were flexible enough to renegotiate their agreement. When interest rates declined and the project neared completion, the parties took advantage of the opportunity to refinance the bonds. When development momentum accelerated and markets improved, the city could afford to reduce tax concessions without losing projects. Development projects become living organisms, and partnership structures need to have the flexibility to quickly adapt to change. The mall agreement demonstrated flexibility by changing six times; however, once it was executed, it lacked a flexible structure that would have allowed for subsequent alterations.

Avoid litigation at almost all costs. Capital Properties's insistence on waiting for condemnation, in order to bid up the price of its land, delayed projects for years and created a hostile environment. Congel's insistence on suing the state for breach of contract would, at best, have extended the project for years, and more likely have led to its complete collapse. And, although it clarified ownership, Lugosch's litigation with a former partner, Alexius C. Conroy, jeopardized financing for nearly a year. Successful development is cooperative, not adversarial, and litigation often diverts funds that would otherwise go into high-quality materials and design.

Connect, connect, connect. Cities are about connection. Warner resolved traffic problems by building 12 bridges. The sky bridge from the mall to the convention center improves connectivity in bad weather but weakens foot traffic along Francis Street. The absence of any entrance at all from the Marriott Courtyard Hotel to Waterplace Park, which it overlooks, removes the park entirely from the hotel's sphere of activity. Nordstrom is isolated because it refused to have a street entrance. The steep concrete steps from the Riverwalk to Providence Place minimize foot traffic between them. The overbuilt, underused concrete labyrinth under the mall and along the river is as much a barrier as a connection: the fact that "a river runs through it" seems more of an annoyance than a cause for celebration.

When projects succeed, trumpet their results. Mayor Cianci was relentless in never missing an opportunity to show the media the fruits of the city's revitalization. The resulting "buzz" brought more tourists and developers to look at the city's achievements—and its potential. The Providence Film Commission takes advantage of every opportunity to feature the city and to accommodate television productions like *Providence* (once, the commission even closed hurricane barriers to keep the river full enough for a filming). Such efforts create the kind of excitement that helps build development momentum.

If developers give to the city, the city will give back. As revered developer Jim Rouse used to say, "If you create places good enough, people will pay for them." Creating places for people keeps people coming back. Cities like to partner with socially responsive developers. The state and the city created the Riverwalk, the development parcels, and the institutional framework. Developers invested to bring people to them. If the place is good enough, people buy condominiums, rent offices and apartments, and patronize shops, theaters, hotels, and restaurants. The taxes repay public investment. The iterative cycle regenerates the city, block by block.

Note

1. Later, St. Florian would become the winner of the controversial Washington, D.C., World War II Memorial design competition.

Project Data: **Waterplace Park and Providence Place**

Land Use Information (Acres/Hectares)

Capital Center District	77/31
Private ownership	48/19
Public ownership	29/12
Providence Place	13.2/5.3

Size of Development Parcels

Parcel	Square Feet/Square Meters	Acres/Hectares
1	204,552/19,005	4.70/1.90
2	91,228/8,475	2.09/0.85
3S	40,033/3,720	0.92/0.37
3W	34,967/3,250	0.80/0.32
3E	23,782/2,210	0.55/0.22
4W	46,329/4,305	1.06/0.43
4E	22,360/2,080	0.51/0.21
5	54,042/5,020	1.24/0.50
6a	276,037/25,645	6.34/2.60
6b	87,120/8,095	2.00/0.80
6c	43,560/4,045	1.00/0.40
7	53,339/4,955	1.22/0.49
7A	76,180/7,075	1.75/0.70
8	36,170/3,360	0.83/0.34
9	71,902/6,680	1.65/0.67
10	274,086/25,465	6.29/2.50
11	158,356/14,710	3.64/1.47
12	24,249/2,255	0.56/0.23
13	290,011/26,945	6.66/2.70
14	97,140/9,025	2.23/0.90
15	90,262/8,385	2.07/0.84
Total	2,095,705/194,705	48.11/19.44

Development Program

Parcel	Planned	Completed	Square Feet/Square Meters
1		Union Station (office and restaurant space; adaptive use) 215-unit Marriott Courtyard Hotel 354-space parking garage Interim parking for 160 cars	150,000/13,935
	Office, retail, and/or residential building		230,000/21,370
2A, 2B	225-unit Hilton Hotel Office space Retail 150 condominiums 500-space parking structure		100,000/9,290 50,000/4,645
3E	190 apartments		
3S		Citizens Plaza (13-story office building with street-level retail)	234,000/21,740
3W	Office building and parking		350,000/32,515
4E	360-space parking structure		
4W	Office building and parking		140,000/13,005
5		Center Place (eight-story, 225-unit luxury apartment building with structured parking for 350 cars)	
6A, 6B, 6C	Townhouses, offices, and/or retail Four-story, 1,200-space parking garage		
7		Amtrak railroad station; 360-space underground parking garage	
8		Gateway Building (four-story office building); 150 underground parking spaces	110,000/10,220
9	Office space Retail space 265-space structured parking		200,000/18,580 70,000/6,505
10, 13		Providence Place mall 4,500-space structured parking	1,300,000/120,775
11 (portion of convention center complex)	A 350-room hotel or an office building	Westin Hotel (363 rooms) 1,700-space structured parking garage	256,000/23,785 (office building)
12	Specialty hotel with upper-level condominiums		
14	Renaissance Marriott Hotel (adaptive use of Masonic Temple)		
15	Office space with ground-level support retail		

Project Costs and Financing (Projected Private Investment, in Millions)

Providence Place	$450
Center Place	47
Citizens' Bank	38
Union Station	30
Boston Financial	18
Marriott Courtyard Hotel	20
Parcel 2 (office, retail, and/or residential)	125
Parcels 3E and 4E (apartments and parking)	55
Parcel 9 retail	75
Total	$858

Projected Impacts upon Completion

Permanent jobs	10,000
Retail space (square feet/square meters)	1,500,000/139,355
Office space (square feet/square meters)	2,000,000/185,810
Number of residential units	500
Number of hotel rooms	1,500
Structured parking spaces	10,000
Total private and public investment	$1,120,000,000

Project Timeline

1981	Capital Center Commission established under a state enabling statute.
1981	Capital Center Plan implemented.
1984	Providence river relocation plan developed.
1984	The city, the state, and the Federal Highway Administration commit to funding the River Relocation Project.
1984	Bill Warner and a group of engineers design the River Relocation Project.
1987	First phase of River Relocation Plan construction begins.
1987	Developers announce plans to construct a $300 million shopping mall near the statehouse.
January 18, 1990	Two of the major developers, Melvin Simon & Associates and Nathan Landow, drop out; separate discussions begin with another developer, Pyramid Companies.
August 1, 1993	Working with a development team headed by Dan Lugosch, Governor Sundlun's administration revives long-dormant plans for the Providence Place mall.
December 12, 1993	The state department of transportation announces that it will use federal money earmarked for traffic congestion to build a 5,000-space parking garage for the mall.
April 28, 1994	Macy's, Lord & Taylor, and Filene's sign on as anchor department stores.
July 27, 1994	The state announces that it will issue $225 million in bonds to finance the mall.
August 5, 1994	In the face of public opposition, the state drops plans to issue bonds.
April 4, 1995	Governor Almond and Mayor Cianci sign a new deal with the developers that shifts much of the risk from the public to the developers.
September 28, 1995	Nordstrom, which had been undecided, announces that it will be one of three anchor stores, replacing Macy's.
November 8, 1995	After weeks of debate, the state general assembly approves a bill authorizing a sales-tax relief package for the mall developers.
October 22, 1996	Mayor Cianci signs a real estate and personal property tax treaty in which the city forgoes up to $141 million

in tax revenues over 30 years. The developers promise to help build a cinema complex downtown.

March 17, 1997	Fleet National Bank and the mall developers commit to a financing agreement to build the mall. Nomura Asset Capital Company also agrees to assist—and later, when Fleet backs out, takes over financing.
March 24, 1997	About 250 people attend a ground breaking ceremony for the Providence Place mall, then scheduled to open in August 1998.
May 28, 1997	After yet another delay, construction begins on the mall site.
August 12, 1997	An ownership dispute flares up between Alexius C. Conroy, a former partner of Bob Congel (Dan Lugosch's former boss), and the development team

lead by Lugosch; during litigation, financing for the mall is threatened.

November 21, 1997	Morse Diesel International, of New York, replaces Gilbane as the mall's building manager.
April 16, 1998	Conroy's suit against Lugosch is settled.
March 24, 1999	A new construction timetable is announced: Lord & Taylor will open in the spring of 2000, and Filene's in October.
June 2, 1999	The mall developers announce that they want to refinance a portion of the project's approximately $460 million debt with help from the state and city. The plan is put off when legislators end their session.
August 20, 1999	Providence Place opens.

Major Project Participants

Office of Governor in Residence
University of Rhode Island
216 University Library
Kingston, Rhode Island 02881
401-874-4000

Commonwealth Development Group, LLC
One Providence Place
Providence, Rhode Island 02903
401-453-2100

Chief of Staff, City of Providence
City Hall
Providence, Rhode Island 02903
401-421-7740

William D. Warner
Architects & Planners
Locust Valley Farm
595 Ten Rod Road
Exeter, Rhode Island 02822
401-295-8851

Friedrich St. Florian, Architect
112 Union Street
Providence, Rhode Island 02903
401-831-8400

Providence Foundation
30 Exchange Terrace
Providence, Rhode Island 02903
401-521-3248

Capital Center Commission
30 Exchange Terrace
Providence, Rhode Island 02903
401-274-8200

Chapman Consulting
600 Cameron Street
Alexandria, Virginia 22314
703-340-1666

Alden Raine Associates
9 Auburn Place
Brookline, Massachusetts
617-738-8960

Peabody & Arnold
One Citizens' Plaza
Providence, Rhode Island 02903
401-831-8340

Kop van Zuid

Rotterdam, Netherlands

Anne Frej

Kop van Zuid is a 500-acre (202-hectare) district of Rotterdam, the Dutch port city that lies at the confluence of the Rhine and Maas rivers. Surrounded by water on three sides, Kop van Zuid was once a thriving port and industrial area ringed by docklands and harbors. But in the years following World War II, Kop van Zuid lost many of its maritime functions, and in the ensuing years, it became increasingly isolated and less and less desirable as a place to live or work.

Though just southeast of the city center, Kop van Zuid was, until recently, cut off from it by the Nieuwe Maas River. Now connected directly to the city center by the strikingly designed Erasmus Bridge, as well as by tram and subway lines, Kop van Zuid has a new image. New offices, entertainment venues, and multifamily housing developments have brought workers, students, visitors, and residents back to the area. The revitalization process, driven primarily by the public sector, has taken considerable time, effort, and public investment. Although publicly financed infrastructure and many large-scale public facilities are now in place, the level of private support that will be forthcoming remains to be seen.

Maritime History

The history of Rotterdam and its neighborhoods is inextricably linked to port and maritime functions. As far back as the early 1300s, a settlement on the site of the present city functioned as a gateway to the North Sea from the north coast of Holland. In the 1800s, with the creation of new waterways and the construction of facilities for the transfer of goods from seagoing vessels to freight barges, Rotterdam strengthened its role as a shipment point for commodities from Germany's Ruhr area. Until the third quarter of the 19th century, most of the development in Rotterdam was focused on the north bank of the Nieuwe Maas River; there was little interest in the area later known as Kop van Zuid. In the 1870s, however, the development of new harbors and warehouse facilities in Kop van Zuid gave it new economic importance. Narrow harbors carved into the land led to the jagged shoreline still present today. By the early 1900s, the island of Feijenoord had been transformed into an active industrial and port area.

Hastily built housing developments in Kop van Zuid became home to many of the workers who came to Rotterdam to work in the harbors; the area also served as the departure point for thousands of

The Zuidkade area is planned as the economic heart of Kop van Zuid. The World Port Center—a high-rise office building, shown here—was completed in mid-2000 and houses logistics companies and the offices of the Municipal Port Authority. © Aeroview

Europeans emigrating to the United States or Canada on one of the ships of the Holland America Line. The company's headquarters building, now a luxury hotel, still stands at the tip of Wilhelmina Pier. During World War II, the area also served as the gathering and transport site for Dutch Jews. From 1942 to 1945, 12,000 people were deported from Rotterdam and its environs to concentration camps.

Shortly after bombing destroyed the city in May 1940, Rotterdam began rebuilding. After World War II, the city's major port functions moved westward, and many of the remaining structures in Kop van Zuid were left vacant. Although the area escaped large-scale demolition, its harbors were no longer able to accommodate modern ships, and Kop van Zuid entered a period of economic decline.

The question of what to do with the deserted harbor area arose as early as 1968. A proposal to create a red-light district was rejected because of objections from the residents of surrounding neighborhoods. In 1978, a residents' association presented a new plan to the municipal council, which was based on transforming Kop van Zuid into a major residential district, with special attention to social housing for lower-income groups.

Rotterdam's economy has always been dominated by port-related uses such as transport, refineries, shipping brokerage, and insurance. In the mid-1980s, the local government began to expand its vision for the city's future, creating policies that were designed to accommodate a greater mix of people and to draw businesses, tourists, and higher-income residents back to the city center. Huge investments were made in order to render the city more attractive, and connecting Kop van Zuid to the rest of the city was an important aspect of this effort. Not only was improved access considered important for the revitalization of Kop van Zuid, but it was also a means of freeing up additional areas for the expansion of the city center.

Planning for Kop van Zuid continued throughout the 1980s and early 1990s. Starting in the mid-1990s, many large-scale infrastructure projects were initiated and completed, including the Erasmus Bridge, TramPlus, and the Wilhelminaplein subway station. New and rehabilitated multifamily residential units continue to grow in number and expand in variety. And, in recent years, the daytime population of office workers at the World Port Center, the Wilhelminahof complex, and the KPN Telecom building has steadily increased.

Housing at the Port

The ambitious development strategy that has evolved over the past 20 years envisions Kop van Zuid as the setting for diverse uses, including shopping and services; residential, business, retail, and entertainment uses; and cultural, educational, and sports facilities. In the most recent plans, the eventual buildout (by 2010) would include 5,300 new residential units; 4,305,705 square feet (400,015 square meters) of office space; 376,740 square feet (35,000 square meters) of commercial space; and 45,000 square meters (484,391 square feet) of educational and institutional uses.

A waterfront setting is not unusual in Rotterdam, so this aspect of the district was not emphasized in the early planning phases. Over time, however, Kop van Zuid's river location has become more significant in plans for the area. To preserve the shoreline, many former harbor areas have been retained rather than filled in. When possible, old warehouse buildings and other structures related to the area's maritime history have been preserved and adapted to modern uses. Other physical elements crucial to the history of the area, such as older quay structures, were retained in order to maintain a traditional character.

Housing creation has been an important goal of the revitalization efforts. Government plans call for over 5,000 new residential units in a variety of sizes and prices. Nonprofit housing associations, rather than private developers, have been most active in this sector: more than 60 percent of the housing in Kop van Zuid is now owned or managed by housing authorities. In recent years, however, these authorities have been partially privatized, and their approach has become more market driven and less focused on the needs of lower-income buyers or renters. It was originally planned that about half the new housing stock in Kop van Zuid would be accessible to lower-

Pedestrian walkways, open spaces, and outdoor seating throughout Kop van Zuid take advantage of its waterfront setting. © *Marcel Loermans*

income residents, but the actual proportion of affordable housing is now estimated to be about 30 percent of the total stock. In fact, in recent years, the residential sector has been the most successful in attracting private sector investment. This pattern has been attributed to a variety of factors, including increased spending power, an overall improvement in economic conditions, the increasing attractiveness of Kop van Zuid, and the greater popularity of the city as a place to live.

In the 1980s, the decline in harbor-related activities led to one of the highest unemployment rates in the country—a situation that was exacerbated by an influx of new immigrants, many without job skills, who settled in the area because of the availability of low-cost housing. To address the problem, the Rotterdam City Development Council initiated, in 1991, a project known as "mutual benefit." The goal of the program was to increase employment opportunities by (1) supporting local entrepreneurs and small-scale businesses and (2) providing construction and redevelopment jobs to local residents. Although employers were encouraged to hire local workers, particularly for large-scale construction projects, the workers' lack of appropriate skills often stymied such efforts.

Creating Distinct Identities

The need to expand Rotterdam's city center became evident in the 1980s. In 1987, looking to the underused areas to the south, the city government—and prominent city planner Teun Koolhaas—developed an urban design plan to connect Kop van Zuid to the city. The plan's broad outline called for improved connections between the two areas and the expansion of residential, commercial, and recreational functions at Kop van Zuid.

A follow-up plan for Kop van Zuid was approved by various levels of government, from local to national, between 1991 and 1994. This plan provided a flexible framework for the redevelopment process by establishing broad guidelines for potential land uses throughout the district. Three important documents—addressing urban planning and design, public open spaces, and the development program—were produced to convey the basic concepts of the land use plan.

Architecture and design have played key roles in the process of improving Kop van Zuid's image. Well-known international and Dutch architects have provided design services for many of the area's prominent buildings. To ensure high standards of design and development within the district, the Quality Team, made up of recognized Dutch and European architects and planners, was established to review plans for proposed projects and advise on their aesthetic aspects.

Each neighborhood or section of Kop van Zuid is intended to have a distinct identity. For the Zuidkade, for example, considered the economic heart of the district because of its visibility and accessibility to the center city, a master plan was generated by Norman Foster Associates, a prominent United Kingdom–based architectural firm. The plan, which emphasized logistics and trade, called for integrated commercial, residential, and recreational uses. The World Port Center, a high-rise office building designed by Sir Norman Foster, opened in mid-2000 and accommodates logistics companies and the Municipal Port Authority offices, which were relocated from the new port area. The new, high-rise KPN Telecom building, designed by noted Italian architect Renzo Piano,

also adds visual importance to the area. Farther south, at the Wilhelmina Pier, a new terminal for luxury cruise ships has been constructed, and the former Holland America Line Hotel has been refurbished as the four-star Hotel New York.

The Entrepot, formerly a warehouse and shipping area, is today largely residential, and the monumental Entrepot warehouse has been converted to lofts, apartments, and retail uses. The city's efforts to create a festival market in the building (as part of a plan to transform the area into a recreation and entertainment district) have been somewhat controversial, however, because of the necessity of using additional public monies to provide financial incentives to prospective tenants and because of fear that the market would compete with small local shops.

The Landtong area is residential and includes a variety of owner-occupied and rental units as well as services for local residents. The Stadstuinen, designed for families, features plentiful open spaces and pedestrian walkways. The Parkzicht residential area is organized around a central park.

Housing has been an important component of government plans for the Kop van Zuid area. The Landtong (shown in the foreground) and Entrepot areas are large and residential in character, with a mix of owner-occupied and rental units. © Aeroview

National Significance

A variety of departments under the authority of the city government are involved in the revitalization of Kop van Zuid, including the Department of Urban Planning and Housing, the Rotterdam City Development Corporation, the Rotterdam Transportation Company, and the Rotterdam Port Authority. One project coordinator represents each of these departments. A project manager oversees the entire effort and maintains direct contact with the various departments and the local political bodies.

ministries—the Ministry of Transport and Public Works and the Ministry of Housing, Regional Development, and the Environment—have made significant financial contributions to the implementation of the plan.

The city government has actively sought public/private partnerships to spread the risk and development costs for projects in the area, but to date, much of the large-scale investment has been financed by the public sector. The Erasmus Bridge, funded jointly by the Dutch government and the municipality of Rotterdam, was completed in 1996. Designed by Amsterdam architect Ben van Berkel, the bridge provides a striking entry portal to Kop van Zuid. Public investments were also made in a new metro

Kop van Zuid (above, center) is a former port and industrial area surrounded on three sides by the Nieuwe Maas River. The Erasmus Bridge (right) now connects this area to the center of Rotterdam. *Right Photo: M. Bergsma/Travel-Images.com*

Because it was designated as a key project in the national government's Fourth Report Extra on Spatial Planning, the revitalization of Kop van Zuid has national significance. Elevating the effort to a national level has made it more visible and has also helped facilitate the acquisition of funds from the central government. Two national

stop at Wilhelminaplein; in TramPlus, a network of tramlines serving the area; and in the Varkenoordse Viaduct.

New government office buildings and educational facilities have brought new life to Kop van Zuid during the day. The Wilhelminahof complex includes tax offices, customs offices, and offices of the justice courts. Ichtus College and the Albeda College Secondary School have added a younger population to the area. Investment has

Project Data: **Kop van Zuid**

Land Use Information

Site area (acres/hectares)	500/202
Number of residential units at buildout	5,300

Building Area by Type of Use

Use	Square Feet/Square Meters
Office	4,305,705/400,015
Commercial	376,740/35,000
Educational	484,391/45,000
Recreational	322,920/30,000

Major Project Participants

City of Rotterdam
Department of Urban Planning and Housing
Marconistraat 2
P.O. Box 6699
3002 AR Rotterdam
Netherlands
31 10 489 6499

Project Timeline

1970s	Early urban renewal activities focusing on social housing
1978	Master plan completed
1987	Teun Koolhaas urban design plan presented
1989	Follow-up plan presented; Dutch central government agrees to contribute financial support
1991	Government approvals process for plan started
1992	Construction of Information Center started
1996	Erasmus Bridge opens; TramPlus in operation
1997	Wilhelminaplein metro station opens
2000	World Port Center and KPN Telecom open
2001	Luxor Theater opens

Rotterdam City Development Corporation
Galvanistraat 15
P.O. Box 6575
3002 AN Rotterdam
Netherlands
31 10 489 6944
Web site: www.obr.rotterdam.nl

also been made in entertainment and cultural venues, such as the 1,500-seat Luxor Theater, which opened in 2001.

A financial incentive program was used to encourage KPN Telecom, a private company, to vacate its office in the city center and to construct a new tower in Kop van Zuid; through the program, the developer received payments for creating renovated apartments in its former office building.

Lessons Learned

Physically integrating Kop van Zuid into the city center and the surrounding neighborhoods—through a new bridge, roads, and public transit systems—was essential to stimulating new development in the early stages.

City officials learned that plans for rapidly evolving areas must remain flexible and responsive to market conditions. When the demand for office development declined because of a downturn in the market and the market for high-quality housing improved, plans were modified to accommodate this change.

Strong leadership and large-scale public investment are important aspects of a major revitalization effort.

Attracting risk-averse private sector players is a difficult process that takes considerable time and effort. In spite of considerable public investment, the private sector has been slow to commit to Kop van Zuid.

Suisun City Waterfront

Suisun City, California

Steve Fader

Suisun City is a small but historic town midway between San Francisco and Sacramento. Founded in 1851, the town sits at the head of Suisun Marsh, which flows into Suisun and Grizzly bays and ultimately into San Francisco Bay. In Suisun City's early days, boats docked there to unload goods destined for the gold rush miners and to bring farm products down the bay to market. The transcontinental railroad, which reached Suisun City in 1869, further reinforced the town's role as a transportation hub. Main Street grew up parallel to the Suisun Channel, and the city's small residential core clustered nearby. And there matters stood for more than a century.

In the years following World War II, the economic base of the region began to change, and the shifts were accelerated by freeway construction in the 1960s. An oil refinery took over the northern end of the Suisun Channel, and metal warehouses crowded the waterfront. "A lot of people didn't even know there was a waterfront there," notes Steve Baker, city manager of Suisun City. "You *could* walk along the waterfront, but you'd have to jump some fences." With industrial uses as their principal neighbors and competing retail centers emerging elsewhere, Main Street businesses declined, and vacant buildings and lots became more and more common.

In the 1970s, a residential project known as the Crescent Neighborhood was constructed adjacent to the town center, but the higher-density project (four dwelling units crowded onto typical single-family lots) ended up as a breeding ground for crime, drug use, and prostitution. Suisun City's "municipal building"—a series of trailers—only reinforced the city's increasingly dejected self-image. "We had the only city hall that was registered with the Department of Motor Vehicles," wryly notes James Spering, the city's mayor since 1986.

In contrast to the disinvestment in the town's core, new residential subdivisions were being constructed at the city's periphery, spawned by the proximity of the freeway and the growing employment base in and around Solano County, which includes Suisun City. Between 1970 and 1999, the town's population grew from 2,600 to 26,750. But this growth was not necessarily good news for Suisun City. Because Suisun City was hemmed in by adjoining towns, Travis Air Force Base, and the marsh, there was little room for new commercial growth to provide the tax base that was needed to service the new residential developments.

The first phase of the marina, with 150 boat docks. In the background is the new Harbor Plaza building, which was built in conformance with the city's design guidelines to relate to the historic structures of nearby Main Street.

All signs pointed to the waterfront, Suisun City's most unique asset. Coupled with the historic Main Street and residential core, it was the key to reestablishing the economic and social health of the city. "We had the water and we had the buildings," notes Jane Day, Suisun City councilperson and an early and continuous supporter of redevelopment.

A Fortunate Turnaround

In 1982, the Specific Plan was prepared for the waterfront area, but it remained no more than a plan. According to city manager Baker, in 1988, the *San Francisco Chronicle* pegged Suisun City dead last in a "quality of life" ranking of the Bay Area's municipalities.

The turnaround in Suisun City's fortunes dates primarily from 1989, when the mayor, James Spering, and the city council took a series of actions to jump-start the redevelopment process: a 13-member citizen's committee was formed, an experienced redevelopment director was hired, and an outside design firm (ROMA Design Group) was brought in to formulate a new plan. Administratively, the city took two actions that proved to be of major significance to the redevelopment effort: (1) it subsumed the city's planning and housing departments under the Suisun City Redevelopment Agency, which resulted in a more streamlined and unified public planning

An aerial view of Harbor Plaza. Designed as the focal point of the Suisun City waterfront, the plaza is the site of concerts, weddings, and other outdoor gatherings.

and 300 landscaped parking spaces; to install new water and sewer lines; and to fund the Facade Improvement Project and related street-scape improvements on Main Street.

The bonds, which initially carried a 7.5 percent interest rate, were refinanced in 1993 at a rate of 5.75 percent, which allowed the city to fund an additional $10 million. To supplement the tax increment financing, the city obtained $6.9 million in loans from the California Department of Boating and Waterways to fund the construction of the marina, and a loan of $500,000 from state transportation funds to renovate the circa-1910 train depot.

The Enterprise Zone Incentive Program was established to spur private sector participation in the redevelopment of the commercial and residential areas surrounding the waterfront. The city offered both monetary and staff assistance. The incentives included

and implementation effort, and (2) it designated the entire city as a redevelopment area, thereby allowing the city to capture the tax increment in the growing residential area and dedicate it to financing improvements in the town center. The city took one further action, of both practical and symbolic import: in 1989, a permanent city hall was constructed in the town center, on a site adjacent to the waterfront.

The 1990 Downtown Waterfront Specific Plan (revised in 1999) has served as the city's blueprint for financing and implementing improvements to the harbor and Old Town. Fifty-eight million dollars in tax increment bonds was issued in 1991 to finance capital-related projects. Proceeds were used to dredge and restore the Suisun Channel and the adjacent Suisun Marsh; to construct seawalls; to purchase and improve properties along the waterfront; to construct a town plaza (called Harbor Plaza), a promenade,

■ Reduced fees (for example, development review fees and business license fees);

■ Permit assistance (which might include assistance in obtaining approvals from Suisun City and in navigating reviews conducted by outside agencies);

■ Design assistance;

■ Flexibility in planning and zoning matters;

■ Land acquisition and development assistance (for example, flexibility regarding financing terms).

In return, the city requires strict adherence to the objectives and spirit of its Downtown Waterfront Specific Plan. In particular, businesses participating in the program are required to follow the design guidelines established for the redevelopment project, which require new development to be stylistically compatible with the existing historic fabric of Old Town. Referring to the city's insistence on appropriate and high-quality design, Steve Baker notes, "Design trumps everything. We want to create something that will outlive us."

Creating a Legacy

There were six central elements in the Suisun City redevelopment project—the Suisun Channel, Harbor Plaza retail, hotel development, office development, residential development, and Main Street retail.

Suisun Channel

The focus of the project's site design is the Suisun Channel. An agreement was reached with the U.S. Army Corps of Engineers under which the channel was deepened, to allow access for larger boats, and silt buildup was removed. The spoils were placed on the adjacent Pierce Island in such a way as to establish new wetlands on the island. The channel's edge is treated in various ways: a standard concrete seawall lines much of its west side, which is adjacent to Harbor Plaza and the seawalk; other areas are lined with riprap (stone rubble); and, in deference to ecology and history, a large portion of the eastern edge of the channel has been retained as a wetland, with native grasses and other vegetation.

In 1994, a 150-berth marina was constructed in the lower part of the Suisun Channel, replacing an older marina that had deteriorated. The new marina opened with approximately 50 to 60 percent occupancy, and reached 100 percent in 2000. Current dock rents range from $134 per month for a 28-foot (8.5-meter) berth to $240 for a 50-foot (15.2-meter) berth. At present, dock rentals do not fully cover the city's combined operating costs and debt service on the construction loan; the shortfall is funded by the redevelopment agency.

In addition to the marina, a 300-foot (91-meter) guest dock and public launch and a 960-square-foot (90-square-meter) harbormaster building have been constructed. The 5,000-foot- (1,524-meter-) long promenade, which borders the channel, is designed for both strolling and boat access, and will ultimately connect the current and future harbor-front uses (the town plaza, restaurants, residences, offices, the hotel, and city hall). A second phase

of docks, planned for the North Basin area, is expected to be constructed in the next few years.

The focal point of the waterfront is Harbor Plaza, which was constructed on the west side of the channel, roughly opposite city hall. The plaza consists of a one-acre (0.40-hectare) triangle inscribed with a paved, semicircular performance area. To stimulate consumer and business interest in the waterfront and Old Town, the city actively programs the plaza and the adjacent seawalk.

The view across Suisun Channel to city hall. Construction of the city hall, in 1991, provided a symbol of the city's commitment to revitalizing its waterfront.

Over 20 festivals and events, including the Waterfront Jazz Festival and the Art and Wine Festival, were held last year, and were attended by more than 150,000 people.

Harbor Plaza Retail

Although the city initially expected the redevelopment project to be built out by a single master developer, no single developer was prepared to take on the sizable and risky project in the recessionary early 1990s. As a result, the city—through its redevelopment agency—has become, in effect, the master developer. In this role, the redevelopment agency has been responsible for physically preparing the land and selling parcels to individual developers and owner-builders.

The agency's role is most clearly demonstrated in the Harbor Plaza retail area, where the city has prepared the land; constructed streets, sidewalks, and surface parking; and prepared individual building pads for sale to others. The prepared lots range in size from 3,600 to 8,800 square feet (335 to 820 square meters), with 2,200–6,000-square-foot (205–560-square-meter) building pads. Lot prices are approximately $15 per square foot ($161 per square meter).

The site design and the sizing of parcels in the Harbor Plaza retail area reflect the city's objectives and expectations for the waterfront project: the small pads allow for smaller, two-story structures of a scale that relates to the nearby historic Main Street structures, and help to ensure that the overall effect will not evoke a shopping center; nor are these small pads likely to be tenanted by large retail chains. Instead, the city encourages the interest of unique tenants, local developers, and owner-builders—entities that will have a particular and hometown interest in the long-term success of the larger initiative as well as in their own projects. The city is also committed to mixed use, and to a live/work concept for the town center. Owner-builders are encouraged to use the upper floor of their Harbor Plaza buildings as their residence, or for office space.

Five commercial buildings have been constructed in the Harbor Plaza retail area to date. Several include outdoor dining on the first floor, and two of these—Bab's Delta Diner and the Athenian Grill—include outdoor dining along the seawalk. Bab's Delta Diner is typical of the owner-builder concept and the city's approach to development. Though the owner, a local restaurateur, had never built a project of this sort, she was interested in opening a restaurant on the waterfront and interested in the live/work option as well. Though considerable redevelopment agency time and resources were required to get the

project built, the effort yielded a unique draw and amenity for the redevelopment project, plus a highly committed tenant and an in-residence owner. In total, there are four live/work businesses in the Harbor Plaza retail area. Currently under design is a 188-seat Buckhorn Restaurant, a branch of the regionally well known Buckhorn Restaurant in Yolo, California.

An aerial view of Suisun Channel, with the town plaza (Harbor Plaza) in the foreground. The channel's edge is treated in various ways, from concrete to riprap to grasses that echo the natural condition of the adjacent Suisun Marsh.

Hotel Development

A 100-room "all suites" hotel across the channel, on the east side of North Basin, has begun grading and utility construction. With an 8,000-square-foot (745-square-meter) conference center, the hotel expects to attract patronage from several markets: business visitors and meetings from the growing base of nearby Solano County offices; visitors to Travis Air Force Base; local special events, such as weddings (ceremonies on the town plaza are increasingly popular); and overflow tourists from the Napa Valley.

Offices

The first phase of a major office project, One Harbor Center, has been completed at the head of North Basin. Developed by the Wiseman Company, a local Solano County developer, the completed first phase consists of a three-story, Class A, 52,500-square-foot (4,880-square-meter) steel-frame structure. The planned second phase is expected to add an additional 75,000 square feet (6,970 square meters) of space. The first phase was 70 to 75 percent preleased at approximately $2.50 per square foot ($27 per square meter) per month, fully serviced—which, according to Doyle Wiseman, principal of the Wiseman Company, represents a rent premium of about 20 percent over similar projects. "People care about where they go to work," comments Wiseman, and the unique waterfront location and walkable retail environment translate into increased rents. The planned hotel, with its conference center, is an added amenity, notes Wiseman, and the nearby train depot and multimodal station may help as well. Building tenants include professional offices and public agencies, typically in the 2,000–10,000-square-foot (185–930-square-meter) range.

The redevelopment agency's incentives for the office project included

■ 100 percent writedown of the land cost;

■ Payment of approximately $250,000 toward land development costs (the project requires 30-foot- [9-meter-] deep concrete caisson foundations);

■ A lease commitment of 16,200 square feet (1,505 square meters) for five years.

In turn, the city will receive a 10 percent profit interest in the operation and sale of the building, with a minimum payment of $500,000.

Residential Development

Early on it was determined that the Crescent Neighborhood was part of the town center's problems with crime, drugs, and prostitution. In 1991, 470 of the dwelling units in the development were acquired and demolished, and 52 were rehabilitated. Tenants were given relocation assistance in the form of Section 8 vouchers. In the mid-1990s, a new, 94-unit development of single-family detached houses was constructed in place of the Crescent Neighborhood. In keeping with new urbanist precepts, streets are narrow, and roundabouts are used to calm traffic; garages are located at the back and are accessed from alleyways; porches and entries front heavily landscaped streets.

A second residential project, a 23-unit live/work development located along the Suisun Channel, just south of Harbor Plaza, is under construction. Developed by the Miller-Sorg Group, a local homebuilder, the Promenade will offer two-story units of approximately 2,800 to 2,900 square feet (260 to 270 square meters), including a 400-square-foot (35-square-meter) first-floor workspace. The intention is for the workspaces to be used for small retail or service businesses or for professional offices.

Main Street Retail

Unlike the Harbor Plaza shops, Main Street consists primarily of older structures, several of which date back to the early years of the town. The redevelopment agency is trying, with some success, to encourage the rehabilitation of the building facades and the revitalization of retail activity. The city offers matching funds for facade renovation and financial assistance for new infill construction. More than a dozen businesses have participated in this program to date.

In addition, the city has encouraged the adaptive use of historic structures. The 1855 Lawler House, for example, an ornate but deteriorated Victorian residence, had been slated to be burned down as part of the fire department's training program; instead, it was moved to a site in the Harbor Plaza area and renovated for offices. The 1876 Bank of Suisun has been converted to a coffee shop, and a third property, the old post office, has been granted new life as a microbrewery and pub. Another notable success is the Harbor Conservatory Theatre; fashioned out of an old grocery store, the facility is jointly operated by the Solano County Community College Drama Department and the Harbor Theatrical Group.

Despite some notable successes, the physical and economic recovery of Main Street is still in an early phase. The street is quite long, and many gaps (vacant lots) remain as a reminder of the area's former deteriorated condition. Demand for retail on Main Street is growing, however, as more and more activity is occurring along the waterfront. Over time, the offices under construction and

Project Data: Suisun City Waterfront

Land Use Information

Site area (acres/hectares) — 260/105

Land Use Plan

Use	Acres/Hectares	Percentage of Site
Buildings	110/45	42.3
Streets and surface parking	90/36	34.6
Landscaping and open space	25/10	9.6
Other (marina)	35/14	13.5
Total	260/105	100.0

Building Area by Type of Use

Use	Area (Square Feet/Square Meters)	
	Existing	Planned
Office	52,500/4,880	75,000/6,970
Retail, restaurant, and service	25,497/2,370	53,000/4,925
Residential	7,757/720[a]	151,800/14,100[b]
Hotel		76,000/7,060
Entertainment (Harbor Conservatory Theatre)	12,600/1,170	
Other (harbormaster building)	960/90	
Total	99,314/9,230	355,800/33,055

Leasable Area by Type of Use

Use	Area (Square Feet/Square Meters)	
	Existing	Planned
Office (net rentable area)	48,000/4,460	
Retail and entertainment (gross leasable area)		33,332/3,095

Number of Units by Type of Use

Use	Existing	Planned
Residential	102	220[c]
Hotel		100 rooms
Other (marina)	150 berths	

Office Information

Percentage of net rentable area leased	85
Average tenant size (square feet/square meters)	2,000–10,000/185–930
Approximate average rents (per square foot/square meter)	$30/$323
Average length of lease	Three to five years

Residential Information

Unit Type	Area (Square Feet/Square Meters)	Number Planned/Sold	Range of Initial Sales Prices
Victorian Harbor	1,022–1,790/95–160	94/94	$130,000–$180,000
The Promenade	2,800–2,900/260–270	23/0	$400,000–$600,000
Harbor Park	1,200–1,700/110–160	55/0	$165,000–$260,000[d]

a. Not including Victorian.
b. The Promenade and Harbor.
c. Victorian Harbor.
d. Sixty-five percent of the units are priced for households earning between 80 and 120 percent of the area median income; the remainder are market rate.

the planned hotel should also provide significant economic stimulus to Main Street.

A Successful Bootstrap Campaign

For a small town, Suisun City's accomplishments are writ large. From a polluted strip of warehouses and a refinery the city has fashioned a successful and inviting waterfront and reversed the tide of deterioration and decay. The effort, essentially a bootstrap campaign, was accomplished primarily by taking advantage of local assets, energy, and talent.

Suisun City reorganized its planning and housing departments under the redevelopment agency to achieve maximum coordination and support for redevelopment, and declared the entire city a redevelopment area to harness the tax revenue on behalf of redevelopment. The city also took the difficult step—both symbolic and concrete—of

Retail Information

Percentage of gross leasable area occupied   100

Tenant Classification	Number of Stores	Area (Square Feet/Square Meters)
Food service	3	6,037/560
Home furnishings	1	1,995/185
Personal services	1	2,200/205
Entertainment (theater)	1	12,600/1,170
Other (marine sales)	1	10,500/975
Total	7	33,332/3,095

Development Cost Information (in Millions)

Site acquisition	$24.5
Site improvement and construction	41.4
Soft costs	9.5
Total development costs	$75.4

Financing Information (in Millions)

Financing source	Amount
Tax increment bonds	$58.0
Bond refinancing	10.0
California Department of Boating and Waterways	6.9
California Department of Transportation	0.5

Project Timeline

1989	Planning started
1991	Site purchased
1992	Construction started
1992	Sales/leasing started
1994	Marine Phase I completed

Major Project Participants

Suisun City Redevelopment Agency
701 Civic Center Boulevard
Suisun City, California 94585
707-421-7309

ROMA Design Group
1527 Stockton Street
San Francisco, California 94133
415-616-9900

building its new city hall in the harbor redevelopment area, demonstrating its commitment to the project.

The city acted as its own developer—improving land, creating parcels, and recruiting buyers and users; although these tasks required enormous amounts of time, skill, and patience, the city was rewarded with maximum control over the results.

The city turned to the talents and energies of the local community to find unique developers and owners who will be committed to the long-term success of the project. Key strategies used to accomplish this goal involved breaking the project and the site into small pieces and fostering live/work development.

Suisun City has focused on its historic building stock and provided incentives to improve unique and historic structures; it has also geared its redevelopment planning to ensure that new development is of a scale and character that are compatible with the existing historic fabric.

Circular Quay

Sydney, New South Wales Australia

Peter Droege

ydney's Circular Quay waterfront area is an extremely popular urban space—pragmatic and simple, yet extraordinarily diverse. This well-choreographed transport interchange is a central focus of Sydney's pedestrian networks and is effectively connected locally, on a metropolitan, and even on a global scale—by car, taxi, bus, rail, and a variety of watercraft, including ferries, pleasure boats, tourist boats, party junks, ocean liners, historic sails, and the ubiquitous and gnat-like water taxis.

There are no large public gathering spaces on the waterfront; instead, it offers a rich network of diverse and interesting paths, streets, water edges, piers, and plazas. From the water's edge the quay is dominated by ferry-packed wharves; behind it is a backdrop of skyscrapers, flanked by the Sydney Opera House and the proud Sydney Harbour Bridge.

With symbolic meaning that extends well beyond its immediate surroundings, the quay is generally regarded as both the birthplace and the living room of the nation. The place speaks to ordinary people as much as to the well-to-do, and to locals as much as to tourists. A highly successful multiparcel, multideveloper, and mixed-use waterfront domain, the quay is a textbook example of a great waterfront. Living, working, and entertainment areas have been skillfully integrated, and historic structures and locations blend seamlessly into the surrounding new development.

The most striking feature of the area, however, is not visible to the eye: the quay does not have a single master plan in place; what exists instead is an understanding between public and private entities, according to which the privilege of exceptional development opportunities is to be paired with a substantial responsibility to contribute to the quality of the public realm.

In the world of internationally acclaimed waterfront developments, Circular Quay is exceptional. Unlike other waterfront areas in Australia, the United States, and elsewhere in the world, it did not emerge suddenly, shaped by a single plan; nor did it move through the typical stages of industrialization, decline, and redevelopment. Rather, it changed gradually—in the pragmatic and decidedly ad hoc ways of a colonial outpost—into what it is today: a place in flux. And although large-scale interventions have recently altered both the sense of place and how it functions, the authorities have sidestepped the risks of master-planned, wholesale redevelopment. (Given the number of players involved and the *realpolitik* of Sydney's brash development culture, this would, in any

The Overseas Passenger Terminal, adjacent to the Museum of Contemporary Art, allows massive oceangoing vessels to dock right in the heart of the city.

case, have been exceedingly difficult to achieve.) A number of public and private landowners, regulatory agencies, and major private and civic institutional players lay claim to one aspect of the area or another.

The key elements of the quay's success are its central location within the urban core; its role as a principal—yet low-key—transportation hub; strong local government leadership in brokering development deals; intense civic and professional interest in future visions for the area; and, last but not least, the gravitational pull of an international architectural monument: the Opera House, Sydney's Bilbao of the 1970s.

A Waterfront in Flux

Sydney Cove, the more formal name for the harbor area that contains Circular Quay, was the initial locus of English settlement in Australia, in 1788. Because of its attractive maritime features, the colony's first ruler, Governor Phillip, selected the site as the headquarters for the first penal colony. In the first century of migrant settlement, these same features led to Sydney's transformation into the principal port of the young colony.

As the earliest site of European settlement, Sydney Cove—more than any other place on the continent—symbolizes the impact of European settlement on Australia's indigenous peoples. The earliest physical evidence of Eora-speaking aboriginal settlements in the area dates back six millennia; but the Cadigal clan, which had thrived on the southern side of Sydney Harbour, was extinguished rapidly through displacement, neglect, and imported disease.

Formal planning for the area began in 1837, when, under the direction of Governor Gipps, Captain George Barney, the colonial engineer, designed Semi-Circular Quay. Funded by gold mine revenues, the curved marine-service structures were completed ten years later. In 1851, the records begin to refer to Semi-Circular Quay simply as Circular Quay. Yet another decade later, the quay was linked to the central Redfern Station by one of Sydney's first horse-drawn trams; in 1879, the trams were replaced by steam engines. During the 1880s, iron and masonry

The historic Rocks area, which forms the western flank of Circular Quay, avoided wholesale redevelopment in the early 1970s and is now a popular tourist attraction and entertainment area.

structure at the quay. Although the structure, which was completed in 1956, was designed to allow as much visibility through the supports as possible, it cut off the historic Customs House (built in 1847) from its prominent harborfront position. Also in 1956, the wharves were reconstructed as flat-roofed pontoon structures and extended along a straight alignment farther into the cove.

works replaced the original 1855 timber wharves, and the jetties were covered with corrugated-iron roofing, decorative ridge caps, and simple timber and cast-iron features. By 1890 the quay supported an estimated 5 million ferry passengers annually.

By the end of the 19th century, the bustling ship traffic and the support structures of Circular Quay had become visual hallmarks of Sydney. In 1901, the newly established Sydney Harbour Trust began to transform the quay, rebuilding wharves (in an attempt to control the rat population) and planting Canary Island palms and fig trees. Construction of the new underground City Circle railway began in 1923, but was not completed until well after the end of World War II.

The completion of Sydney Harbour Bridge, in 1932, led to a substantial decline in ferry use, and to the decline of the quay as well, until it became what one report referred to as "probably the . . . untidiest front door" of any city in the world. This state of affairs motivated the state government to establish, in 1936, the Circular Quay Planning Committee. In that same year a new Maritime Services Board (MSB) absorbed the Sydney Harbour Trust, and the new MSB building replaced the Old Government Commissariat Store, which dated to 1809. Although much of the new City Circle line was underground, efforts to save costs led to the construction of a cheaper, elevated station

The opening of the Sydney Opera House, in 1973, marked the beginning of the revival of Sydney Cove. The building's design and position heighten the harbor front experience, turning the city toward the water in a dramatic and radical way.

The revival of Circular Quay progressed slowly over the following decades. In 1961, the International Passenger Terminal opened on the west side of the quay, making the area the first point of arrival for waves of largely British and European migrants. In 1957, a change to the Height of Buildings Act prompted the demolition of small-scale gabled bond stores, which were replaced by a row of three narrow, high-rise office structures—efficient but undistinguished. ICI House and Unilever House opened in 1958, and Lend Lease House followed in 1961. This side of the quay—now formal, urban, and dense—was still lushly planted with exotic and local varieties of flora.

The most significant milestone, perhaps, was the opening, in 1973, of the Sydney Opera House. Construction had been in progress throughout much of the sixties, but no one had envisioned the enormous impact on tourism that the opera house would engender: designed not only to measure up to but to reinforce the spectacular harbor location, the opera house soon emerged as one of the 20th century's architectural highlights.

Throughout the 1980s and 1990s, the area around the opera house was transformed into a dynamic and complex entertainment district. And the historic Rocks area, which forms the quay's western flank (the opera house is positioned at its eastern edge), is now a popular tourist attraction and entertainment area.

Other changes included the establishment, in 1993, of the Museum of Contemporary Art (MCA) in the abandoned MSB Building, and the approval, in 1994, of the large-scale redevelopment of ICI House, Unilever House, and Lend Lease House, a project that was to include an exclusive hotel, a restaurant, and a residential complex. These developments marked the transformation of the area from a diverse but rather utilitarian hub with some significant cultural functions into a full-blown entertainment district. They also raised the stakes in some important, longstanding conflicts—such as those between the pleasure crafts and the oceangoing ships, between Sydneysiders from poorer neighborhoods and the "cappuccino set," and between the daily commuters and the throngs of tourists queuing up for the ferries to Toronga Zoo, Manly Bay, and Watson's Bay.

Three Dimensions of Redevelopment

The ongoing redevelopment of Sydney Cove can be described in terms of three parallel dimensions. One dimension consists of the individual development projects; instead of being guided by any single vision or master plan, these projects are monitored rather casually through the quasi-democratic processes of public discussion and consultation, and through various other regulatory procedures that are designed to optimize the value—both public and private—of development.

The second dimension is the process through which targeted infrastructure is maintained and upgraded. The

Sydney Harbour Foreshore Authority (SHFA) is responsible for protecting and enhancing the natural and cultural heritage of Sydney's inner harbor foreshore through place management and development, heritage conservation, urban renewal, and tourism. In 1998, the SHFA commissioned a set of initiatives that are carried out by another state-government body, the Department of Public Works and Services. The SHFA hopes to renovate or redevelop existing infrastructure in key areas, adding highly designed finishes in the process. The SHFA hopes to accomplish this task, in part, by guiding the capital investments of stakeholder agencies such as Sydney Ferries, an organization that operates under the aegis of the New South Wales State Department of Transport. Through this effort, the SHFA also seeks to improve Circular Quay's function as a transportation interchange that brings together, in one small area, commuter ferries, tour boats, water taxis, city buses, tour buses, taxis, and rail.

The last dimension is that of management and maintenance, a domain that extends beyond basic quasi-public functions to embrace retail planning and management, leasing arrangements, and development services. This effort is being pursued by the SHFA as part of a new corporate direction; in another waterfront part of the city, Ultimo-Pyrmont, the SHFA is overseeing the development of strategic infrastructure, such as fiber-optic cabling, in order to promote the area as a high-tech location.

Precincts and Projects of Circular Quay

The work undertaken on a number of development parcels illustrates the long-term, incremental approach that has been used to upgrade and revitalize Sydney Cove and Circular Quay. The Overseas Passenger Terminal, the careful rehabilitation and infill development undertaken

The view, from Dr. Mary Booth Park, of the Sydney Harbour Bridge, the opera house, and Sydney Cove.

on the western edge, and the larger-scale reconstruction of what is known as East Circular Quay are good examples, as are the refurbishment and rebuilding of the current Museum of Contemporary Art, the upgrading of the terminal structures and their retail and technical components, and the reconstruction of the opera house.

The Opera House and Its Environs

The Sydney Opera House, completed in 1973, is not only the key architectural icon for Circular Quay, Sydney, its harbor front, and urban Australia, but is a symbol of waterfront development everywhere. The opera house has inspired cultural projects worldwide, from China to Spain. Drawing over 1 million tourists annually, the opera house is the major anchor for all the features and facilities of Sydney Cove. Two things make the opera house outstanding: its design and its position on the Bennelong Point, a promontory that juts out into Sydney

Harbour and provides extraordinary views of the central business district and Sydney Harbour Bridge. The combined force of the design and location helped turn the city toward the water in a dramatic and radical way. The completion of the opera house marked the beginning of the revival of Circular Quay and Sydney Cove as a whole.

The Sydney Opera House Trust owns the opera house and parts of the precinct immediately surrounding the building. In late 1999, the trust hired Jorn Utzon, the original designer, to work with Richard Johnson, the renowned director of Johnson, Pilton & Walker; together, the designers were to develop a renovation plan that would protect the original design intent and be in keeping with current needs. The long-term strategic building plan developed by Utzon and Johnson established a scheme for the renovation of the interior, the exterior, and the associated perimeter spaces.

The refurbishment will partially retain the building's internal components (which were designed by the city's architect, Peter Hall, after Utzon's unhappy departure

The Park Hyatt Hotel

The success of the Park Hyatt Hotel, at Campbell's Cove, on the western side of Circular Quay, was the product of close interaction between the developer, the architect, and what was then known as the SCRA, the Sydney Cove Redevelopment Authority.[1] There were three keys to the success of the project: maximizing the return on the premium waterfront location, ensuring that the project came to be identified with its setting, and avoiding the risk to corporate image that can result from developing a highly exposed site in an unsuccessful way.

Conceived and developed in 1989 by CRI Limited, the project resulted from a bid and a consequent development effort tailored to the design envelope and guidelines provided by the SCRA. Since its opening, the Park Hyatt has achieved the highest room rates in the city while maintaining an average occupancy level of 80 percent—also among the highest in the city.

It can be argued that the hotel's performance is due largely to the location, the privileged view, and Sydney's vibrant hotel market. But location alone does not guarantee success. While modest at first glance, the hotel greatly increased the sense of complexity, drama, and excitement in the area. By taking a contextual approach to the urban design, the developers avoided the potential risk of community objection. (Few things are worse for corporate image than an awkward architectural solution in a highly exposed public site.)

The project embodies the best practices in architectural design for the public domain and makes the best of what was already an extraordinary site. Its low-slung massing and the curves of both the building and the waterfront promenade, along with the consistency in architectural articulation and design detail, render the Park Hyatt the experiential counterpoint of the Sydney Opera House, perched at the opposite side of Circular Quay. Perhaps

during construction). Special attention will be paid to improving accessibility. In addition, a retail, restaurant, and entertainment environment will be created to accommodate the enormous tourist stream that was never envisioned in the original concept for the opera house.

An application for listing as a World Heritage site (a list sponsored by UNESCO) has been prepared and is pending the resolution of public funding and other long-term management issues. That application, together with the statement of heritage significance and Jorn Utzon's design principles, will place the future redevelopment of the opera house on a firm footing. (Utzon won the 2003 Pritzker Prize for his design of the Sydney Opera House.) However, one important issue that remains to be addressed is how the structure and its immediate surroundings can be made to fit even better into the larger context of the quay.

most important, the project has come to be virtually synonymous with the larger urban jewel surrounding it: the Rocks and West Circular Quay. The Park Hyatt benefited from the successful adjoining area of the Rocks, and contributed value in its turn.

The building has stood the test of time: it is as fresh and up-to-date as when it first opened. Nevertheless, there are certain design flaws, including a facade that is impervious to public use; pedestrian access to large stretches of the waterside, which dampens the experience; and a needlessly homogeneous approach to the staging of hotel spaces. To balance the homogeneity, smaller restaurants were added within the building envelope in 2000 and 2001. These restaurants have enriched the waterfront enormously, adding to the diversity, appeal, and success of Sydney Cove's waterfront areas.

The Park Hyatt demonstrates the value of successful synergy between intelligent urban design, effective civic leadership, and corporate sensitivity. The result—a win-win situation for the public and private participants—enhanced both their images and provided an important public amenity.

East Circular Quay

Unlike the Park Hyatt, the development of East Circular Quay was less than a success. In 1999, when a new block of apartments rose up alongside the opera house, the response was a massive public outcry. The building was the first of a set of buildings, initially approved in 1993, that were intended to replace a tall, narrow strip of commercial office blocks that dated back to the late 1950s and early 1960s. The original plans called for a hotel and for retail and residential uses, but the project was later renegotiated without the hotel component. Dubbed "the Toaster" by the press because of its unusual appearance, the apartment building provoked an immediate hubbub—including a serious call for its demolition, despite the fact that it was largely complete. Public petitions and open letters were filed from around the world, rallies

were staged, and demonstrations were held. A California businessman even offered to purchase the structure and substitute for it a tall new building at the edge of the central business district (CBD), but the only alternative site proved too difficult to acquire.

Ultimately, it was not the new building that upset the populace but the belated realization that there had been an opportunity not to have a wall of buildings at all. Despite six years of public discussion and design review, no one had anticipated the magnificent view of the Royal Botanical Gardens and the Old Government House that would be revealed when the old office buildings, which had long been vacant, finally fell. This, combined with the fresh reality of private residences a stone's throw from the opera house, filled tourists and locals alike with a tremendous sense of loss. Other proposals that had been tendered earlier for the site—one of which called for the development of gardens and parklands and would have reserved new buildings to the edge of the CBD—were now recalled.

But the storm settled as quickly as it arose, thanks largely to the unique, hands-on approach to deal making of Frank Sartor, Sydney's lord mayor, and to the skills of another civic design leader, Paul Keating, who was then prime minister. Sometimes referred to as "Australia's Prince Charles," Keating is a committed amateur urban designer as well as a civic power broker who, along with Sartor, worked out an agreement with the developers—the Colonial Mutual insurance group and Mirvac, a publicly listed residential development company—under which the apartment buildings would be of lower height, and the historic Customs House, located directly south of the Circular Quay rail station, would be refurbished for public use (It is now the home of the popular City Exhibition Space.)

A pedestrian walkway beginning at the base of the new buildings and extending to the opera house was transformed into a two-story arcade several hundred yards in length. (When it opened, sporting a number of bars, restaurants, shops, and a boutique cinema, civic leaders and public-opinion leaders not only buried the hatchet, but some even began to speak lovingly of the development.) Where there was a full-height gap between the territories of the two developers, a walkway to the park side of the development was retained.

Despite the ominously looming facades and the general bulk and "privatized" air of the new buildings, which seemed to tower massively over the fragile quay, they did indeed prove to be much lower in height than their predecessors. Nevertheless, the new buildings had to command a considerably wider berth in order to accommodate spacious luxury apartments with grand views of the harbor and park.

Development to more profitable residential depths made it necessary to claim the old covered walkway that had been intended to shelter the stream of tourists as they moved from the central quay area to the opera house. Because the walkway was public space, the developers had to acquire the air rights from the city. The city government, in turn, joined the group overseeing the design and construction of the project, and, as part owner, gained a seat on the body corporate strata council (the building owners' cooperative).

Other Developments

A number of other related projects are worth mentioning. The dramatic, popularly supported rescue, in the 1970s, of the picturesque Rocks historic district, which was threatened with destruction by wholesale redevelopment, was critical to the rise of a major cultural and tourist attraction and to the preservation of a major source of Sydney Cove's current vitality. The Rocks is the site of some of Australia's earliest urban structures. The wool stores of Campbell's Cove are but the most prominent quayside face of the Rocks: their conversion into restaurants has been an important step in the incremental transformation of Sydney Cove.

Another project that had a powerful impact on Circular Quay was the refurbishment of the wharves themselves, a move that relegated much of the thriving, but visually distracting, fast-food business to other parts of the quay, and sanitized the messy world of ferry support. For better or worse, this refurbishment—completed in 2000, in time for the Olympic Games—gave the structures a more sober and cosmopolitan appearance that was enhanced by sleek steel-

At the Rocks, the site of some of the earliest structures in urban Australia, the conversion of buildings into restaurants has been an important step in the incremental transformation of the city as a whole.

and-glass additions. The wharves were designed by the preeminent Queensland architects Kerry and Lindsay Clare, who had been retained by the Department of Public Works and Services as creative-talent-in-residence.

On the west side of the quay, the Overseas Passenger Terminal that, in the 1980s, replaced the original 1961 structure, has allowed massive oceangoing vessels to come right into the heart of the city, a breathtaking sight to behold. (Sydney Ports owns and operates the structure.) A study commissioned by the Department of Public Works and Services has proposed that the public spaces on the terminal's southern side be refurbished and commercially supported with new restaurant space. And, despite the desirability of having spectacular ocean liners arrive right in the city center, there is likely to be increasing pressure to open up this large site to more active and commercially profitable uses. Discussions are already underway involving the replacement and relocation of the passenger arrival facility, which is only one of a number in operation within the general reach of the CBD.

Also on the western side, but farther to the south, sits the Museum of Contemporary Art (MCA), hard against the edge of the CBD and the Rocks and occupying the structure that once housed the Maritime Services Board. In recent years, the MCA has experienced great difficulties: it lost its university endowment, and neither the state nor local governments were willing to provide outright financial support. In 2000 and 2001, the University of Sydney entrusted the city with the task of exploring options for the future of the facility. The city made various attempts to raise funds from government and industry and developed several architectural proposals, one of which involved the addition of a new wing dedicated to the art of the moving image. Several rounds of international design competitions were completed. One of the leading options calls for the structure simply to be razed, and to be replaced with a large, mixed-use development that would also house the institution in more suitable space; the proceeds, tax, and income from the development would be used, in part, to offset the costs associated with operating the museum.

Flanking Circular Quay on its east and west sides are two distinct cultural districts. On the east, a continuous and powerful domain stretches from the opera house to the Botanical Gardens, past the Old Government House, and on to the newly expanded Conservatory of Music, the State Library, the Domain parklands, and the Art Gallery of New South Wales; as it continues deeper into the city, the district encompasses the refurbished Sydney Hospital, the Hyde Park Barracks, St. Mary's Cathedral, Cook and Phillip Park, and the Museum of Australia. On the west side, the Rocks constitutes a single cultural precinct with a large number of historic sites and important institutions, and the Museum of Contemporary Art is in a sense an important component of that precinct. These larger contexts are waiting to be seized as clues to a new future for the quay as the most direct open-space link between the eastern and western flanks of the city.

Lessons Learned

The success of recent strategies and developments in Circular Quay hinged on continuous civic attention, the creation of suitable institutions to match emerging needs, and a shrewd championing of projects by various local and national leaders. The area's successes emerged from a fragmented and ad hoc approach. The newly mooted, updated strategic plan that the Department of Public Works and Services commissioned covers only part of the Sydney Cove waterfront; it excludes the opera house and the East Circular Quay areas, largely because of conflicts between the jurisdiction of the city of Sydney and the state-owned SHFA. It seems inevitable that all public authorities and major private players involved need to institute a master programming process to address the area's extraordinary civic potential, without sacrificing its exceptional diversity, vitality, and civic openness.

The final lesson illustrated by Circular Quay is that there are five fundamental elements necessary for a successful urban waterside space:

■ A central, well-connected location;
■ Easy access to a multitude of transportation systems;
■ Broad access to a variety of income groups engaged in a range of activities;
■ Proximity to major tourist attractions;
■ Preservation of authenticity.

All images in this case study are courtesy of Tourism New South Wales.

Note

1. The SCRA, the City West Development Authority, the Darling Harbour Authority, and the Australian Technology Park—all state-government–owned development and management corporations—were recently integrated into the Sydney Harbour Foreshore Authority (SHFA). The SHFA now owns and manages virtually all the public spaces of the defined Sydney Cove/Circular Quay redevelopment zone. Exceptions are the territory of the Opera House Trust; the public spaces along the East Circular Quay development; the spaces associated with the Overseas Passenger Terminal, which are owned by Sydney Ports; and a small adjacent park belonging to the National Parks and Wildlife Service.

Project Data: **Circular Quay**

Project Timeline

1932	Sydney Harbour Bridge completed		1973	Sydney Opera House completed
1958	ICI House and Unilever House open		1989	Park Hyatt Sydney opens
1961	International Passenger Terminal opens		1991	Museum of Contemporary Art completed
1961	Lend Lease House built			

Major Project Participants

CRI Limited
Sydney, New South Wales
Australia

Johnson Pilton Walker
Sydney, New South Wales
Australia
Web site: www.jpw.com/au

Kim Utzon Architects
Copenhagen, Denmark
Web site: http://www.utzon.dk/

Museum of Contemporary Art
Royal Exchange
Sydney, New South Wales
Australia
Web site: www.mca.com.au

Sydney Harbour Foreshore Authority
The Rocks, New South Wales
Australia

Grosvenor Place
Sydney, New South Wales
Australia
Web site: www.shfa.nsw.gov.au

Sydney Ports
Sydney, New South Wales
Australia
Web site: www.sydneyports.com/au

Sydney Opera Trust
Royal Exchange
Sydney, New South Wales
Australia
Web site: www.soh.nsw.gov.au

Harbourfront

Toronto, Ontario Canada

Beth Benson

Toronto's waterfront has always been a place of change, a place where nature meets culture and where hopes and dreams are debated and lived. Far from its beginnings, in 1793, as a small settlement on the shores of Lake Ontario, Toronto is now known as one of the most ethnically diverse cities in the world and as one of the most desirable places to live, work, and visit. Toronto's population is currently 2.4 million, and the city expects to add up to 1 million residents over the next 20 years. The Toronto city region, with 5 million people, has become Canada's economic center and is recognized by the United Nations as "one of the most multicultural cities in the world."

Toronto's continued reputation as one of the world's finest cities is closely linked to the redevelopment of its 28-mile (45-kilometer) waterfront—a project that is poised to become the showcase of this internationally renowned city. Harbourfront, Toronto's signature waterfront project, has been developed through public and private investment over the past 30 years. The lessons of the Harbourfront experience are helping to inform the next phase of the city's waterfront planning and development process and to more clearly establish the roles and responsibilities of government, citizens, and the private sector.

A Vibrant and Eclectic Area

Situated at the heart of Toronto's downtown central waterfront, the Harbourfront area occupies a narrow, 92-acre (37-hectare) strip of land and water lots (land that is covered by water some of the time), just over one mile (1.6 kilometers) long and varying in width from approximately 600 to 1,320 feet (183 to 402 meters). The area is bounded by York Street on the east and Stadium Road on the west, and is squeezed between the Lake Ontario shoreline to the south and Lakeshore Boulevard to the north. To the north of the site are the former railway lands and the main rail corridor, and one-third of a mile (0.5 kilometers) further north are the towers of downtown Toronto.

Public programming and services now run the length of the project area, along the water's edge from York Street to Stadium Road, south of Queens Quay West. Most of the activity is concentrated at the eastern end, on York Quay, where Harbourfront Centre provides a vibrant and eclectic year-round selection of cultural, educational, and recreational programs for both adults and children. Each year, more than 4,000 events are held there, attracting more than 3 million visitors.

West, the public buildings are interspersed with parks and open space, allowing full public access to the water's edge and many views—both of the harbor, lake, and islands to the south and of the towers of the city's central financial district to the north.

A Unique Waterfront Park

For more than 90 years the central waterfront was Toronto's main industrial, rail, and port center. By the 1960s, however, the area was not only obsolete for these uses but had also become isolated and decayed, cut off from the life of the city by outmoded infrastructure, environmental degradation, and the inaccessibility of the shoreline. When the city government initiated plans for the area's future, market conditions clearly demanded that the next phase of waterfront development would be a mixture of private and public uses, with a balance of residential and commercial land use.

Residential buildings, such as these condominium buildings, face the northern edge of Harbourfront, along Queens Quay West. *Urban Strategies Inc.*

An almost continuous line of predominantly residential buildings now defines the northern edge of Harbourfront, along Queens Quay West. All the buildings are privately owned, and range in height from eight to 14 stories at the western end to 37 stories at the eastern end, closest to the downtown. On the south side of Queens Quay

In the early 1970s, as part of the first phase of the redevelopment program, private high-rise commercial and residential buildings were constructed at the water's edge, immediately to the east of what was to become the Harbourfront site. Citizens perceived these buildings as blocking public access to the water, however, and were concerned that the central waterfront would become a private domain for private profit—with little, if any, public use. The voicing of these objections proved to be a turning point for the Toronto waterfront.

In 1972, in response to public concern, the Canadian government acquired 92 acres (37 hectares) of land and water lots that became known as the Harbourfront lands. The intent was to help change the course of Toronto's waterfront redevelopment by creating an urban park that would guarantee the people of Toronto continuous public access to the waterfront. However, the land acquisition was undertaken without consultation with the province or local governments, a move that set the stage for difficult negotiations and led to delays in the creation of a development plan on which all stakeholders could agree. Citizens demanded participation in the planning as well as in the implementation of the project.

In 1978, after several years of intergovernmental negotiation and public consultation, the federal government created a quasi-independent development agency, Harbourfront Corporation, to manage the development of Toronto's premier waterfront park. The corporation was given a dual mandate by the government: to develop the site and to provide public programming. Given the economic prosperity of that period, it was expected that the Harbourfront Corporation would generate revenues from its real estate development activities and become self-sufficient within seven years. Revenues from the development would be used to partly subsidize the programming and would also contribute to the provision of park space and open space.

The Harbourfront Development Framework that was devised to guide design, programming, and both public and private investment was not a traditional master plan but a more flexible instrument that would allow for creativity and change as long as they were in keeping with the overall concept. The Harbourfront Corporation would submit each project to the city of Toronto for its planning approval, and to the federal government for the approval of public funding.

During the creation of the Development Framework, the concept for the "unique urban waterfront park" that was to be the heart of Harbourfront evolved: initially planned as a passive green space, the park developed into something more active, which would blend traditional parkland and open space with a variety of cultural, recreational, residential, and commercial activities. The goal of the Development Framework was to achieve the complete rejuvenation of Harbourfront as a people-oriented, mixed-use urban area. The buildout program was to be based on nine key principles:

■ To attract private investment, the Harbourfront Corporation would make upfront public investments in infrastructure (roads, sewers, etc.). Private developers who successfully competed for the right to develop the planned residential and commercial developments would receive long-term ground leases (66.5 years), and the lands and buildings would revert to the Crown at the end of the leases.

■ Harbourfront Corporation would achieve self-sufficiency within seven years.

■ Harbourfront would be an identifiable community, providing live/work opportunities.

■ Public access to the waterfront and the surrounding area would be improved, as would integration with the city and the railway lands to the north of the Harbourfront area.

■ A strong mix of activities would be provided, making a place for a cross-section of the community.

■ Development would demonstrate respect for climatic conditions by, for example, using buildings and covered walkways to shelter open space, and making use of indoor space.

- All building design would demonstrate respect for views and vistas.
- Ground-level space would be devoted to public uses.
- Existing buildings would be restored, renovated, or preserved wherever possible.

In 1980, when the Toronto City Council passed the Harbourfront Part II Official Plan and Zoning By-Law, it put the Development Framework into effect. The Official Plan and By-Law provided general guidance for the use and density of each major part of the site, for a total of 5.9 million square feet (548,125 square meters) of development. Detailed subarea plans, allocating uses and densities to specific sites, soon followed.

Early Success

In its early years, Harbourfront was a great success: increasing numbers of people were drawn to the site by imaginative and creative programs, aimed at all age groups, whose costs were subsidized by the federal government. The federal government spent $54.6 million to assemble the Harbourfront lands and invested $40.2 million on parks, infrastructure, and other site improvements.[1] Most of this investment preceded private sector involvement in the project. Ottawa also subsidized operations in the early years, but by 1976 the federal government insisted that Harbourfront Corporation become financially self-sufficient by the mid-1980s.

The second turning point for the waterfront came during 1982–84, when Toronto struggled with a hard-hitting recession. During the early 1980s, Harbourfront Corporation continued to strive for financial self-sufficiency by pursuing private residential development, and set aside its original development concept to allow the construction of five high-rise residential buildings on the north side of Queens Quay West. Public objections to the addition of more high-rise buildings on the waterfront—and public disappointment with the Harbourfront Corporation's failure to complete the park and promenade projects—led to strong public demands for more parks, and for develop-

The 1980 Development Framework mandated the rehabilitation and reuse of existing waterfront buildings. Here, a power plant has been renovated for use as an art gallery. *Urban Strategies Inc.*

ment authority to be placed in the hands of local government. Harbourfront Corporation had lost the public trust.

In 1990, the federal government responded by dismantling Harbourfront Corporation and gradually divesting its land holdings. The lands south of Queens Quay West were transferred to the ownership of the city of Toronto. In 1991, under a long-term lease, a nonprofit charitable organization, Harbourfront Centre, was established to oversee the programming and operation of the city's land from York Street to Stadium Road, south of Queens Quay West. Most of the rest of the original Harbourfront lands (that is, on the north side of Queens Quay West) was sold to private interests.

Harbourfront Today: Managing the Public Realm

The goals that were set for Toronto's Harbourfront project in 1980—ensuring public access to the water's edge; creating new parks; building a lively, stimulating, well-designed,

Real Estate Development Put Harbourfront on the Map

Harbourfront Corporation's parks, public programming, and initial development projects radically changed the image of Toronto's waterfront. The early real estate developments were of high quality and widely acclaimed. The renovation of the Terminal Warehouse and the construction of the Admiral Hotel and the King's Landing condominiums have been held up as good examples of urban design and renewal.

The conversion of the Terminal Warehouse is particularly noteworthy. Located at the eastern edge of Harbourfront, the 1928 warehouse was purchased and renovated by Olympia & York in 1982. With a capital cost of $60 million, the project was, at the time, one of the largest renovations of an industrial building in North America. The Canadian architectural firm Zeidler Roberts Partnership transformed the warehouse into a mixture of office, retail, performance, and condominium space by redesigning the interior space and adding four new floors to the original eight. The result was over 471,000 square feet (43,755 square meters) of prime rentable space on Toronto's waterfront. The building—renamed Queens Quay Terminal, and offering a mix of stores, restaurants, offices, and residences, as well as a dance theater—quickly became known as a popular destination for residents and tourists. Now owned by Gentra Inc., and managed by Brookfield Properties, Queens Quay Terminal demonstrates how innovative design and private investment can not only transform a building but also serve as catalysts for reinvestment in the surrounding area.

The goal of ensuring public access to the water's edge has been met all along the waterfront, such as with this facility, used as an international market. *Urban Strategies Inc.*

and people-oriented place; and providing high-quality cultural, recreational, and educational programs—have been largely achieved over the past 23 years. The success of Harbourfront reflects a strong and persistent public demand for a waterfront that is accessible, connected, diverse, attractive, affordable, and green. It also reflects an evolution in governance and accountability, which was required to ensure that the vision was achieved—and that sufficient revenue could be raised to achieve it.

Harbourfront Centre's mandate is to organize and present public activities and events and to operate a ten-acre (four-hectare) site encompassing York Quay and John Quay, south of Queens Quay West. The Centre's professional staff reports to a community-based, 26-member volunteer board of directors. Harbourfront Centre's multipurpose facilities now include several theaters, an art gallery, a dance theater, outdoor concert venues, craft shops and studios, an ice rink and canoe pond, and meeting rooms.

Harbourfront Centre works closely with arts and ethno-cultural groups and is recognized as an international center for cultural exchange, where new frontiers in the arts and creative expression are encouraged. The wide array of affordable programs, produced with the participation of more than 450 community groups each year, gives a large cross-section of people a sense of ownership of Harbourfront Centre.

Harbourfront Centre also manages facilities to support a diverse range of marine activities: two marinas, with a combined total of 300 berths; provision for water taxis and tender services for yacht clubs; and docking facilities

Harbourfront Centre's multipurpose facilities include an ice rink. The iconic CN Tower is a visible landmark to the west. *Urban Strategies Inc.*

The waterfront promenade is part of the 220-mile (354-kilometer) Waterfront Trail, which connects 30 Canadian communities on Lake Ontario. *Urban Strategies Inc.*

at John Quay, for visiting pleasure craft from around the world, and at York Quay, for commercial vessels offering harbor and lake cruises. In addition, the Centre provides marine programs of its own and participates in or organizes frequent events throughout the summer season.

The waterfront promenade that runs the entire length of the Harbourfront site is a link in the 220-mile (354-kilometer) Waterfront Trail, which connects some 30 communities on the Canadian shore of Lake Ontario. Forty acres (16 hectares) of lakeside city parks are being developed along the promenade, offering a variety of experiences within close proximity to each other; visitors' options range from the bustling vitality of the quayside restaurants at York Quay and Queens Quay Terminal to the tranquil

beauty and elaborate design of the Toronto Music Garden, which was inspired by the music of Bach.

Other public amenities at Harbourfront include public marine facilities and a hotel on Maple Leaf Quay, as well as a community center and a school on Bathurst Quay. Also at Bathurst Quay is a ferry service across the 400-foot (122-meter) Western Gap, which lies between Toronto's City Centre Airport and the mainland.

In late 2001 the federal government transferred to the city the final funds it had committed to the development of the Harbourfront parks system, a move that stimulated an important public consultation process that addressed planning for the whole central waterfront, the future of the

Harbourfront parks, and linkages between the waterfront and surrounding communities and parks, including the railway lands. The results of the public involvement to date indicate that the first priority is to maintain the existing uses; within this priority, stakeholders want a traditional urban park design, complemented by more green space and the preservation of waterfront views.

Many members of the public have said that Harbourfront needs a new, unifying "Big Idea." Almost universally, stakeholders agreed that the music garden is a wonderful park and a special place, but that it needs to be complemented and connected to other unique park spaces to really make a difference. *Looking* was one of the most frequently identified activities for the Harbourfront urban parks system—being able to look at boats, at the water, and at the vitality of the city is a highly valued activity that translates into designs that protect views and enhance connections. Predictably, access to the public spaces and being able to move easily through the area—along the water's edge, on foot, in a wheelchair, on a bike, or while using in-line skates—is another priority for the public. Finally, the public would like to see stronger landscape links between the various venues and Harbourfront's pocket parks.

The Centre's annual operating revenues ($22.7 million in 2003) are derived from sponsorship and foundations (20 percent); parking and site fees (28 percent); event admissions (14 percent); facilities rental, such as the Premiere Dance Theater and Harbourfront Centre Theatre (6 percent); government programming grants (11 percent); federal government investment (18 percent); and the city (3 percent). The Centre's permanent staff of 130 expands to 400 during the summer months. A 2000 study showed that Harbourfront Centre annually returns $132 million to the region, provides 1,240 person-years of employment, and returns $24 million in taxes to the government.

A New In-Town Neighborhood

Over the past decade, a broad mix of urban housing that reflects Toronto's diverse population—including social housing, affordable co-op housing, market-rate rental apartments, and luxury condominiums—has been developed along the northern edge of Harbourfront. With some 4,400 units in place and an additional 635 under review by the city of Toronto, residential development is nearing buildout. Units range in size from 506 square feet (47 square meters) for a studio to 947 square feet (88 square meters) for a two-bedroom. Although the new developments do not include affordable housing units, the city's current review of its Central Waterfront Plan (adopted April 2003) will revisit the need for affordable housing in the western part of the area, on Bathurst Quay.

Changing the Course

In retrospect, two distinct phases emerge in the implementation of the Harbourfront plan, both of which were closely linked to the two main economic cycles that influenced development throughout Toronto. In the first phase, during the economic boom of the late 1970s and early 1980s, Harbourfront Corporation was able to dramatically change the image of Toronto's central waterfront, turning it into a desirable destination for residents and tourists alike.

The corporation's initial development strategy was to open up development opportunities across the whole site by negotiating long-term (66.5-year) ground leases with developers for individual development sites. At the same time, the corporation undertook a rapidly expanding program of public activities on the waterfront; it also moved toward its goal of financial self-sufficiency. Within a short time, the corporation had entered into contracts with a half-dozen developers for the design and approval of almost half the allocated density, and additional contracts were in the approval pipeline.

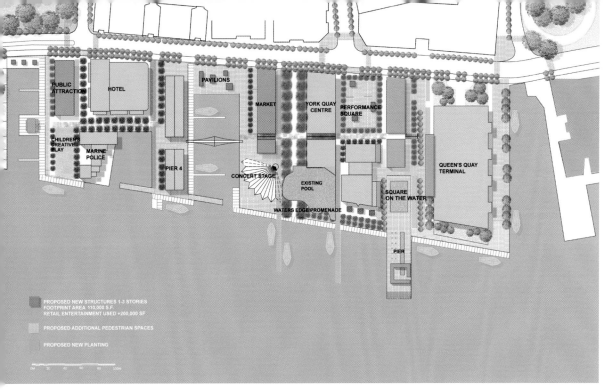

PUBLIC
ATTRACTION

HOTEL

PAVILIONS

CHILDREN'S
CREATIVE
PLAY

MARINE
POLICE

PIER 4

MARKET

YORK QUAY
CENTRE

PERFORMANCE
SQUARE

QUEEN'S QUAY
TERMINAL

CONCERT STAGE

EXISTING
POOL

SQUARE
ON THE WATER

WATERS EDGE PROMENADE

PIER

PROPOSED NEW STRUCTURES 1-3 STORIES
FOOTPRINT AREA 110,000 S.F.
RETAIL ENTERTAINMENT USED +200,000 SF

PROPOSED ADDITIONAL PEDESTRIAN SPACES

PROPOSED NEW PLANTING

Harbourfront Centre's master plan of 2003 for the ten acres (four hectares) south of Queens Quay West and between York and John quays.
Harbourfront Centre

By 1983, however, the economic boom had turned into a recession; the real estate market lost momentum, and the Harbourfront Corporation's drive to achieve self-sufficiency within the seven-year target was threatened. Endeavoring to meet its commitments by adjusting its priorities, the corporation elected to focus on the social housing component of the project until stronger market conditions returned. Five high-rise buildings were constructed.

In the eyes of the public, however, the corporation appeared to be turning away from its commitment to provide public parks and cultural programs. In response to the public's demands for change, all three levels of government, and the community at large, became involved in an extensive policy and planning review. Between 1987 and 1991, project development came to a halt while the issues were debated, and solutions developed.

Public opinion was clear. Citizens wanted guaranteed public access to the full length of the water's edge at Harbourfront and assurance that the planned 40 acres (16 hectares) of parks and outdoor open space would be completed; they also wanted Harbourfront's affordable and diverse cultural programming to continue. Although the federal government continued to underwrite Harbourfront's programs while the review was underway, the government also felt that it had accomplished its initial objective—that is, to change the course of Toronto's waterfront development—and did not wish to continue as the long-term owner of the site.

As the settlement was being worked out, the second economic downturn occurred, arriving quite suddenly in 1989. Toronto was among the hardest hit centers in the country, and the effects lasted a number of years.

A New Organization, New Tools

The review resulted in a fundamental reorganization of the whole project. The Harbourfront Corporation was dissolved in 1990, and in 1991, its programming function—along with the associated buildings—was turned over to a new, nonprofit charitable organization called Harbourfront Centre, governed by a 26-member local board of directors.

Harbourfront Corporation's development function was assigned to a new and temporary land corporation, Queens Quay Land Corporation, which was given a mandate to dispose of all land assets not required for public purposes. Land for public purposes, including the waterfront promenade, the parks, and all utilities, as well as the ten acres (four hectares) on York Quay allocated as a base for programming, was transferred from the federal

The elevated Gardner Expressway continues to act as a physical and psychological barrier between the waterfront and the city of Toronto. At center left, north of the viaduct, is the Skydome, with its retractable roof in closed position, and the base of the CN Tower.
Urban Strategies Inc.

government to the city. The city thus became the landlord of Harbourfront Centre.

In 1991, the city council adopted a revised Harbourfront Part II Official Plan and Zoning By-Law for the Harbourfront area, which set out site-by-site densities, heights, and setbacks; provided for community facilities; and designated 40 acres (16 hectares) of land to be developed as parkland and a water's edge promenade. The plan also prescribed the transfer of density from the south side of Queens Quay to the north, which permitted the 40 acres (16 hectares) to be protected. The city council also approved a set of design guidelines covering open spaces, view corridors, the relationship of buildings to the surrounding streets, building scale and orientation, pedestrian comfort, the quality of the streetscape, and the accommodation of cyclists. While protecting the public interest, the city council set the stage for a new wave of private development.

Because of the economic conditions, the Queens Quay West Land Corporation gradually sold off sites for residential development at substantially reduced prices. Since there was no market, however, developers and investors held off on construction until demand picked up; it was not until 1995–96, after the Toronto economy had recovered, that residential (condominium) construction at Harbourfront resumed. The pace of development by the private sector has been rapid since that time.

Harbourfront is now a vibrant part of Toronto's waterfront community; a residential area of choice for a broad cross-section of the market; a center of cultural, recreational, and educational programming; and a destination for Torontonians and tourists alike. It is viewed as a distinctive neighborhood, rather than as a special enclave managed by an agency of higher government.

Together with the surrounding neighborhoods, Harbourfront has now achieved the critical mass necessary to ensure convenient access to a full range of urban services, and to weather economic cycles. Separating the development function from public programming was one of the keys to its success.

As with any complex development project in the core of the city, there are ongoing issues that focus attention on the need for sustained program and capital funding, improved public transit and parking, and improved physical connections to the surrounding urban fabric. Another emerging issue is the potential conflict between the growing residential community adjacent to the vibrant, congested area on the waterfront's edge.

For two principal reasons, Harbourfront has not yet been fully integrated into the fabric of the city. First, the rail lands are still under development, and the road network that will connect them to the city is not yet complete. The second and more significant reason is that the elevated Gardner Expressway continues to be both a physical and psychological barrier between the city and Harbourfront. There are now prospects, however, that the expressway will be replaced by the combination of an upgraded regular road network and an expanded regional transit system. This scheme is under discussion by the city, the province, and the federal government as part of a much larger initiative to further revitalize Toronto's 28-mile- (45-kilometer-) long waterfront. However, it is likely to be at least ten years before this substantially improved system will benefit Harbourfront.

Achieving Critical Mass

The experience of Harbourfront holds important lessons about waterfront development that touch on political, planning and design, and financial issues.

The Role of Government

Most Torontonians would agree that without the involvement of the federal government after the first wave of development, in the late 1970s, city residents would have been cut off from their central waterfront by a wall of private high-rise buildings. Most would also say that Harbourfront as it is today, with its blend of residential buildings, parks, open space, commercial activity, and programming, is a highly valued part of their waterfront.

That the federal government precipitated action in 1972 was, in an important sense, an accident of the political situation. In different circumstances it could have been the city or the province that intervened, or a combination of governments that joined together. The lesson is that governments have an important role to play in waterfront development because the public interest is often at stake. However, unilateral action on the part of a higher level of government is seldom productive. Success depends on effective relations with local government, and confrontation between different levels of government can be avoided where development is based on a shared vision that is rooted in community-based objectives.

Private Sector Involvement

The second lesson of Harbourfront bears on the management challenges involved in a complex, long-term waterfront project. In structuring the Toronto Waterfront Revitalization initiative, the three levels of government considered various implementation options, including the past Harbourfront experience. They concluded that in view of the project's overall complexity and scale, government would be unable to meet the challenge alone. Private sector skills, creativity, and financial resources were critical to the success of the project. The chosen vehicle for managing the revitalization was a special-purpose development corporation with strong mechanisms of accountability to ensure that local objectives were met from the start.

The Evolution of the Public/Private Partnership

The creators of the Harbourfront Corporation intended it to manage a partnership between the public and private sectors. However, what emerged was not as much a partnership as a standard, hands-off real estate deal in which the corporation simply sold land to private developers on the basis of a competitive process.

The Harbourfront Corporation offered no special incentives to attract developers' participation in the project. The attraction was based, instead, on the potential for profitable development created by a favorable real estate market and by the site's desirable location, near downtown. The attractiveness of the site was also enhanced by the success of the corporation's early programming efforts, which drew large numbers of people to the site and sparked new public interest in the waterfront.

Initially, when the Canadian developer Olympia & York won the competition to redevelop the Queens Quay Terminal, the corporation's approach, which was to provide limited assistance and guidance, seemed successful. The architectural quality and the imaginative building program the developer brought to the project significantly boosted the corporation's reputation in the industry and with the public, and strengthened Harbourfront's image both locally and internationally.

However, in the years since, the public sector has moved away from large deals with single developers, choosing instead to work with more developers on smaller increments of the plan. For example, the lands not required for public purposes, which were developed more recently, have been sold to a variety of developers and investors. The residential developers have generally responded well to the design guidelines that the city issued in 1991, and have paid closer attention to design and building quality. More than 20 developers and construction companies have been involved in the development of Harbourfront over the past 20 years. Collectively they have made a big contribution to Toronto's central waterfront—by, among other things, respecting the essential character of this important waterfront location, strengthening the area's unique local qualities, and creating a sense of organic growth.

Lessons Learned

The Harbourfront experience offers three lessons that should inform the next steps in the transformation of Toronto's waterfront.

First, over the life of the project, the economic cycle may affect plans, capacities, and schedules in ways that cannot be completely predicted in advance, and that may force adjustments. Development agencies must be able to adjust the phasing of development and programming to take account of cycles in the real estate market.

Second, the Toronto civic movement and the public in general can be expected to follow progress closely, and to hold the development corporation accountable if it appears that the public interest is not being respected. The development corporation and its government and private sector shareholders will need to keep the public well informed, stay tuned to public opinion, and avoid surprises.

Third, finding an appropriate balance for multiple objectives will be a key management challenge. The corporate goals of financial self-sufficiency and short-term profit should not jeopardize other objectives.

Every city has a unique civic culture and history, and every urban waterfront has its own special challenges and opportunities. There is no single formula for waterfront regeneration, and no single model for implementing waterfront projects. Nevertheless, cities learn from one another. Just as Torontonians continue to compare their waterfront with those of other cities, Harbourfront offers useful lessons for those who care about the future of urban centers—and about the role of public spaces and cultural programming in ensuring their vitality. Continued investment in the public realm, insistence on high quality in landscaping and in the built environment, and effective public/private partnerships will be the keys to Toronto's success in its continued waterfront renaissance.

Note

1. Unless otherwise noted, all dollar amounts in this case study are in Canadian dollars.

Project Data: **Harbourfront**

Land Use Information (Acres/Hectares)
Site area   92/37
Parks and open space   40/16

Land Use Plan
Terminal warehouse
(square feet/square meters)   471,000/43,755
Number of housing units
(completed/planned)   4,400/635
Unit sizes
(square feet/square meters)   Studios 506/45
                                         two-bedroom units 947/88

Project Timeline
1972   Canadian government acquires Harbourfront lands
1978   Harbourfront Corporation created
1980   Toronto City Council passes the Harbourfront Part II Official Plan
        and Zoning By-Law
1991   Harbourfront Centre established
1991   Toronto City Council adopts the revised Harbourfront Part II Official
        Plan and Zoning By-Law

Project Contact
Harbourfront Centre
235 Queens Quay West
Toronto, Ontario M5J 2G8
Canada
416-973-4600
Web site: www.harbourfront.on.ca

Concord Pacific Place

Vancouver, British Columbia Canada

Steve Fader

oncord Pacific Place is an ambitious, mixed-use, master-planned waterfront redevelopment project located in the downtown core of Vancouver, British Columbia. The 204-acre (83-hectare) project, which stretches some 1.8 miles (three kilometers) along the north shore of False Creek, responds to several identified objectives of the city of Vancouver: the new community is woven into the fabric of the adjacent city grid; it provides public access to the waterfront along its entire length and view corridors throughout the project; it is in many respects a self-sufficient community, with a range of neighborhood retail, services, and amenities; and it is demographically diverse, with a mix of housing that includes both family-oriented and affordable units.

At completion, the 20-year project will house some 15,000 people in almost 9,200 dwelling units. Seven neighborhoods are being developed, each with a combination of townhouses and low- and mid-rise flats. The project will also include approximately 47 towers, ranging in height from 15 to 38 stories. At buildout, the project is expected to include two schools, four daycare centers, a community center, 50 acres (20 hectares) of public parks and open space, three marinas, and a complement of retail and office space.

Now more than ten years into construction, Concord Pacific Place is, as its name implies, a "place" in Vancouver. A seawall with pedestrian and bicycle paths now lines most of the 1.8-mile (three-kilometer) shoreline, and three major waterfront parks have been built. The community center, converted from an old railroad roundhouse, has been completed, as have two daycare centers. The first of the three planned marinas is nearly complete, and approximately 60,000 square feet (5,575 square meters) of neighborhood retail space has been developed. Of about 9,200 planned dwelling units, approximately 3,393 have been constructed, including 436 affordable units. The market-rate housing units are generally sold prior to the commencement of construction.

Bringing Housing to the Core

The Concord Pacific site was first developed in the 1880s as the terminus of the Canadian transcontinental railroad. The site was used for industrial purposes but by the 1960s had deteriorated and was mostly abandoned. The city of Vancouver began its planning efforts for False Creek in the late 1960s, and in 1974 rezoned most of the land, transforming it from heavy industrial use into a comprehensive development district that would allow for multiple uses. With an eye toward

The towers of Concord Pacific Place are typically connected by low-rise structures that encircle the block and define the private open space within. *James K.M. Cheng Architects*

later redevelopment, the provincial government acquired the Concord Pacific site and cleared it for use as the location of Expo '86, the 1986 World Exposition.

In 1988 the city issued the *False Creek Policy Broadsheets,* which articulated the city's goals of bringing housing to the downtown core and spelled out the planning principles that have governed the development of Concord Pacific Place. The provincial government's decision to sell the property to a single developer, rather than to carve out packages for multiple developers, was also critical to the project. In response to a 1988 request for proposals, Concord Pacific Group Inc. (formerly Concord Pacific Development Corporation) was selected as the master developer for the site. The selection was based, in part, on Concord Pacific's proposed land acquisition cost and development plan, its experience as a large-scale developer, and its financial strength.

The agreement with the province provided for a land acquisition price of $320 million (to be paid in several installments) and required the developer to pay for and construct all required infrastructure for the project with the exception of Pacific Boulevard, the major thoroughfare through the site, which was constructed by the city.[1] The developer was also required to pay for and construct all the agreed-upon amenities for the project except the two schools, which will be built by the local school district on land deeded by the developer. According to Matthew Meehan, Concord Pacific's vice president for planning, the city was clear in its approach: except for site remediation, "all the risks and uncertainties [of development] were to be shouldered by the developer."

The development process for large-scale redevelopment in Vancouver starts with the official development plan (ODP). Once it was designated as the master developer, Concord Pacific spent the next two years formulating and negotiating an ODP for the False Creek North property. The city of Vancouver worked closely with the developer in this process, notes Larry Beasley, Vancouver's codirector of planning, in what amounted to a "cooperative planning approach" between developer and municipality. The effort, adds Beasley, entailed hundreds of workshops with the public, over 50 public meetings, and substantial ongoing collaboration with city staff.

The resulting ODP, which was adopted by the city of Vancouver in 1990, is a detailed document that lays out proposed land uses, densities, building heights, and development principles, all of which are used as the basis for area-specific rezonings. The seven organizing principles articulated and detailed in the ODP require that the proposed development

- Integrate with the city;
- Build on the setting;
- Maintain the sense of a substantial water basin;
- Use streets as an organizing device;
- Create lively places that have a strong image;
- Create neighborhoods;
- Plan for all age groups, with a particular emphasis on children.

The ODP provided concept plans for street patterns and public walkways, proposed land uses, subareas within neighborhoods, sites for community facilities, marina locations, view corridors to be preserved, and axial focal points; it also set numerical targets for the distribution of family-oriented and affordable housing within each neighborhood.

The next step after the development of the ODP is the area-specific rezoning—which, in the case of Concord Pacific Place, applied to the project's seven neighborhoods (including some 16 subareas). The third step is the devel-

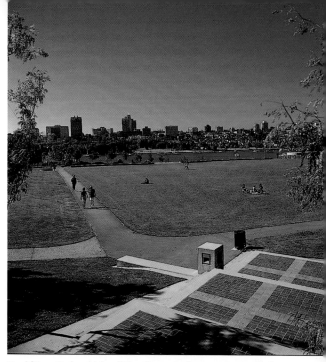

David Lam Park, which adjoins the waterfront and seawalk, is one of three major parks at Concord Pacific Place. Dedicated open space amounts to 42 acres (17 hectares) of the project's 166 land acres (67 hectares).

opment permit, which addresses larger-scale urban design issues. The final step involves obtaining a building permit for a specific structure.

Creating a Lively Place

As the site plan makes clear, Concord Pacific Place is designed to extend the city to the waterfront. Vancouver's existing street grid has been continued virtually to the water, where it is intersected by a cross street grid that conforms generally to the contours of the shoreline. Developing the site this way accomplished several goals: the project is clearly part of the city, and not a separate or walled enclave; the public is symbolically encouraged to visit the waterfront and the community in general; views of the waterfront are protected, and the scale and character of the city are maintained. Pacific Boulevard, the major cross street that runs from one end of the long, linear site to the other, is designed to meld the city grid with the waterfront edge and has been developed with commercial spaces at street level and housing above. As one moves back from the water's edge, the spaces are clearly layered: first is a continuous stone seawall, then a 15-foot- (4.6-meter-) wide brick-paved walkway, then a five-foot- (1.5-meter-) wide landscaped median, then a 15-foot- (4.6-meter-) wide bicycle path. In some cases, raised planters along the side of the bike path denote and physically separate the private realm from the public. From this line, an area of raised terraces, bounded by low railings and landscaping, provides a transition space to the housing—a kind of front stoop. In other areas, public parks directly adjoin the waterfront walkway, allowing for both active and passive recreation by the water's edge.

Throughout the project, low- and mid-rise construction provides a nearly continuous facade along the streets. This street wall, which is lined with varying combinations of retail uses and townhouses, gives an urban feel to the

The seawalk along the 1.8-mile (three-kilometer) length of Concord Pacific Place has defined zones for strolling and bicycling. Public art, required by the official development plan, enlivens the scene.

project and further delineates the public and private realms. Where the low- and mid-rise housing lines the entire street grid to form a rectangle, it creates an inner courtyard for the private use of residents. In some areas, where public streets do not penetrate through the project, mews have been developed. These pedestrian passageways, which are open to the public, are also lined with low-rise housing, allowing surveillance of these areas by residents.

The major portion of Concord Pacific's housing, however, is located in mid- to high-rise towers set strategically to maintain certain view corridors and to maximize views for residents. Most of the towers are located at the intersections of streets, and some are situated to terminate axial views.

Because the towers are set back from the property line, their mass is not fully apparent at street level. Thus, the foreground view at street level is of the scale and rhythm of the townhouses and the retail uses, and the towers' bulk becomes apparent only in the longer view. Explaining the perception of density, Concord Pacific's Meehan notes that "it isn't the height—it's what happens on the first three floors." In line with this philosophy, the Concord Pacific development plan provides for ground-floor retail and commercial uses along Pacific Boulevard, along Davie Street (which is the axial street leading to the primary waterfront marina), and along Marinaside Crescent, which is adjacent to the pedestrian and bicycle path.

Architecturally, the towers and townhouses at Concord Pacific are all strongly modernistic in design. Brick, steel, and concrete detailing—inspired by the industrial look of the adjacent historic Yaletown warehouse district—has been used widely, particularly at the lower building levels. Above, the towers are dominated by glass curtain walls. Inspired by the water and by boating imagery, many have undulating glass facades and rooflines. The highly articulated tower forms are modulated by projecting balconies and rooms, and by the rhythmic patterns of mullions within the glass facades.

Constructing a Community

With the exception of the Roundhouse Community Centre building, the Plaza of Nations building, and the British Columbia Place Stadium, which is on the east end of the site, little was retained from Expo '86. The first phase of construction focused on environmental remediation and the construction of the seawall. Both False Creek Basin and the adjacent lands were contaminated from a long history of industrial uses. Remediation, which continues on an area-by-area basis, has involved soil decontamination, the development of subsurface drainage systems to capture and treat potentially contaminated subsurface drainage, and the redirection of sewer outfalls to treatment plants. Construction of the seawall, which has also proceeded in phases, required minor dredging and filling to make the contour of the shoreline more regular.

The province retains responsibility for environmental remediation. Otherwise, notes Meehan, potential developers would have demanded deep discounts in the price of the land in order to protect themselves against the unknown costs and liabilities associated with contamination. Under an agreement with the province, Concord Pacific excavates the land, but where contamination is found, the additional cost of complying with requirements for the special handling and disposal of contaminated materials is billed directly to the province by the excavation contractor. The site and its historic uses had been thoroughly investigated and documented before construction began, and no major surprises arose during excavation. To date, the province has spent $35 million on remediation.

Beyond site work, most of the construction so far has focused on housing, supporting amenities, and neighborhood retail. Little of the office or the major non-residential portions of the project has been constructed.

The development module for the market-rate housing has typically consisted of an entire block, including perimeter townhouses and two to four towers. Parking is provided in below-grade garages, and the low-rise garage roof often serves as a podium for a swimming pool and other amenities. In some cases, the townhouse units have direct, private stair access to garage parking. In accordance with requirements for the protection of views, the towers have slender profiles and relatively small floor plates, allowing for just four to eight units per floor in most cases. Virtually all units have exterior terraces.

In addition to the ample communitywide amenities, many of the residential projects offer health club facilities, concierge services, meeting rooms, and computer rooms. Mini-theaters (ten to 25 seats) can be booked for private gatherings and are becoming more common, as are overnight guest rooms, which can also be reserved. Fiber-optic cable has been laid throughout Concord Pacific, and high speed computer connections are available to all residences.

The tall, slender towers of Concord Pacific Place are carefully sited to maintain view corridors from the city to the waterfront and from the waterfront to the mountains to the north.

Affordable housing at Concord Pacific is set at 20 percent of all dwelling units and is built through a partnership among the developer, the city, nonprofit organizations, and the provincial or federal government. The non-market-rate buildings are spread throughout the site and are mostly indistinguishable from the market-rate structures. Because the city prefers to limit the number of dwelling units in each non-market-rate building, the affordable-unit buildings are typically ten stories or less.

The first marina at Concord Pacific Place was completed in 2002. Located at the foot of Davie Street, the Quayside Marina has 115 slips and accommodates boats between 30 and 120 feet (9.1 to 36.5 meters) in length. Amenities for boaters include secure, gated access; an on-site dockmaster; restrooms; showers; laundry facilities; a solid waste and recycling center; and pump-out services. Off street parking is available in a below-grade structure adjacent to the loading and dropoff zone. Prior to construction, 90 percent of the 115 berths were sold to boaters

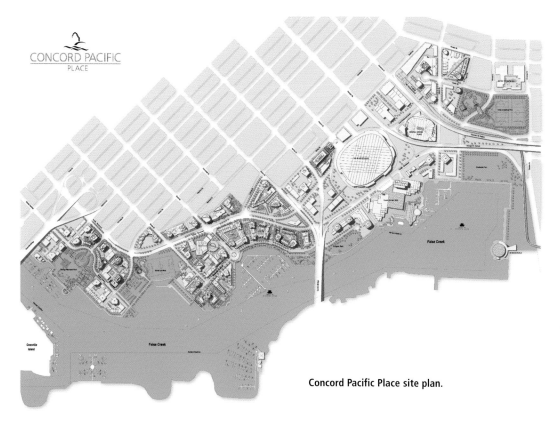

CONCORD PACIFIC
PLACE

Concord Pacific Place site plan.

in a stratified, condominium-like concept. The cost of a 50-foot (15.2-meter) slip, not including the monthly maintenance fee, was set at $169,900. Tracie McTavish, director of sales for Concord Pacific, notes that nearly all the slips were sold to boaters unconnected to the Concord Pacific Place residences, but as the community has matured, many of those who have purchased residences have shown an interest in purchasing a boat slip as well.

In addition to the private boat-launching facility, the Quayside Marina includes a 500-foot- (152.4-meter-) long floating public pier, and a launch for nonmotorized craft. The Aquabus Ferry service, which plies False Creek, will add a stop at the Quayside Marina. Two additional planned marinas, located at either end of Concord Pacific Place, are expected to add 120 slips to the project total.

Concord Pacific Place is designed to be a walkable community. All parts of the project are connected via the pedestrian and bike path and the parks and mews that adjoin it. Retail uses and restaurants are located on Pacific

Boulevard and in adjacent Yaletown; closer to home, neighborhood services, including a supermarket, are provided in the center of Concord Pacific, near the marina. The supermarket, called Urban Fare, is a 27,000-square-foot (2,580-square-meter) facility aimed at an upscale urban demographic. Tucked into the base of one of the residential blocks, Urban Fare is high-tech in interior design, and includes a café and delicatessen.

The one- to three-bedroom housing units at Concord Pacific Place range in size from 527 to more than 4,000 square feet (50 to 370 square meters). About half of all units sold to date have two bedrooms, a den or nook, and two baths. Prices range from about $140,000 to $2.5 million; the two-bedroom units are in the $192,000–$699,000 range.

The Concord Pacific residences are presold, typically through "presentation centers." Initially, because the notion of presales was new to the Vancouver market, most of the

Project Data: **Concord Pacific Place**

Land Use Information (Acres/Hectares)

Site area	204/83
Land	166/67
Water	38/15

Land Use Plan

Use	Acres/Hectares	Percentage of Site
Buildings	91/37	44.6
Streets and surface parking	14.5/5.9	7.1
Landscaping and open space	60.5/24.5	29.7
Other (water)	38/15	18.6
Total	204/83	100.0
Floor/area ratio	2.86 (based on 101 acres/40.8 hectares: land area net of streets and public open space)	

Gross Building Area (at Buildout)

Use	Square Feet/Square Meters
Office	1,615,000/150,040
Retail	877,000/81,475
Residential	9,750,000/905,805
Hotel	350,000/32,515
Total	12,592,000/1,169,835

Retail Uses

Existing gross leasable area (square feet/square meters)	60,155/5,590

Residential Uses

Existing	3,799 (3,363 market rate; 436 nonmarket)
Planned	9,197 units

Marinas

Marina	Number of Slips
Marina #1	115 (existing)
Marina #2	60 (planned)
Marina #3	60 (planned)
Total	235

Retail Information

Tenant Classification	Number of Stores	Gross Leasable Area (Square Feet/Square Meters)
General merchandise	6	9,905/920
Food service	5	35,147/3,265
Personal services	7	7,372/685
Financial	2	7,731/720
Total	20	60,155/5,590

Concord Pacific residences were purchased by Canadian and overseas investors. As the amenities were constructed and the community began to take visible shape, demand shifted to more local sources, and purchases for primary residences increased. McTavish notes that the community has reached a critical mass: for the past year, entire projects have been selling out within a few months of the project launch. According to McTavish, the developer's objective is to provide high-quality accommodations at attractive prices, thereby accelerating buyer acceptance—and, ultimately, shortening the development horizon.

The range of housing and prices offered at Concord Pacific Place has attracted a wide variety of buyers. Buyers are mostly Vancouverites, and include first-time buyers, families, empty nesters, and move-down buyers. Although some purchases are still for investment (with each new building launch, some existing residents buy additional units for investment), the majority of purchases are for owner occupancy.

Lessons Learned

The experience of Concord Pacific Place demonstrates that public and private development interests at the waterfront are not mutually exclusive. Through careful site planning and urban design, it is possible to preserve public access to the waterfront, as well as views to and from the waterfront,

Residential Information (Market-Rate Units)

Unit Type	Unit Size (Square Feet/ Square Meters)	Number Sold/ Leased	Initial Sales/Rental Prices
One-bedroom	527–649/50–60	209	$139,800–$182,900
One-bedroom plus den/nook	668–999/60–93	1,025	$149,800–$270,000
Two-bedroom, two-bath, plus den/nook	840–1,708/80–160	1,680	$192,000–$699,000
Three-bedroom or larger	1,195–4,038/110–375	459	$283,000–$2,500,000
Total		3,393	

Development Cost Information

Site acquisition cost	$320,000,000
Site improvement costs	100,000,000+
Construction and soft costs	258,000,000
Total estimated development costs at completion	$3,000,000,000

Development Schedule

1988	Site purchased
1988	Planning started
1992	Construction started
2008	Estimated completion

Major Project Participants

Concord Pacific Group Inc.
Vancouver, British Columbia
Web site: concordpacific.com

James K.M. Cheng Architects
Vancouver, British Columbia

The Hulbert Group
West Vancouver, British Columbia

Roger Hughes Architects
Vancouver, British Columbia

Hancock Bruckner Eng & Wright
Vancouver, British Columbia

Other Key Concord Pacific Group Development Team Members

Terry Hui, President and Chief Executive Officer
Henry Man, Chief Operating Officer
David Negrin, Senior Vice President, Development
Peter Wong, Senior Vice President, Construction
Dennis Au-Yeung, Vice President, Finance
Dan Ulinder, Senior Vice President, Marketing and Sales

Larry Beasley
Community Services Group
Vancouver, British Columbia

and to satisfy the market and security needs of private housing development. "The cooperative planning model between developer, city, and the public has been essential in achieving these results," concludes Beasley.

At Concord Pacific Place, compact layouts, a mix of uses, and a measure of density allowed the creation of a truly urban, pedestrian-oriented community, lessening the need for automobile ownership and use. Concord Pacific has been built to the minimum required parking ratios; according to the project developer, however, the project is so strongly oriented to pedestrians and to transit use that even the minimal amount of parking provided exceeds the level of need.

The sense of urbanity and comfortable density at Concord Pacific depends on the eye-level perceptions of the project's continuous low-rise street facades. Says Meehan, "What's guiding your vision is the lower three floors." At the same time, the unbounded space at the water's edge may offer an especially appropriate location for high-rise development. "If there's any place that density won't feel so dense," Meehan continues, "it's by the water." The freedom to build intensively is the engine that enabled the developers to provide public amenities in a waterfront setting; as Meehan notes, "The way you get the parks [and other amenities] is to go up."

Note

1. Unless otherwise noted, all dollar amounts in this case study are in Canadian dollars.